Chester I. Barnard and the Guardians of the Managerial State

Portrait of Chester I. Barnard. (Photo courtesy of New Jersey Bell, a Bell Atlantic Company)

Chester I. Barnard and the Guardians of the Managerial State

William G. Scott

University Press of Kansas

Published by the University Press of Kansas (Lawrence, Kansas 66049), which was organized by the Kansas Board of Regents and is operated and funded by Emporia State University, Fort Hays State University, Kansas State University, Pittsburg State University, the University of Kansas, and Wichita State University

Library of Congress Cataloging-in-Publication Data

Scott, William G.
    Chester I. Barnard and the guardians of the managerial state / by
William G. Scott.
        p.   cm.
    Includes bibliographical references and index.
    ISBN 0-7006-0550-9 (hard cover : permanent paper)
    1. Barnard, Chester Irving, 1886–1961.   Functions of the
executive.   2. Executives.   3. Management.   4. Industrial sociology.
I. Title.
HD31.B363S37   1992
658.4—dc20   92-9978

British Library Cataloguing in Publication Data is available.

Printed in the United States of America

10 9 8 7 6 5 4 3 2 1

The paper used in this publication meets the minimum requirements of the American National Standard for Permanence of Paper for Printed Library Materials Z39.48–1984.

To the memory of John Franklin Mee

Quis custodiet ipsos custodes?
—Juvenal

Contents

Preface   ix

Acknowledgments   xiii

Abbreviations   xvii

Introduction: The Voice of the New Managerial State   1

1 The Managerial Age   9

2 The Management Revolution   25

3 Barnard's Harvard Circle   40

4 The "Empirical" Barnard: A Biographical Sketch   61

5 Barnard's Intellectual Debts and His Epistemology
   of the Social Sciences   88

6 The Search for Behavioral Control: The Individual
   and the Small Group   104

7 Engineering Consent in Formal Organizations   118

8 The Leadership Attributes of the Management Elite   134

9 The Moral Obligations of the Elite   145

10 The New Order of National Power and
   Organizational Governance   157

11 The Exhaustion of Managerialism   169

Epilogue: The Management of Crisis and Tribulation   185

Notes   189

Selected Bibliography   217

Index   225

Preface

Chester I. Barnard's vision of national institutions reconstructed with managerial values was formed during the critical interwar decades of the 1920s and 1930s. His teachings concerning the social control of employees and the efficacy of corporate management elitism were influential then and thereafter, but never more so than during the last ten years. His reputation rose dramatically among management scholars in the 1980s, and there is every indication that this trend will continue in the 1990s.

Nevertheless much has changed since he wrote his major book, *The Functions of the Executive*, more than fifty years ago. Although this paradigmatic statement still informs the theory, the research, and the practice of management, I believe that now such reliance on Barnard's orthodoxy is a serious defect of the field. Therefore I feel his work warrants a fresh look. This book has three aims: to reinterpret Barnard's important concepts through an analysis of his writings, to examine the confluence of historical events and ideas that shaped his managerial values and ideology, and to assess the future of those values that he was so successful promulgating. I hope that students, scholars, and practicing executives in business management and public administration will be interested in and profit from this inquiry.

I am not a historian so I make no claims for the elegance of my historical methods or my excursions into biography. This book is neither a full-blown history nor a biography. Rather it is written in the manner of social commentary much as David K. Hart and I wrote our last book. But this volume fills spaces that we left mostly open. *Organizational Values in America* was about the present; this book is about the past and about the future of Barnard's ideas about managerialism.

Barnard's ideology of a managed America is seldom learned by students, mostly unacknowledged by management scholars, and overlooked by historians. I have written this book in the hope that it will compensate somewhat for the misunderstanding of a significant person who, between the wars, established with other notable individuals the parameters within which American institutions were modernized. Barnard created much of the intellectual capital upon which the management field still draws.

I first read *Functions* in 1954 as a doctoral student in a seminar conducted by Professor John F. Mee at Indiana University. In that same seminar I also read Herbert Simon's book *Administrative Behavior* and Peter Drucker's just published *The Practice of Management*. The wartime disjunction that separated them from Barnard's book, published in 1938, made it appear to me at that time to be hopelessly old-fashioned. I have since changed my mind.

In any event, I did not study Barnard systematically for many years after I graduated from Indiana. I spent most of the 1960s and early 1970s toiling in the tribal gardens of my field's normal science. While I made routine references to *Functions* in articles and books, I did not dwell on Barnard's theories nor did I give much thought to those important issues of the period that captured his attention and influenced his ideas.

It was 1976 when Barnard again surfaced in my attentions. I had been assigned to teach a core MBA course in management. My first problem was finding a textbook that challenged graduate students. After thrashing around in the under-brush of standard texts in the field, I decided to go to the source and use Barnard's *Functions*. The more I taught this book, dragging my grumbling students with me, the more I appreciated the depth and intricacy of Barnard's thought. I also real-ized, after penetrating his prose and difficult arguments, that he was pleading for a particular value system and for a special form of social hierarchy. He thought that professional corporate managers were the "better sorts" of leaders who would, in exchange for power and privilege, guide the managerial state into that good future of prosperity and harmony envisioned by the Progressives around the turn of the century.

Once I grasped the essence of his aims, I was hooked, and in the 1980s I published a number of articles, most of them jointly written with my colleague Terence R. Mitchell, that analyzed certain specialized topics in Barnard's book. This work convinced me that there was a need for a larger study to reassess some of Barnard's views set against the background of those decades, between 1920 and 1950, when he was at the peak of his intellectual vigor and public influence.

So in the late 1980s I began my Barnardian odyssey, and it took me from Seattle to the centers of learning and power on the East Coast. This territory, bounded on the north by Boston and on the south by Washington, D.C., was where Barnard spent his life and where most of the archival material pertaining to him is found. This journey was the most rewarding and pleasant of my professional career. Its outcome is now in your hands.

The reader will find that Barnard's views ranged widely across the social sciences and moral philosophy, intertwining what he believed was the best of them in his theories of management. Barnard painted with very broad strokes, and consequently a study of his ideas and values must be interdisciplinary. This is a risky undertaking because specialists in fields such as sociology, psychology, social psychology, economics, and philosophy might claim that my treatment of their areas is a bit thin. Furthermore, professional historians could criticize me for not exploring in adequate depth how and why the period that was most influential on Barnard's thought connected with the formation of his ideas. So if the reader is anticipating a detailed microhistory or a penetrating technical analysis of various social science disciplines, he or she may be disappointed. All of that requires a different book.

However, readers should be alerted to what they may expect to find herein. First, I intend to show that Barnard was in the ideological mainstream with other opinion leaders who argued for national collectivization in the form of a managerial state. The factor that made Barnard different from the rest of the intelligentsia of the time was that he, as a spokesman from corporate America, believed that professional managers in the private sector should collectivize America on their terms, as unencumbered as possible by the inconveniences of accountability. Unlike Walter Lippmann, who thought that the legislative branch of government must exercise control over the managers, Barnard scarcely mentioned it. While I recognize the potentially great part that the legislature could play in making policy and setting national agendas, Barnard was not so convinced. He was mainly interested in the regulatory functions of government's executive branch.

Second, Barnard's organizational and personal connections were critical to the development of his theories, ideals, and values. I will discuss some of these connections with Harvard University, ATT, and the Rockefeller Foundation as well as acquaintanceships that were important to his career.

Third, Barnard's intellectual life was unique for a corporate executive. He read widely and used much of what he read in his speeches and writing on management. Unfortunately, an inventory of his library is not available. However, he acknowledged many of his sources, and consulting them allowed me to flesh out Barnard's central concepts.

Fourth, nearly half of this book is a textual analysis of Barnard's written work: an interpretation of his primary ideas about the individual, the informal organization, the formal organization, cooperation, management virtues and moral responsibility, business-government relationships, and organizational power.

Finally I raise the *quo vadis* question regarding Barnard's contributions and legacy to management and to America. And here I acknowledge that I have an axe to grind about present conditions that Barnard had anticipated but in no way condoned. I refer to the deterioration of management competency and integrity in practice that has gone hand in hand with a decline in the public acceptance of managerial philosophy and values. One has to wonder about the extent to which Barnard's ideas concerning the centrality of the managerial elite in American life contributed to this state of affairs. Or, alternatively, whether or not violations of Barnard's ideals of perfection led to the failure of his dreams for a cooperative commonwealth of abundance and tranquility. These speculations admit no definitive answers, but if this book encourages thoughtful readers to see Barnard anew and question his views, then this effort will be justified.

In the light of these comments, I am ambivalent about Barnard. On the one hand, I am suspicious of the concentrated organizational power that he advocated, and I detest an elitism based upon it. I find the subordination of an individual's moral character to the imperatives of contrived organizational collectives, which he also recommended, a repugnant idea. On the other hand, his intellect, his vast accomplishments in the affairs of business, government, philanthropy, and public service, his prodigious writings, and his profound personal integrity impress me beyond telling. He is a giant in the field of management and he was a major figure in public life during the strategically important years when this country modernized. He deserves our attentive consideration if for no other reason than to reevaluate his philosophy and learn from it what we might want to pursue or avoid in the future.

WGS
Seattle, February 1992

Acknowledgments

Many have generously contributed their ideas, time, and financial support to the research and writing of this book. While I am anxious to recognize their contributions, not all of these helpful people and institutions endorsed my arguments and conclusions.

Five close colleagues furthered this inquiry in specific and significant ways. Terence R. Mitchell, Edward Carlson professor of business administration at the University of Washington, and I coauthored three articles about Barnard between 1985 and 1990. These articles are the backbones of chapters 6, 7, 8, and 10. Chapter 11 draws in part from two other articles that Mitchell and I wrote. These five articles, cited below, shaped much of my thinking about Barnard's theories, his intellectual range, and his contributions to the field of management. Mitchell's analytical abilities and his thorough knowledge of the behavioral science literature are reflected in these chapters.

My collaboration with David K. Hart, J. Fish Smith professor of free enterprise studies at Brigham Young University, on *Organizational Values in America* and on an article that appeared in *Society* magazine helped me immeasurably to frame the introduction and last chapter of this volume. I shamelessly borrowed the title for chapter 11 from this article. I owe Hart a special debt for my education in political philosophy and for his principled position on ethical individualism. His good humor in finding obscure references in his extensive library saved me many hours of research.

William Alberts, professor of finance at the University of Washington, did a financial analysis of New Jersey Bell Telephone Company that gave me an impression of its performance during Barnard's presidency. Alberts's interest in my work, even though we are not in the same field, has been gratifying.

David Norton, professor of philosophy at the University of Delaware, read chapter 10 with a sharp critical eye and cautioned me against making excessive claims about Barnard's drift into existential philosophy. He also gave me valuable

advice about various aspects of moral philosophy that I discuss in this chapter and
in other places throughout this book.

For nearly two years, when he was a visiting professor at the University of
Washington, William B. Wolf, professor emeritus of Cornell University, and I had
a running debate about the meaning of Barnard's work. Although we shall never
agree on interpretation, these conversations forced me to defend my position and
hone the arguments presented herein. Wolf is a worthy adversary on the subject of
Barnard because he has studied his thought in detail and was one of the first
contemporary scholars to recognize his importance to modern management.

In addition to these friends are people with whom I have corresponded and
have had telephone conversations. Barnard's grandchildren, Julia and Jared
Welch, recounted for me some of their memories of their grandfather, and they
also provided very important documents and photographs that assisted me to
round out the biographical chapter of this book. H. Roy Hershey, who worked at
New Jersey Bell Telephone Company during most of Barnard's years as president,
told me some wonderful anecdotes that shed light on Barnard's personality as seen
from the perspective of a subordinate employee. Bernard Barber, professor emeritus of Barnard College, took L. J. Henderson's course, Sociology 23, Concrete
Sociology, as an undergraduate at Harvard. His recollections of that course and
Barnard's lecture in it were useful information that helped my development of
chapter 3. Professor Barber also read an early draft of that chapter and his valuable comments were incorporated in revision.

Primary archival data were critical for this study, and I am grateful to those
archives and archivists who were so helpful: the Baker Library, Graduate School
of Business Administration, Harvard University; the Rockefeller Archive Center;
the Archives of the National Science Board; the National Archives; the American
Telephone and Telegraph Company archives; the records of New Jersey Bell
Telephone Company, a division of Bell Atlantic Company; and the archives of the
Northfield–Mount Hermon School.

All the people who worked in these archives were unfailingly helpful. However
several stand out because of the special nature of my requests. Sheldon Hochheiser at the ATT archives familiarized me with their system so that I was able to take
maximum advantage of the time I spent there. He also followed through by
providing me with additional information when I left the archives. Hazel Dove at
New Jersey Bell Telephone exceeded the call of duty by assembling documentation that pertained to Barnard's presidency of that company. And Linda Batty, the
archivist at Northfield–Mount Hermon School, found documents for me that
related to Barnard's early education and to some of his later exploits. I appreciate
the grant made to me by the Rockefeller Archive Center that permitted my return
there for further study.

Portions of some of the chapters contain material from articles that I published
in various scholarly journals. The editors of these journals and my co-authors have

graciously given me their permission either to quote or to adapt the material for this book. The source and authorship of these articles together with the chapters in which the subject matter is used follows:

Introduction and Chapter 11—William G. Scott and David K. Hart, "The Exhaustion of Managerialism," *Society* 28 (March–April 1991): 39–48; Terence R. Mitchell and William G. Scott, "Leadership Failures, the Distrusting Public, and Prospects of the Administrative State," *Public Administration Review* (November–December 1987): 445–52; and Terence R. Mitchell and William G. Scott, "America's Problems and Needed Reforms: Confronting the Ethic of Personal Advantage," Academy of Management *Executive* 4 (August 1990): 23–35.

Chapter 6—Terence R. Mitchell and William G. Scott. "The Universal Barnard: His Micro Theories of Organizational Behavior," *Public Administration Quarterly* 9 (Fall 1985): 239–59.

Chapter 7—William G. Scott and Terence R. Mitchell, "The Universal Barnard: His Macro Theory of Organization," *Public Administration Quarterly* 11 (Spring 1987): 34–58.

Chapter 8—William G. Scott and Terence R. Mitchell, "The Universal Barnard: His Meta-concepts of Leadership in the Administrative State," *Public Administration Quarterly* 13 (Fall 1989): 295–320.

Chapter 10—Scott and Mitchell, "The Universal Barnard: His Meta-concepts," and William G. Scott, "The Management Governance Theories of Liberty and Justice," *Journal of Management* 14 (Summer 1988): 277–98.

Time is an author's most valuable commodity, and I am grateful to Professor Borje Saxberg, head of the management and organization department, the University of Washington, for arranging my schedule so that I had large blocks of unencumbered time during the writing phase of this project. I also appreciate my school's funding of travel connected with this research.

Robert D. Cuff, York University, and Jack Rabin, Penn State University, reviewed the manuscript. I am in their debt for comments and suggestions for improvement. Cuff was adamant about clarifying the focus of the book, and Rabin stressed the importance of the legislative branch of government in the managerial state. The shortcomings of this book are my doing, not theirs.

Michael Briggs is an inspired editor at the University Press of Kansas. His continued faith in this project carried me over some difficult periods with suggestions that were always on the mark. I deeply appreciate his editorial help and also his informal role of consulting psychologist.

My electronic literacy ended with crystal radio sets so word processing with personal computers is beyond my comprehension. However, Joannie Shearer, who is a magician with these machines, made up for this character defect of mine and prepared draft upon draft of the manuscript. Many thanks, Joannie.

Finally, Karyn Kawahara, my graduate assistant, attended to the endless details that pile up when a manuscript is in the final stages of preparation. Her work on the bibliography and the index is praiseworthy.

Abbreviations

ASME	American Society of Mechanical Engineers
ATT	American Telephone and Telegraph Company
ATTA	American Telephone and Telegraph Company Archives
BL	Baker Library Graduate School of Business Administration, Harvard University, Barnard Collection
CEO	Chief Executive Officer
GSB	Graduate School of Business Administration, Harvard University
LSRM	Laura Spelman Rockefeller Memorial
NA	National Archives
NIRA	National Industrial Recovery Act
NJBT	New Jersey Bell Telephone Company
NJBTR	New Jersey Bell Telephone Company Records
NMHA	Northfield–Mt. Hermon School Archives
NRA	National Recovery Administration
NRC	National Research Council
NSB	National Science Board
NSBA	National Science Board Archives
NSF	National Science Foundation
PACH	Public Administration Clearing House
RAC	Rockefeller Archive Center
RF	Rockefeller Foundation
SSRC	Social Science Research Council
USO	United Service Organizations
WIB	War Industries Board

Introduction: The Voice of the New Managerial State

If the twentieth century has been the American century, then that has been due, in no small part, to management. But management as an institution, an occupation, and a subject of study has languished in a neglected corner of public opinion, being neither widely understood nor highly regarded. It loses out in the competition for national attention to diplomacy, politics, science, and military affairs. Unable to engender much public interest or enthusiasm, except when ethical transgressions and technical ineptitude are too much to ignore, managers are often seen as boring apparatchiki who do excruciatingly dull things in organizations.

Yet managers run America. Through their shadow organizational empires they more deeply and directly affect everyday American life than do the media celebrities in their glamorous, high-visibility jobs. Even so, few contemporary writers since the end of World War II, with the exception of Peter Drucker and Alfred D. Chandler, Jr., have presented management in the light of its true importance: the primary organ of modernization that created an America for the twentieth century.

As this century ends, the advantages and the shortcomings of managed America have become apparent. Our faith in the free market system was vindicated by the collapse of the command economies in Eastern Europe and the Soviet Union, and our military success in the Gulf war erased the depression over the Vietnam War, but the jubilation caused by these historic events is tempered by a lack of international competitiveness, management incompetence and corruption, a stagnant economy, and a growing separation between managers and the employees they are supposed to manage. So in the 1990s, with many Americans spiritually, morally, and economically displaced, there is pessimism about the future. What sort of passage will our republic make into the new millennium?

History cannot answer this question; its trajectories do not lead to a predetermined future. However, knowledge of the past reveals something about why we are as we are now and suggests what we might want to avoid and to repeat. This is the spirit in which this book approaches its two main themes: America's transi-

1

tion, early in the century, into the modern age of the managerial state and Chester I. Barnard's contributions to its formation and expansion between the two world wars. Barnard's ideas, products of the Progressive era, indelibly marked today's America with the stamp of managerialism.

Managerial states were cultural mutations[1] developed by advanced nations to solve their problems of economic destabilization and institutional modernization. Formed after World War I, these unique organizational artifacts were thought to be rational instruments for efficiently allocating resources and for responding, in a measured way, to national emergencies. Their contours were shaped by the imperatives of national progress and corporative collectivism. Regarding the last, historian Richard P. Adelstein has observed that "like its collectivist counterparts in Europe, American *managerialism* vigorously asserted the primacy of an abstract, reified collective. . . . But to this it added a distinctive commitment to social engineering—the conscious, scientifically informed control of complex social processes and outcomes in the service of a collectively defined purpose."[2]

Strictly speaking, those purposes were not collectively defined, if that meant that national policies resulted from citizen participation in democratic processes. Instead, such policy agendas were set by leadership elites who decided what they thought best served the collective interest. Those elites in Europe in the interwar period were found in the Communist, Fascist, and Nazi parties.

America differs from this pattern, because politicians and government officials do not dominate our managerial state. At first, it was quite the other way around. Private interests were supreme in the 1920s, but that changed when Franklin D. Roosevelt took presidential office in 1933. However, the case was not black or white even during the 1920s and 1930s, since our system of national governance never has been an exclusive preserve for either public or private interests.

Instead, a system of shared power evolved among managerial peers who at the top level of organizations represented widely varying interests. Sometimes those interests were compatible, but other times they conflicted. Nevertheless, this arrangement produced national priorities and agendas due in large part to the stability of our national institutions and the permeability of our social hierarchy.

The nature of our managerial state may be best described as a sort of peer pluralism.[3] Compared to other nations, the power to determine the national agenda was fairly evenly, if not perfectly, divided among elitist managers. This arrangement, however, disguised the essential dynamics of American rulership, wherein the contest among elitists was over the matter of moral authority. Put another way, this contest concerned which institutions or subgroups of their leaders were to be first among equals. So, although institutional power seemed roughly balanced, the moral authority to set the tone and to decide the direction of national policy was not. Historically, the location of that power changed cyclically, depending on the political atmosphere. As political scientist Kevin Phillips argued,[4] the site of moral authority depended to a great extent on whether public opinion and voting behavior favored strong government intervention or autonomy of the private sector. Furthermore, according to Phillips, shifts between these sectors occurred regularly as a reaction of one against the excesses of the other. These swings tended during this century to differentiate liberals from conservatives, Democrats from Republicans, although now such distinctions are so blurred as to be nearly meaningless.

However, early in the century an epic change occurred of vastly greater importance than these cyclical movements. A professional management leadership cadre with a distinct ideology gained power in national affairs and has kept it for more than seventy years. A number of people wrote about this new class of managers and have labelled it the power elite, the inner circle, the planning elite, and the significant people. But historian Guy Alchon's term, the technocratic professionals, seems closer to the mark.[5] Applying rational techniques developed by behavioral scientists and using data supplied by institutional economists, these professionals attempted to modernize American institutions after World War I. Collectively they held, and still hold for that matter, the top organizational jobs in business, government, labor, education, trade associations, philanthropy, and research institutes. In such positions, they were the custodians of our national agenda as it evolved in the 1920s and 1930s.

Because the managerial class was an unprecedented social phenomenon, it needed a new legitimacy to justify its power. The old forms such as property ownership, democratic election to office, or charisma simply were not applicable. And so there began a search to find different grounds for legitimizing management's right to rule the nation. The public administration scholar Dwight Waldo was notable in this respect because he may have been the first to attach the guardian concept to professional managers. He claimed that government officials needed an "unusual natural endowment of physique, stamina, and qualities of personality" that made them attractive, winning and enduring.[6] In addition, they had to be intelligent, educated, and wise above all. Thus, in those virtues of character and physical strength, Waldo's ideal administrator emulated the qualities that Plato advised for his Guardians. Similar virtues were proposed for corporate managers, and Barnard's list of them preceded Waldo's by a number of years.

Of course the idea of guardianship implied leadership legitimacy. Plato's Guardians had the right to rule because of their specialized knowledge of the Good. They were experts, and their arcane learning accompanied by the skills to put it into practice in the polis were acquired by education and rigorous training of a few selectively bred individuals. Those who successfully completed their training entered the martial class of the Guardians, and from it, after a final winnowing, an elite of leaders was drawn. Their legitimacy to rule was based on their cognizance of the ideal forms. Armed with the knowledge, skills, and the wisdom of age, the Guardians could then release the people from the bondage of their ignorance and aid them to develop the virtues of character necessary for worthy citizens of the state. Interpreting Plato as though he had been a developmental psychologist, philosopher David L. Norton observed, "Plato supposed that individuals, having been initially placed and role-trained by Rulers, would in the course of their subsequent development arrive independently at the self-knowledge by which to judge their placement."[7] If the citizens decided that the Rulers had placed them poorly, they would replace the placers by denying them sustenance. Therefore, the Guardians did not have absolute power since they were ultimately accountable to the citizens, who were enlightened by self-knowledge.

This leadership image had considerable legitimizing potential, for who could doubt the efficacy of an expert leadership elite that dedicated itself to the welfare of others and was ready to sacrifice itself in the process of doing so? As a luminous ideal, guardianship shed an aura of legitimacy on the technocratic management professionals, and the concept is still touted for that purpose.[8]

The parallel between management and the Guardians is compelling, especially as a justification for management's social position and organizational function. Indeed management thought of itself in Guardian terms; competence, moral integrity, and rational stewardship became the coins of the managerial realm. The people who practiced management were fit and lean physically, morally superior, and expert in the ways of their profession. By Barnard's time, the management elite—and it made no difference whether they worked in the public or private sector—believed that they knew far better than anyone else what was good for the republic and for its individual citizens.

Politicians had little doubt that professional management was the custodian of the republic's fate. Herbert Hoover wrote in 1934 that "the manager's restless pillow has done more to advance the practical arts than all the legislation upon the statute book."[9] And, in the same year, Franklin D. Roosevelt said, "But government [the executive branch] is essentially the outward expression of the unity and the leadership of all groups. . . . Government . . . must be the leader, must be the judge of the conflicting interests of all groups in the community."[10]

And also in 1934, Walter Lippmann summarized the situation in his characteristically lucid way: "Between Mr. Hoover and Mr. Roosevelt there was, in 1932, no issue of fundamental principle as to the responsibility of the modern state for the modern economy. Both of them recognized the responsibility. They differed as to how it could be best discharged, but not on the underlying question as to whether the attempt ought to be made to discharge it."[11]

Hoover and Roosevelt agreed on two fundamental points, even though they disputed the location of moral authority in the managerial state. First, they believed that the managerial specialists who controlled the great public and private organizations should be the leaders of America. Second, they realized that structurally the most suitable kind of national governance was a form of "free collectivism." It permitted the nation's managers to have the most flexibility to cooperate in the design and the implementation of social and economic policies that would be helpful for overcoming the depression. In Lippmann's opinion, this approach to institutional reform was consistent with American traditions of voluntarism and contrasted favorably with the "absolute collectivism" then prevalent among totalitarian governments in Europe. Lippmann concluded:

> The great issues of the contemporary world, as between conservatives and progressives, fascists, communists, and social democrats have to do with the kind of collectivism, how it is to be established, in whose interest, by whom it is to be controlled, and for what ends. But about the underlying premise of all these policies, which is that the continuity of an ordered life is a collective responsibility, there is not debate.[12]

Management, therefore, had a political voice almost from the start of this century, beginning with Woodrow Wilson's. But it had not produced an ideological voice from its own ranks. Granted that Frederick W. Taylor and the rest of the scientific managers expressed their views, but they were management consultants, by and large. Management really needed an exemplar who spoke authentically from the organizational trenches. That became Barnard's destiny and the chief reason for his supreme importance to management's historical passage into modern prominence.

With a bent for philosophy and theory, a strong ideological position, a taste for scholarship, and an evangelical sense of professional calling, Barnard was a corporate executive unlike those before and after him. However, these attributes would not have been enough to set him apart then, or to make him a significant figure now. His corpus of influential writings distinguished him, an accomplishment that was unusual for a person in his position. His books, monographs, transcribed speeches, and articles are a remarkable testimony to his singular stature in management. Barnard held that corporate management, with its allies in philanthropic organizations and premier private universities, must have the moral authority to rule and to modernize the nation. The single most important ideological goal of Barnard's work was to reaffirm Hoover's vision of a cooperative state directed and inspired by the "better sorts" who came from the private and voluntary side of the republic's life. Barnard set himself to the task of delivering this message, but that posed difficulties.

Barnard often complained that standard English could not express the subtleties of management reasoning. So he created a new voice that communicated managerial concepts that were beyond the ordinary experiences of common folk. Therefore, what scholars and practicing executives said about management had to be put in a specialized, philosophical way with little regard for the graceful phrase or for the conventional meaning of common words. In this respect, and whether he knew it or not, Barnard followed the advice of Charles Sanders Peirce, the great Harvard philosopher of pragmatism, who had argued, while Barnard was yet a young man, that "the philosophist must be encouraged—yea, and required—to coin new terms to express such new . . . as he may discover . . . [philosophy] thus has a peculiar need of a language distinct and detached from common speech."[13]

Herein lies the reason for much misunderstanding of Barnard by the people who comment on his work. Most critics agree on one thing: Barnard was a terrible writer. The flaw in this judgment is that it is based on one sample, *The Functions of the Executive*. Because this was Barnard's major work, critics seldom bother to look beyond it, but if they did, they would find that Barnard wrote for two audiences. One was a popular audience, composed of students, businesspeople, fellow employees in the Bell System, and the public at large. The second was an academic or a scholarly audience made up of teachers, researchers, university administrators, and thoughtful individuals on boards of philanthropic organizations. Barnard wrote clearly for the first group, but for the second his prose was frequently dense and convoluted. Barnard's book falls into the latter category, and it would seem that he followed one of Peirce's dictums closely: "In order to be deep it is requisite to be dull."

Throughout his book Barnard used phrases—such as efficiency and effectiveness, or the zone of indifference—that employed ordinary words to mean extraordinary things. Although he defined his terms, they still confuse readers. Students, for example, always mix up effectiveness and efficiency. When Barnard launched into the philosophical stratosphere with statements like, "So among those who cooperate the things that are seen are moved by the things unseen. Out of the void comes the spirit that shapes the ends of men,"[14] his meaning is particularly obscure. If one doesn't know that Barnard worshiped cooperation, the reader cannot know that this statement was the closest Barnard ever came to "theology" in his writing.

So we read in Kenneth Andrews' introduction to the thirtieth printing of *Functions* an apology for Barnard's awkward style. Andrews explains that happens when a nonacademic strains to write a scholarly treatise. In addition to neglecting to mention that academics are not renowned for the elegance and crispness of their prose, Andrews also missed the main point. Professor William B. Wolf, a notable Barnard scholar, came closer when he argued that Barnard used specialized language to bring precision of thought to management. This interpretation is correct as far as it goes.

But Barnard had more in mind than merely to heighten the precision of management language. His new words and meanings were designed to control discourse in order to establish and to preserve management's ideological purity. George Orwell commented on this instrumental use of language in two notable essays,[15] arguing that the control of thought through the control of words was the best way to secure ideological orthodoxy.

Although Barnard never had such a grandiose expectation for his work, his rhetorical enterprise was successful, as members of modern academic fields, such as business management and public administration, are unable to think and to converse in ways that are incompatible with his views about the general superiority of a managed society and the great amount of discretion that managers need to run it. For example, since 1956, when the *Social Science Citation Index* started to count such things on an annual basis, until 1990, there were over 1,400 citations of Barnard's work, and most of them refer to his major book. But Barnard's spirit also lives in management practice. His rhetoric about management's discretion to exercise almost absolute power in organizations is a recurring theme in modern management discourse because it supports the political, economic, and social legitimacy of this favored class. Such words and phrases as *discretionary power, cooperation, mutuality of interests, integration and stability, consent to authority,* and *faith in good management intentions* define a rhetorical situation in which management and its clients have the same expectations, which causes them to create realities consistent with the ideological imperatives of managerialism.[16]

On a less galactic plane, Barnard's innovative contributions to management set the course for the future development of the field. It owes Barnard a debt for his theory of decisionmaking that inspired Herbert Simon's Nobel-prize-winning work on the subject. Barnard also modified classical organization theory to legitimate management authority on the grounds of functional skill not hierarchical position. He was the first management writer to integrate social psychology into a general theory of management and organization. He understood organizational culture and wrote about controlling it in order to achieve obedience to management's orders. Finally, he had a political vision of private sector hegemony that restated Hoover's "new era" Progressivism in management terms. Barnard's psychological theories of motivation and behavior, his sociological theories of cooperation and complex organizations, and his political ideology of privatism and voluntarism qualified him as management's first universal scholar and protagonist. He showed explicitly why America ought to be led by the management guardians; they alone could foster a new age of cooperation, prosperity, and stability in a world seemingly coming apart after the Great War.

Such was in part Barnard's legacy to us, and therefore he cannot be ignored. But this is not to suggest that he has been, for among present management scholars are those who adulate him, others who find inspiration in his ideas, many who accept his views without question, and a few who vehemently oppose what he stood for.

An academic cottage industry based on Barnard's book sprung up almost immediately after it was published. Since then this industry has grown; citations of his book have increased in frequency over the years. But in addition to these acknowledgments is the trend toward longer commentaries. Most of these were written in the 1980s, and they continue to appear in the 1990s (see this book's bibliography). So Barnard's reputation as a management thinker has risen considerably in the last ten years. However, amidst this flurry of recognition the context of the period in which he wrote has been neglected. My purpose is to call attention to his work once again.

The first four chapters treat the major influences that shaped his thinking. Chapter 1 is about the development of the American managerial state and its ideology. Chapter 2 describes the management revolution in terms of heightened professional and class awareness. Chapter 3 considers the contribution of the Harvard Circle, an unusual group of people who had a profound influence on management education, research, and theory, as well as on Barnard's own ideas. The biographical sketch of Barnard's life in chapter 4 is an essential transition between the larger influences in his environment and the more specific ideas he proposed about management. Although inadequate as biographies go, this chapter is designed to answer a few questions about Barnard's background and important associations. Of special importance in this regard were the thirty-nine years he spent as an executive with ATT. Chapters 5 through 10 treat various Barnardian theories. Chapter 5 traces, as much as possible, the sources of Barnard's chief concepts and presents his epistemology of the social sciences. Chapter 6 begins our inquiry into his theories with the smallest units of his analysis, the individual and the informal organization. The formal organization, the subject of chapter 7, covers Barnard's sociology of complex organizations. With these two levels of analysis considered, the way is opened for a discussion of Barnard's broader concepts, and they include the ideal attributes of character for elitist managers, chapter 8; the moral responsibilities of that elite, chapter 9; and in chapter 10, the politics and government of the new managerial order. Finally the question of the future significance of Barnard's work has to be raised. This question is not so much about the validity of his management concepts per se, but more about his defense of managerial ideology. In this century, managerialism has budded, bloomed, and faded. Since Barnard had so much to do with the way that it rose, one must also wonder about the defects in his vision that may have contributed to managerialism's decline. This is the work of chapter 11.

1

The Managerial Age

Contemporary historians use such terms as *reconstitution*,[1] *reconstruction*,[2] and *modernization*[3] to describe the interwar period. These words produce a feeling for the fundamental transformation of American institutions and leadership that was in motion then. Alchon put it bluntly that World War I, by highlighting the needs for industrial coordination, created in the 1920s "the institutionalization of a 'technocratic bargain' between social science and managerial institutions."[4] This bargain was an essential element in Herbert Hoover's New Era of "techno-corporatism," with its central project the coupling of social science to management. Many social science research studies and some philanthropic policies for funding projects were designed to ensure the triumph of the managerial state.

Shortly after World War II, such eminent management scholars as Dwight Waldo, Herbert Simon, and Peter Drucker proclaimed the success of that state in their public administration and business management books.[5] And the business historian Alfred D. Chandler, Jr., capped it all off with the statement in 1977, "Rarely in the history of the world has an institution grown to be so important and so pervasive [as management] in such a short period of time."[6] By any measure, the twenty years between the two world wars were the most important in management's history, because that was when its theoretical grounds were established and its ideological values were formed.

THE IDEOLOGY OF MANAGERIALISM
AND THE AMERICAN DREAM

At no time during the nineteenth or twentieth centuries was the reputation of the businessman higher than in the 1890s, the Gilded Age of American capitalism.[7] Successful business leaders were lionized as exemplars, proof that the dream of affluence was open to anyone with pluck and luck. Their wealth gave them influence, and they strode in the corridors of American power, certain that their position was unassailable. Who could ever displace such titans as John D. Rockefeller, Cornelius Vanderbilt, Andrew Carnegie, Henry Clay Frick, and J. P. Morgan? While some critics, such as Thorstein Veblen and Ida Tarbell, exposed their foibles, these businessmen's suzerainty seemed impervious to significant threats. Consequently, it was startling that they were rather easily displaced by professional managers as the new ruling class.

Underneath the baroque glitter of the end of the last century, strong currents of reform were moving. The more perceptive could discern the shape of a coming new age. Henry Adams wrote of his return to New York in 1904:

> The city had the air and movement of hysteria, and the citizens were crying, in every accent of anger and alarm, that the new forces must at any cost be brought under control. Prosperity never before imagined, power never yet wielded by man, speed never reached by anything but a meteor, had made the world irritable, nervous, querulous, unreasonable and afraid. All New York was demanding new men, and all the new forces, condensed into corporations, were demanding a new type of man . . . for whom they were willing to pay millions at sight.[8]

As Adams implied, many doubted that the traditional business elite had either the foresight or the integrity to advance the cause of progress for the majority. As their popular esteem diminished after the turn of the century, the old czars of business and government, tainted by private greed and public corruption, were less able to counter the vision of the Progressive reformers in Henry Adams's age.

Although the name most commonly associated with the Progressive movement is that of Theodore Roosevelt, Woodrow Wilson was far more significant. As early as 1887, when he was a young professor at Bryn Mawr, Wilson published a prescient and influential article entitled "The Study of Administration."[9] He argued for the reform of the civil service by the professionalization of government administrators. He contended that the improvement of the "organization and methods of our government offices" could be achieved through the application of the "science of administration," as it was being invented, developed, and applied by the great businesses and the management associations in those days.

Even though the Progressives differed widely in their opinions, they agreed on the need for the reform of government and business institutions with rational management based on scientific principles. Most of all, the Progressives concurred, those in leadership positions needed to be competent and to have impeccable moral integrity.

In the years leading to his presidency, Wilson was an outspoken critic of the insensitivity of the traditional business elite. Herbert Hoover wrote "[Wilson's] philosophy of American living was based upon free enterprise, both in social and economic systems."[10] For Wilson, then, professional management was to be an instrument of reform for the institutions that he cared for, "The object of administrative study is to rescue executive methods from the confusion and costliness of empirical experiment and set them upon foundations laid deep in stable principle."[11] Those principles that Wilson identified were the Progressive ideals of efficiency, science, rationality, competency, and moral integrity.

So as the outmoded leadership of the past lost favor, the reputations of the imperious men who represented it collapsed and their power declined. But who were the "new men" who replaced them? Some, particularly Veblen, had predicted that they would be engineers, and certain numbers of them were, such as Hoover. However, for the most part they were from the middle and lower classes— individuals distinguished by an education in the new discipline of management and experienced in the new organizational tasks of the manager.

Demography was one reason for the democratization of the managerial class. The social base of management had to be broadened since there were not enough old aristocrats to fill the top jobs becoming available in the growing numbers of American organizations. Therefore these positions were no longer solely preserves for the sons of the wealthy. As America's former aristocracy of industrialists, merchants, financiers, and landowners gave way, their places of power were taken by people rising from the ranks of the petite bourgeoisie, farmers, urban industrial workers, and technicians.[12] Their legitimacy was not based on property ownership, inherited wealth, and election to popular office but on the control of property, professional credentials, merit-based appraisal methods, and the widely held belief among Americans in the efficacy of managerial expertise for creating higher standards of living. The new managerial class seemed progressive, democratic, and American.

This shift of power to professional management was imperceptible at first. But a new epoch had dawned, and as it accelerated, it changed institutional relationships. These new leaders tended to not call attention to themselves. So in quiet and unspectacular ways, the managerial state grew with a leadership mandated to modernize the nation and to reconcile the inherently conflicting values of democracy and efficiency, freedom and technology, and personal and functional morality.

Managerialism was born within this context, and it has persisted as a constant historical theme throughout this century. The economist William Alberts's metaphor "golden eggs and tranquility"[13] captures the essence of its ideology: its pledge to provide the people with the good fortunes of social harmony and material affluence. In the words of Alberts's metaphor this meant that professional managers had to lay the golden eggs of material abundance and see to it that they successfully hatched, for from them came the tranquility of national consensus. Looking through this ideological lens, management leaders saw themselves as the guardians of American modernization and the stewards of the organizational engines that brought peace, prosperity, and progress to the country. The productive husbanding of the critical relationship between consensus and materialism, therefore, was the litmus test of management's legitimacy.

The managerial class believed that it could accomplish this end on its own, provided there were appropriate institutional arrangements that permitted cooperation among top managers for coordinating their organizational policies, that emphasized technical merit and competency in rewarding individual managers with power and privilege, and that ensured that the vast discretionary powers of top managers were bounded by an ingrained ethical sense of what was right. Given these preconditions, the public could be assured that its managerial rulers would do well what it wanted them to do. To achieve this congruity of aims between the leaders and the led was the purpose of a novel American political formula.

The political philosopher Gaetano Mosca held that the first step in obtaining political legitimacy was for leadership to gain the public's acceptance of the moral principles for which it stood. He wrote, "One is not governed on the basis of material or intellectual force, but on the basis of moral principle."[14] As mentioned above, material progress and social harmony were those principles in America. National leaders defined them with concrete policies that put great weight on using resources efficiently, achieving material well-being for citizens, securing social stability based upon equality and welfare, pursuing national self-sufficiency, and advancing the nation's hegemony in the world. As the political scientist John H. Schaar wrote, "The test of legitimacy . . . meant just about what it always has meant: security and national abundance."[15]

The international search for such formulas began around the turn of the century but was hastened by World War I and the wrenching economic and political crises that followed it. Devastated European nations sought new political approaches for reconstructing their social orders. Bolshevism, fascism, and national socialism emerged in the Soviet Union, Italy, and Germany. These revolutionary movements carried ill winds that blew across the Atlantic ocean to America. Ideologically challenging, they confronted the American values of individualism and capitalism. Wallace B. Donham, dean of the Harvard business school, warned that the prosperity of the 1920s had obscured, "temporarily, fundamental conditions of real seriousness."[16] He argued that this grace period, during which American radicalism had waned, should be used by the American business group to reconstruct the social order with a working philosophy that had an idealistic basis "far away from the materialistic basis that it was at present constructed." Donham's statement was published in 1927; his fears were soon confirmed.

Threats from abroad seemed palpable at the time. While Mussolini's popularity in America is hard now to imagine, foreign propagandists could claim, with some truth, that their governments' totalitarian doctrines and cults of personal leadership settled domestic unrest, solved social problems, restored economic stability, and improved the material lot of their citizens. Hitler did end the crushing unemployment in Germany early in the 1930s; Lenin destroyed a hated autocratic regime; and Mussolini got the beggars off the streets of Rome. These totalitarian states appeared to have found political formulas that seemed to unriddle the intractable social and economic puzzles that beset nations in the desperate days of the 1920s and 1930s.

Some Americans were enthusiastic. The journalist Lincoln Steffens rhapsodized in his pro-Soviet autobiography, "I have been over into the future . . . and it works."[17] Even Barnard, a conservative corporate executive, was stirred by the Soviet Union and recorded his impressions in a pamphlet that chronicled his thoughts about Leningrad and Moscow when he visited them in 1939.[18] He observed that these cities were orderly and clean, few police were in sight, there was an absence of signs of extreme poverty, and the people seemed in good health. The only discordant note about daily life was the placement of loudspeakers bellowing propaganda on every main intersection. The noise disturbed Barnard.

However, he had little patience for Marxian economics. He wrote, "Marx was writing bunk and he was a good enough economist to know it."[19] Furthermore, Stalin's regimentation of Soviet society appalled Barnard, but he thought it would work as long as "people believe that it is a system that serves their private interest."[20] He acknowledged that the Communists' "organizing principle" seemed to function for them and that it enabled the Communist party to amalgamate an ethnically and racially diverse people, so securing its citizens' cooperation in nation building. The party was successful with its political formula because of the galvanizing power of its moral principles and because of the willingness of party leadership to endure great personal hardship to advance them. This fortified Barnard's view that people needed such principles to bond their commitment to a cooperative undertaking. The problem was to develop an American political formula with peculiarly American moral principles and values that would create cooperative unity in this country.

But the American quest for a new political formula was not solely a reflexive response to foreign threats. America needed to change its social order to cope effectively, on its own terms, with the demands of modern times. It found such a formula in an institutional network composed of traditional organizations run by professional managers under the oversight powers of the legislative branch of government. The politicians and the managers who were involved in the practical affairs of establishing a national agenda seemed to share with Americans at large the conflicting values of capitalism, collectivism, cooperation, equality, and individual freedom.

THE RISE OF THE MANAGERIAL STATE

The animus of the managerial state is corporatism. It has been associated with the political formula imposed on Italy by Mussolini in the 1920s, earning for it an unhappy identification with fascism. However, it can be seen in a more neutral light. Corporatism is a form of national organization in which the leaders of major institutions and occupational associations work together cooperatively, either voluntarily or pressed by government, to make and to fulfill national policy goals.

America got its first sample of corporatism during World War I, when the main national priority was to mobilize the country's resources for an all-out war effort. The old and wasteful ways of peacetime had to yield to a war imperative. This imperative required cooperation among institutional leaders and sacrifices from individual citizens. Further, it demanded the application of rational management practices that increased industrial productivity. This in turn catapulted professional managers into positions of power because they alone had the specialized knowledge and technical skills to administer and to coordinate the huge interconnected institutional apparatus, known as the "war system."

Upon entering the war, President Wilson lost no time establishing the necessary executive agencies and boards, under the aegis of the federal government, to regulate essential sectors of the economy. Agencies were set up that controlled prices, wages, hours of work, material resources, markets, and a multitude of other matters that concerned the war effort. Among these agencies was the Food Administration, headed by Herbert Hoover. This agency had regulatory powers to license and control farmers and businesses, to buy and sell produce, and to stimulate production of food commodities. It had the authority to control the prices of food directly at the consumer level, but it did not. Under Hoover the agency introduced an advertising campaign that successfully encouraged the public to restrict its consumption of strategic commodities. This self-imposed, patriotically inspired rationing impressed Hoover, proving to him the value of the people's voluntary cooperation for "their own satisfaction and the nation's profit."[21]

The War Industries Board (WIB) was the industrial counterpart to Food Administration. It mediated between the government and private corporate contractors of military supplies and equipment. Difficult as the work of the Food Administration was, the task of the WIB was exponentially more complicated. Wall Street financier Bernard M. Baruch inherited a mess when he became chairman of the WIB in 1918. In late 1917, allied military leaders were concerned that the spring offensive planned for 1918 would fail because of a breakdown in the supply system.

Baruch assumed broad powers when he took over the WIB. His tactics—combining threats, cajoling, and clever manipulative ploys, with no small amount of personal financial risk (his maneuvers left him vulnerable to lawsuits)—were generally successful. He was able at least to open some of the bottlenecks that blocked the production of strategic supplies, particularly gunpowder and motor vehicles. He also achieved a standardization of many commodities such as automobiles, tires, and farm plows, which resulted in the conservation of raw materials for military use.

Baruch headed the WIB for just eight months. It was disbanded when the war ended. However, his service to government was not over. He was heard from again when Franklin D. Roosevelt was elected president.[22]

The hastily constructed war system was the first serious American attempt to suspend some of its traditional, deeply rooted populist prejudices against monopoly, giantism, collectivism, and statism. The war system made cartelization seem patriotic. It discouraged individual entrepreneuring as selfish and unworthy behavior when cooperation for the good of the nation was required. And, finally, it granted to the federal government unprecedented authority to centralize its administrative control over much of the economy. Thus, despite its improvisations, the war system produced prodigious amounts of war materiel and transported it from American shores to France. This accomplishment, when coupled with the infusion of fresh American troops on the Western front, foretold the defeat of the Central Powers.

As historian Ellis Hawley has pointed out, the war system stimulated America's quest for a new managerial and organizational order.[23] Although its life was brief, the war system made a considerable impression on the people who worked in it, some of them already public figures who would rise to even greater prominence in the following decades. They, like Baruch, went to Washington during the first term of Roosevelt's New Deal. Others had distinguished careers in industry. Barnard worked with the U.S. Telephone Commission and his mentor, Walter S. Gifford, the executive director of the WIB under Baruch, later became president of ATT.

As Gifford and Barnard, many corporate managers served the war system. After the war these same managers returned to their companies and influenced the direction of American modernization. Historian Robert D. Cuff wrote of them: "The WIB men of World War I directed one of the most ambitious attempts at institutional coordination in American history. Sophisticated in ideology and skilled in their managerial ability, they set out to mobilize the country's economic resources for war and to protect its industrial economy for peace. They achieved a great deal in the short time available to them and built up a fund of experience and knowledge for crisis managers of the future."[24]

Alchon observed that the bureaucratic structures of the war period contributed to the development of managerialism in four specific ways. First, they allowed social scientists to establish themselves as "disinterested professionals" serving a public cause that bridged the "gulf between scientist as observer and scientist as planner." Second, the merger of public and private interests for the sake of the war effort highlighted the importance of a national cause for entrenching in power management leaders who seemed to transcend politics and selfish interests. Third, the war system created a network of personal and professional associations among organizational technocrats that carried over into the postwar period. And fourth, the system encouraged the collection of information that promised to improve the vision of management decisionmakers by adding the "eyes" of statistics.[25]

More generally, the war system acted as a kind of administrative laboratory in

which government and business officials saw the policies of industrial coordination and planning, decision centralization, and rational management succeed on a
massive cross-institutional scale. Business executives had, of course, realized the
benefits of these policies but were hampered from putting them widely into
practice by antitrust laws and public opinion. The war system suspended these
restrictions for a short time, and it added the force of the federal government to
coordinate national policy. This experience with corporatism quickened the pace
of the United States toward its managerial state.

Post–World War I Developments

Of all the world's leaders of this period, Mussolini may have been the first to have
a clear idea of the principles and structure of the modern managerial state. He
thought of it in a way that can be crudely described as a matrix organization
applied to an entire nation. While still a primitive notion, one axis of this matrix
contained the vocational associations of the working and professional classes
while the other arrayed the major syndicates of industrial and financial cartels.
Presiding over this matrix, and participating in it, was the central government, in
turn vitalized by a dynamic leader.

Although Mussolini has been justly maligned for his bombast, fecklessness,
and cruelty, he was, nonetheless, a visionary intellectual of some substance and
flexibility. He dreamed of resurrecting ancient Roman glories in a modernized
Italy, and he saw the means for doing it in the fascist government he installed
when he took control of the country in 1922. In greater or lesser degrees, both the
democratic and totalitarian nations of the West, including the United States,
followed Mussolini's organizational model. Their leaders wanted a system that
would wrap up in one neat package of cooperation all of the major institutions of
a modern industrial state. Consequently, the managerial state rose to prominence
because it seemed the optimum instrument to achieve national progress and to
respond to destabilizing crises that could detract from it. Most Western nations
came to this conclusion rather quickly; Mussolini, however, was the first world
leader to sense the direction of the new order and act decisively on it.[26]

Government structures, however, should not conceal the fact that these managerial states were essentially administrative apparatuses through which national
ideological and political goals were pursued. But they were not morally equivalent, and they differed widely in terms of national goals. So it was consistent for
Americans to recoil in horror at the descriptions of how Stalin used the Soviet
state apparatus to exterminate the Kulaks and to purge officialdom in the Communist party during the 1930s, while accepting with relative equanimity the New
Deal reforms that Roosevelt wrought by government during the same period.
Consequently, although the interdependent image of national institutional arrangements and the machinery for managing them was similar, the ideological

ends of nations in the 1920s and 1930s varied greatly, depending upon their history, culture, and leadership goals.

The New American Order: The Hoover Era

While Lenin, Stalin, and Mussolini worked their schemes in the 1920s, Herbert Hoover was publicizing and implementing his rendition of the managerial state in the United States. Hoover got his first taste of the corporative state in action with his work with the Belgian food relief program and then with the war system's Food Administration agency. These were important experiences for him because they demonstrated the power of national management, cooperation, and voluntarism. But beyond this, Hoover learned about making plans and implementing controls on a national scale. Extrapolating from Food Administration to the war system as a whole, Hoover concluded that an "associative state" was essential to secure future American prosperity and progress.

Philosophically, Hoover was no statist. He believed that centralized government would extinguish American individualism. Nevertheless, the war system's promise of greater social efficiency through cooperation appealed to Hoover's humane and engineering instincts. The problem was to encourage the cooperation of organizational leaders without government playing a dominant part in policy-making of the private sector, except in its opposition of monopolies.

Yet his economic policies were not laissez-faire. As secretary of commerce for eight years in two administrations, he formulated many government programs that included conservation, public education, housing, waste prevention, agriculture, and child health.[27] He used the power of the federal government to threaten boycotts against the English rubber and Brazilian coffee cartels. These countries had monopolized those commodities and sent their prices skyrocketing in the United States. Hoover was not beneath taking retaliatory measures that would withhold American cotton from the English market and financial investment from Brazil. He sought the cooperation of American cotton producers and Wall Street bankers to lend support to these countermeasures.[28] In both domestic and foreign policy, as historian Melvyn P. Leffler has noted, Hoover emphasized "the interdependence of the modern world, . . . the use of experts, . . . and private voluntary cooperative action."[29] There was little in government in which Hoover did not have his hand during the Harding and Coolidge administrations.

Hoover has been described as a government interventionist and as an industrial corporatist. These attributions are correct as far as they go, but he also preached a circumscribed role for federal government that stemmed from his deeply held belief in individualism. However, Hoover's individualism did not include destructive competition or the uncontrolled pursuit of personal advantage. He wrote in his slim but important 1922 book, *American Individualism*,[30] about what he believed were the two "deadlines" that had to be drawn in American life: the deadline of state regimentation on the one hand and the deadline of rampant individualism on the other hand. These deadlines were the polar points on his ideological continuum, and he stated that neither was appropriate policy for the United States when moving into the new era that he envisioned.

He instead imagined an era in which interdependent private organizations voluntarily forged cooperative arrangements among themselves, with the federal government lending a helping hand to encourage those efforts. Hoover expected marvelous results from such voluntary cooperation: greater productivity, reduction of waste, improved living standards, and an effective American response to foreign ideological challenges. He wrote, "There are in the cooperative great hopes that we can even gain in individuality, equal opportunity, and an enlarged field for initiative, and at the same time reduce many of the wastes of over-reckless competition in production and distribution."[31]

This interesting blend of individualism and voluntary cooperation in the quest for efficiency and social justice was the essence of Hoover's philosophy of the American managerial state—a species of Progressive conservationism that molded his approach to domestic and foreign policy issues. Using a scientific apolitical rhetoric, he encouraged a form of corporatism that was uniquely American. He saw in it the opportunity for American individualism to blend with a national network of institutional cooperation guided by expert managerial leaders coming mainly from this country's dominant organizations in the private sector. Cooperation under this regime's moral authority would produce, in the long run, the greatest benefits for all Americans.

Hoover's cooperative ideal was shared by many members of the intelligentsia, although they differed among themselves about the nature and degree of influence that government should have in national affairs. The philosophical problems that concerned them had to do with the relationship between the individual's need for freedom versus society's need for order. Although not a novel issue, the way that those who were active in public life treated this relationship was revealing. Barnard, for example, repeated in 1938 Hoover's admonitory "deadlines," stating that Americans should not tolerate those who argue for systems of vast regimentation or unbridled freedom.[32]

Elaborating on this point in a 1940 speech, Barnard said, "Our most important liberties are not freedom of democracy but freedom from government—democratic or otherwise."[33] In a book review published six years later, he explained: "The most general condition of freedom is that of order. We cannot have freedom without order. We apparently cannot have order and all our freedoms too."[34] On the surface, these views may seem almost like Orwellian doublespeak: "freedom is slavery." However, Barnard had a Hooverian reconciliation of these contradictory ideas. His alternative, like Hoover's, was the voluntary association and cooperation of the American managerial elite, whose leadership would provide an "ordered freedom" for the people. There was too much similarity between Barnard's and Hoover's positions on this matter to be a coincidence.

Hoover's philosophy was gravely tested during the depression, as that calamity intensified during his presidency. His efforts to find work for the unemployed failed and the economy did not respond to his policies. Hoover lost credibility and was defeated in the presidential election of 1932. Franklin D. Roosevelt promised the country a "new deal" to replace Hoover's "new era." But through all this, the continuity of the managerial state was not interrupted, and it evolved along the lines that were established for it during the twelve years of Hoover's reign.[35] Hoover's policies, and more importantly his conception of the nation's corporative realpolitik, stamped the American managerial state with its distinctive hallmark of voluntary cooperation among those peer decisionmakers who ran its major interdependent institutions.

The New American Order: The Early Roosevelt Era

The crash of 1929 and the ensuing depression signalled the end of decades of excesses that began with the robber barons in the 1880s and ran through the wild speculations in the 1920s. After the votes were tallied in 1932, a clear mandate had been given for an activist-interventionist government to cope with the economic emergency as well as to protect labor and to stimulate a working relationship between it and business, to seek equality among citizens through taxation and welfare, to stabilize the social order by creating a more just and efficient political economy, and to increase government services. It was a large order, but Roosevelt claimed that his New Deal could fill it, and the voters had faith in that prospect. They wanted a crusading public sector led by the federal government that would end the woes of the depression by putting "America back to work." Private enterprise was singled out as the cause of the economic hardship, and the alternative seemed to be a clean, reform-oriented government, led by a person with the charm and magnetism of FDR.

While the New Deal introduced major structural and functional changes in the country, a value shift also occurred that had profound implications for the American managerial state. The balance of moral authority moved from private to public leadership. Barnard had seen this coming and had argued that the professional managers of the largest and most powerful American corporations had to be as dedicated, energetic, and committed to reform as their administrative counterparts in government. Only then could they hope to reassert their rightful leadership authority that was being dangerously preempted by the zealots who Roosevelt appointed to government posts.

Roosevelt knew how to pick advisors for his first term. Some of them had served in the old WIB—Baruch, for example, as well as Gen. Hugh Johnson who became chief of the National Recovery Administration (NRA). Others were liberal-minded economists and lawyers, many of whom were from the academic community at prestigious eastern universities—Rexford Tugwell and Adolph Berle from Columbia and Felix Frankfurter from Harvard (who brought with him into government a number of young attorneys who were collectively known as his "little hot dogs"). Roosevelt, furthermore, enlisted the aid of industrialists and heads of trade associations to help him in the task of reform by drafting and enforcing legislation to reverse the dour economic trends. It was not surprising, for example, that the Chamber of Commerce and the National Association of Manufacturers applauded the passage of the National Industrial Recovery Act (NIRA). They, or their closely associated representatives, had a hand in writing most of the provisions of this new law. With the exception of section 7a pertaining to collective bargaining, this act was prepared by business leaders working collaboratively with the officials of the new administration.

The NIRA and its administrative arm, the National Recovery Administration, were examples of the new government's intention to preserve the continuity of the American managerial state and to breathe life into its corporative animus. It did two things immediately: it suspended antitrust laws for two years, and it vested broad discretionary powers in the executive branch of government. But it also made explicit and legitimate the network of institutional collaboration that had been a shadow government in this country from the end of World War I. The industry codes that the NRA supervised were the mechanisms of this undertaking. These codes were framed in such a way that each industry's self-interest was specified. Most of the trade associations, which were instrumental in writing these codes, demanded price-fixing power and market allocations for companies within each industry. In return for these privileges they had to consent to collective bargaining and to minimum wages and hours for workers. Furthermore, in many instances the trade associations themselves became the authorities responsible for ensuring compliance to the codes by their member firms. Thus, one representative of the New York coat and suit industry could say, "When the NRA came we were all ready for it."[36] He meant that labor and industry had the working relationships and the organizational machinery for complying with the law before its enactment. The garment industry in New York was an ideal place for NRA corporatism to flourish, since it had a history of cooperation among independent companies, trade associations, and labor unions. As historian Dwight Robinson recorded, it was indeed prepared to translate this experience into the code provisions required by the new law.[37]

The NRA was successful in capturing the popular attention. Its logo of a blue eagle was quickly adopted and exhibited on many products of the period. It informed the public that the product purchased was made by a company that observed the code of the industry. The implication was that management was doing its part to help the nation recover from the depression.

However, the NIRA was more than industrial codes and positive-thinking propaganda. It symbolized a shift in the moral authority of national leadership to a crusading government. Americans were enticed by the benefits promised by the new activism of government, especially of the kind that the NIRA represented.

The influential New Dealer, Rexford Tugwell, concluded his book, *Industrial Discipline*, with the words:

> What is required in view of the nature of industry is a recognition of the desirability of large scale and of concentration. . . . Such a recognition would cause us to abandon attempts to prevent association and to enforce conflict. . . . An industrial administration of some sort, being supreme in this field, might use its superior knowledge and power to devise a system of affairs in which each unit would be complementary to each other one, in which cooperation, rather than . . . conflict, should be the organizing principle.[38]

Although Hoover abhorred monopolies and was not as confident as Tugwell about the value of government intervention, he would have agreed with him about cooperation and the use of expertise in managing organizations efficiently on an industrywide basis.

Tugwell's philosophy of industrial combination and coordination under federal government authority was the early approach for New Deal reform. However, it was thwarted when in 1935 the Supreme Court declared the NIRA unconstitutional. Roosevelt, a consummate pragmatist, shifted direction. He moved next to reorganize the executive branch of the government. In 1936 he commissioned the Committee on Administrative Management, chaired by Louis Brownlow and including Luther Gulick and Charles Merriam.[39] The purpose of the committee, according to Stanley M. Milkis, was to create a bipartisan "administrative presidency" that would neutralize party politics and bypass the other two branches of government.[40] As Luther Gulick put it, the great need of the times was to transform the federal government into "a superholding company of economic life."[41]

This reorganization strategy was partially successful. By the late 1930s Roosevelt achieved many of the reform goals he sought in his first term. However, the solution to the depression still eluded him. It took World War II, not government reorganization, to solve it. Nevertheless, the single most important landmark of growing federal power in the American managerial state was the Brownlow report, *Administrative Management*. From its recommendations and subsequent executive actions, the national debate over the locus of moral authority in America was brought to center stage.

THE REALITY OF THE AMERICAN MANAGERIAL STATE

Modern views of the managerial state are narrow restatements of the New Deal reform legacy. The present orthodoxy in the fields of public administration and business management holds that the managerial state (often called the administrative state) is characterized by activist government composed of specialized agencies, usually on the federal level, empowered by law to regulate, promote and control economic, welfare, and military policies in the public interest.

The American reality departs from this interpretation in a very important way. Our managerial state is a system of shared institutional power held by an elite class of professional technocratic peers. While not denying the prominence of government, this reality is centered upon the dynamic and creative aspects of the elite rulership in a pluralistic network that includes many different organizations and institutions. Major figures in government and business conceived of it precisely in the terms of such cooperative alliances during the early stages of its formation.

For example, the sociologist George C. Homans and his coauthor Charles P. Curtis, Jr., contemporary observers in the 1920s and 1930s, approved of what they were witnessing. They wrote, "The governmental elite includes not only those holding the higher posts in the administration but also, in modern societies, the powerful financiers, industrialists . . . and the high ranking officers of the military forces."[42] Homans and Curtis articulated a view broadly held in the ruling circles. Most of those in this circle realized that more was at stake than simply efficient structural arrangements. The contest was over the locus of power and the preeminence of moral authority among those in the leadership elite.

Donham claimed in a 1927 article that management leaders in business had the obligation of national stewardship thrust upon them because they controlled the great corporate engines of finance, distribution, and production. He said that the giant corporation "must be reasonably trustworthy since it has met the test of survival." He concluded that "it inevitably tends therefore, to choose trustworthy men for its organization . . . the type of men who are trustworthy in dealing with the public."[43] In Donham's opinion the competitive world of business ensured that the best would rise to the top as the result of a Darwinian survival struggle that eliminated the immoral and incompetent. But Wilson and Franklin Roosevelt had a different idea. They felt that federal executives were morally cauterized by public service since its aim was to advance the public interest.

This debate about moral authority was of supreme importance because the public favor garnered by one side or the other determined, at least temporarily, the distribution of political and economic power within the managerial leadership class. The issue, fortunately, has not been permanently settled. Historically, moral authority has alternated between public and private sector managers. This shifting balance of power within the elite network has been a source of vitality for the American managerial state from its inception, and together with congressional oversight, a protection from tyranny.

But each polemicist argues for a cause, so it is no surprise that those who favor the public sector have written warmly about its virtues. The public administration scholar John Rohr observed: "The administrative state is in reality the welfare/warfare state we know so well. Despite its warts and wrinkles, it has provided the underpinnings of the free, decent, and prosperous society most Americans have enjoyed for the past half-century."[44] Hoover, as might be expected, was less sanguine about the beneficence of government activism. He wrote: "The perpetual howl of radicalism is that it is the sole voice of liberalism. . . . These men would assume that all reform and human advance must come through government."[45] Although Hoover wrote these words in 1922, there are now many who support policies of deregulation and privatization who would heartily agree with them. The rhetoric of this debate is not hollow because it reflects the essence of American political discourse during this century.

Although Wilson-Roosevelt and Hoover-Barnard-Donham came from opposing camps on the moral authority issue, they had similar appreciations of the structural and cooperative nature of the managerial state. They agreed on the terms of the debate. They accepted the fact that the managerial state had to be ruled by managers of skill and knowledge. But much more than this, they believed that the managerial elite functioned as America's harmonizing agency, giving it a form of ordered freedom that would resolve the social antagonisms that arose from competition. Peace and social harmony through cooperation were meta-ideological goals that were as important to Barnard and his conservative circle as they were for the liberals. And so it fell to the planners and organizers in the professional management class to reconstruct America.

But there were some distressing criticisms of the emerging managerial order. For example, James Burnham in 1941 asked the readers of his book *The Managerial Revolution* to consider the rise of the managerial class as a dialectical process that resulted in a new economic system that would be neither capitalistic nor socialistic.[46] Managerialism, and the class system it spawned, was something different, and as all class systems exploit, the managerial class would exploit as well. Hindsight shows how correct Burnham was in his general assessment of the economic organization and the social hierarchy that evolved in advanced nations before World War II.

Burnham was by no means first to object to managerialism. As early as 1910, management's rising power had been challenged when Wilson warned of the unrestrained power of some top corporate executives.[47] By 1927 William Z. Ripley worried that managers had an uncomfortable amount of control over corporate assets.[48] In 1933 Adolph A. Berle and Gardiner C. Means corroborated Ripley's qualms in their famous study, *The Modern Corporation and Private Property*.[49] Harking back to a Wilsonian principle, they concluded that America would be best served if its corporations were guided by public policy. If not, the public interest would be held hostage to the private cupidity of managers. The Berle and Means study provided Burnham with the sort of data he needed to support his argument that executives' control of access to corporate resources would enable them to expropriate those resources for their own purposes. In Burnham's opinion the likelihood of private cupidity among managers was far greater than was the chance for their selfless corporate stewardship.

Burnham has had many critics, and George Orwell was one of the first of them. Orwell could not abide class theories because of his deep political commitment to social democracy. Since Burnham's thesis depended on elitist premises, he was fair game for Orwell. Summarizing Burnham's ideas, he wrote:

> Capitalism is disappearing, but socialism is not replacing it. What is now arising is a new kind of planned, centralized society which will be neither capitalist nor, in any accepted sense of the word, democratic. The rulers of this new society will be the people who effectively control the means of production: that is, business executives, technicians, bureaucrats, and soldiers, lumped together by Burnham under the name of "managers." These people will eliminate the old capitalist class, crush the working class, and so organize society that all power and economic privilege remain in their own hands.[50]

In his rejection of Burnham's thesis, Orwell captured its essence with considerable accuracy. Blinded by his own ideological predispositions, Orwell may not have had the perspective to interpret correctly the sweeping events that fundamentally changed power relationships within some industrial nations from around 1920 onward. Alternatively, Burnham wrote about these power shifts during the interwar period with remarkable insight. Some scholars now acknowledge that Burnham was right and that Orwell's criticism of him was misplaced.[51]

Regardless of whether Burnham was right, the dissenting opinions of those who preceded him struck at the issue that was the heart of managerial legitimacy, the congruity of management's interests with those of the public. No one was more aware of this than Barnard. He rushed to the defense of corporate management, especially in *The Functions of the Executive*, and tried to legitimate its leadership role in America. Therefore, first and foremost, Barnard's work must be understood as an ideological attempt to restate the Progressive case for the consistency of the American dream with the managerial order in the face of criticisms by those who saw managerialism as something less than a blessing upon the land.

Concurrent with the emergence of the managerial state was a management revolution in techniques and attitudes that promised to fulfill Progressive ideals through the application in organizations of new social engineering technologies and through a heightened awareness among managers themselves of their obligations as the guardians of the national agenda.

2

The Management Revolution

Frederick W. Taylor in 1911 called the management revolution a "mental" revolution because it reordered the way management thought about itself and its methods for bringing prosperity to employees, customers, and investors.[1] Dwight Waldo later characterized this new thinking by management as heightened "self-awareness."[2]

This radical transformation had two aspects. First, management became aware of itself as a profession with concepts, research methods, and specialized techniques of practice that could be studied, taught, communicated, and improved by the acquisition of scientific information regarding human behavior, management functions, and organizational structure. Second, and of equal importance, managers became aware of themselves as members of a distinct class set apart from others by their possession of arcane knowledge and position within the structure of organizational power. The time line shown in Figure 2.1 records some of the major events that led to this transformation, and by 1941, thanks to Barnard and Burnham, the essential theories of the management revolution were in place.

HEIGHTENED PROFESSIONAL AWARENESS

The invigorating myths and sagas that surrounded the old order had lost their appeal well before World War I. In its place, Progressivism drove national reform in a loosely defined, diverse movement linked initially to city and state "better government" campaigns of the 1880s.

Progressivism quickly expanded its scope beyond government because it held that science, rationality, efficiency, competence, and moral integrity should apply to the management of all public and private organizations. The public was assured by Progressive spokesmen that if managers pursued these enlightened reform ideals, the nation would prosper.

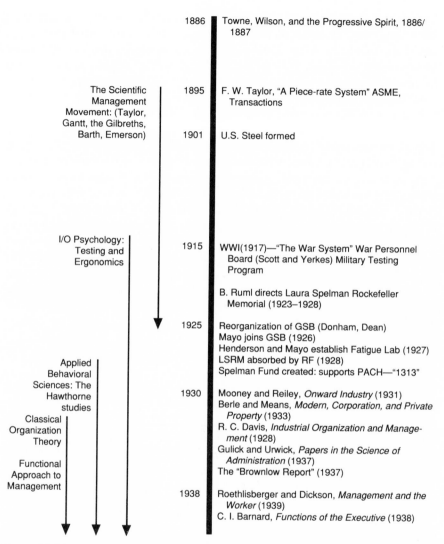

The Scientific Management Movement: (Taylor, Gantt, the Gilbreths, Barth, Emerson)

I/O Psychology: Testing and Ergonomics

Applied Behavioral Sciences: The Hawthorne studies

Classical Organization Theory

Functional Approach to Management

1886	Towne, Wilson, and the Progressive Spirit, 1886/1887
1895	F. W. Taylor, "A Piece-rate System" ASME, Transactions
1901	U.S. Steel formed
1915	WWI(1917)—"The War System" War Personnel Board (Scott and Yerkes) Military Testing Program
	B. Ruml directs Laura Spelman Rockefeller Memorial (1923–1928)
1925	Reorganization of GSB (Donham, Dean) Mayo joins GSB (1926) Henderson and Mayo establish Fatigue Lab (1927) LSRM absorbed by RF (1928) Spelman Fund created: supports PACH—"1313"
1930	Mooney and Reiley, *Onward Industry* (1931) Berle and Means, *Modern, Corporation, and Private Property* (1933) R. C. Davis, *Industrial Organization and Management* (1928) Gulick and Urwick, *Papers in the Science of Administration* (1937) The "Brownlow Report" (1937)
1938	Roethlisberger and Dickson, *Management and the Worker* (1939) C. I. Barnard, *Functions of the Executive* (1938)

Figure 2.1. The management revolution: A time line of growing self-awareness (1886–1938).

The Progressive Origins of Management's Professionalization

Two remarkable statements were made in the 1880s that demonstrated the impact of Progressivism on management thought. The first was Henry Towne's address to the American Society of Mechanical Engineers (ASME) when he became its president in 1886;[3] the other was Woodrow Wilson's essay on efficiency in government published in 1887.[4] The title of Towne's speech, "The Engineer as an

Economist," captured one of Progressivism's essential ideals, efficiency. By linking management to engineering and economics, Towne, in a masterful stroke, joined the three in the common theme of technical rationality that had the purpose of increasing efficiency by manipulating the ratio of organizational outputs (goods and services) relative to organizational inputs (human, financial, and material resources)—E = O/I !

Towne, an industrialist, did not intend to make an intellectual tour de force. His immediate goal was to encourage the "shop managers," who were members of the ASME, to participate more actively in the association's affairs. Specifically, he wanted managers to submit to ASME meetings papers that examined management problems, interests, and practices. Although the initial response to Towne's urging was modest, five papers in nine years and all dealing with economic incentive plans for workers, eventually his wish was fulfilled. In 1895 Frederick W. Taylor presented to the annual meeting of the society his paper titled "A Piece-Rate System."[5] Management was never the same after it. This paper introduced the concept of differential payments for piecework and changed forever the way management designed wage incentive plans. But Taylor's ideas had a broader impact. He demonstrated that science could address and solve management problems, launching the scientific management movement on the same reformist trajectory as Progressivism.

The Scientific Management Movement

As most revolutions, management's had its tract writers. They were the Progressive-minded pioneers of scientific management who began to proselytize for their ideas of efficiency well before World War I. These people—Taylor, the Gilbreths, Emerson, Gantt, Cooke, and others—had a clear vision of the reforms they wanted to achieve in the management and organization of work. Such reforms had to be based on science, since it alone could increase efficiency. Efficiency, in turn, would raise productivity, lower costs, end want, solve labor problems, and lead to American supremacy in world affairs. Thus, their vision was entirely in accord with the moral principle of golden eggs and tranquility that was central to the political formula in this nation.

While their ideas might seem theoretical, these pioneers were practical people, actually management consultants, who hired themselves out to solve concrete business and government problems. Often decrying mere "theorizing," they wanted to increase the efficiency, productivity, wages, and profits of the factory, office, and retail store. Frank Gilbreth experimented successfully with motion study and work simplification.[6] When his discoveries were added to Taylor's time study system, the science of management created a new specialization, time and motion study. Frank's wife, Lillian, was the first American to try to put personnel management on a scientific basis. Her 1914 book, *The Psychology of Management,* discussed the application of scientific principles to personnel selection, place-ment, and training.[7]

However, in one of history's quirks, the scientific management pioneers are remembered more for their theory and research than for their work as efficiency experts. By fact gathering and concept validation, however crude, they estab-lished positive science as the epistemology of choice in management. Further-more, their emphasis on productivity set a normative tone for years to come by underscoring the necessary relationship between materialism and social consen-sus, otherwise known in the management field as the doctrine of "mutuality of interest."[8] Thus, productivity and social harmony became the yardsticks that measured management success and legitimacy.

However, these theoretical ideas were probably more appreciated in Europe than in America during this time. Walter Rathenau in Germany made rationaliza-tion somewhat akin to theology; Antonio Gramsci thought that Fordism, his word for rationalization, was necessary in Italy to banish its vestiges of feudalism; and Nikolai Lenin argued that Taylorism, though a capitalistic invention, should be used to further the proletarian revolution in Russia.[9] Consequently, professional management, inspired by science and materialistic values, was one of the few ideas that America exported to the Old World.

But the practical side of scientific management excited the American public, and it learned about it in the popular press. For example, public attention was captured in 1910 by the Interstate Commerce Commission's hearings on railroad rate making through the Eastern railroads' petition for increased rates. The attor-ney opposing the railroads, Louis D. Brandeis, later to become a justice on the Supreme Court, attacked them at their most vulnerable point. He claimed that the railroads could save a million dollars a day by using scientific management principles. This argument, according to Skowronek, "allowed a politically inse-cure and institutionally limited ICC to take refuge in a strong displinary posture in administrative regulation."[10] The railroads lost their appeal for higher rates, and scientific management garnered considerable publicity.[11] Several magazines asked Taylor to write articles on the subject for them, and Taylor settled on *The American Magazine* to publish a series.

As the fame of scientific management spread, the efficiency measures Taylor preached were endorsed not only by business leaders but also by spokesmen for educational and religious organizations. For example, the National Education Association and the High School Teachers Association recommended that schools hire efficiency experts. A superintendent of schools in Newton, Massachusetts, even reduced the number of pupil recitations to a common denominator so that the efficiency of teaching one subject could be compared to another. He deter-mined that the fiscal investment required to teach a pupil enough to give 5.9 recitations in Greek equalled 23.8 pupil recitations in French, 12 in science, and 47.7 in vocal music. What was taught was not important, but rather its relative cost compared to other subjects.[12]

Some church leaders were also seduced by the efficiency craze. One New York City pastor proclaimed from a billboard advertisement: "Come to church! Public worship increases your efficiency."[13] Another theologian wrote in an influential article about the churches' need for efficiency: "The age in which we live, more than any preceding one, emphasizes the divine principle of utility. This manifests itself in specialization of work, economy of material, time and excellence of product."[14] Bruce Barton, an advertising executive in the 1920s, portrayed Jesus as a young executive who forged twelve men of the lower ranks into the most efficient management team of all time.[15]

The popular enthusiasm for scientific management waned by the late 1920s. Its exaggerated claims, scientific pretensions, mean-spirited paternalistic applications, and improbable generalizations about the defective character of workers reduced its credibility. Taylor's discourse on the pig-iron handler is a classic illustration. He averred:

Now one of the very first requirements for a man who is fit to handle pig iron as a regular occupation is that he shall be so stupid and so phlegmatic that he more nearly resembles in his mental make up the ox than any other type. The man who is mentally alert and intelligent is for this very reason unsuited to what would, for him, be the grinding monotony of work of this character. Therefore, the workman who is best suited to handling pig iron is unable to understand the real science of doing this class of work. He is so stupid that the word "percentage" has no meaning for him, and he must consequently be trained by a man more intelligent than himself into the habit of working in accordance with the laws of this science before he can be successful.[16]

Taylor also responded to novelist Upton Sinclair, who wrote a scathing criticism of scientific management in *The American Magazine* after the publication of Taylor's series. Taylor replied to Sinclair's allegations that scientific management exploited workers:

A long series of experiments, coupled with close observation, has demonstrated the fact that when workmen of the calibre of the pig-iron handler are given a carefully measured task, which calls for a big day's work on their part, and that when in return for this extra effort they are paid wages up to 60 percent beyond the wages usually paid, that this increase in wages tends to make them not only more thrifty but better men in every way; that they live rather better, begin to save money, become more sober, and work more steadily. When, on the other hand, they receive much more than a 60 percent increase in wages, many of them will work irregularly and tend to become more or less shiftless, extravagant, and dissipated. Our experiments showed, in other words, that for their own best interest it does not do for most men to get rich too fast.[17]

These two passages illustrate most of the failings of scientific management. But were it possible to give just one reason for its dimming popularity, that would have to be its inadequacy to solve the human problems of motivation and productivity solely by economic incentives and work organization. Management needed the broader vision provided by industrial psychology to tackle these matters.

Industrial Psychology

The National Research Council (NRC), formed in 1916 as part of the war system by the National Academy of Science and the Engineering Foundation, had the purpose of mobilizing the scientific resources of the nation. The NRC charged its committee on psychology to develop a selection and placement program for military recruits and draftees. NRC psychologists led by Robert M. Yerkes for the committee and by Walter Dill Scott for the adjutant general office's committee on classification of personnel were responsible for testing nearly 1.75 million men during World War I.[18] Although both Scott and Yerkes had used intelligence tests in industry before the war, the large-scale application of the Stanford-Binet test of intelligence by the government convinced management of industrial psychology's potential for improving business's personnel practices. Psychology's perspective on the "human factor" seemed more complete, satisfying, and scientific than Taylor's "stupid and phlegmatic ox" hypothesis.

Thus, the modern era of industrial psychology was born, and it had two major branches. The first was the aforementioned testing branch that quickly expanded in the 1920s to include tests of aptitude, personality, job preference, manual dexterity, as well as more advanced tests of intelligence. The second branch, an early form of ergonomics, studied the work environment's impact on the physiological and psychological aspects of productivity. Psychologists of the 1920s, of whom Elton Mayo was a pathfinder, studied the relationship between physical fatigue (measured by blood pressure and pulse rate) and the level of employee productivity. Other research looked at the relationship between drug and alcohol use and attention spans. Many studies were designed to measure the effect of job environment variables, such as noise, plant layout, and dirt, on accidents, absenteeism, and turnover. Experiments were also conducted on the effects of color, sound, light, and even music on worker productivity and satisfaction. But this burst of energy in industrial psychology was just one aspect of the general movement of the social sciences into prominence, thanks to the decision of the Rockefeller Foundation to go ahead, full speed, with their support of them.

The Rockefeller Philanthropies and the Social Sciences

In 1923, the Laura Spelman Rockefeller Memorial (LSRM), established by John D. Rockefeller in memory of his first wife, decided to fund research in the social sciences. Under the direction of Beardsly Ruml, one of the truly great academic entrepreneurs of this century, the LSRM committed its resources to research and scholarship in such fields as sociology, psychology, economics, political science, history, and anthropology.

Ruml had two objectives. First, he hoped to create social science research facilities in universities of note in this country and in Europe, and second, he wanted to increase the pool of able people working in these fields.[19] Early grants from the LSRM were made to university social science departments. Those universities in turn allocated the funding, at their discretion, to established faculty members. Grants were also made directly to promising individual scholars who applied to the Memorial. And finally the Social Science Research Council (SSRC) received Memorial funds to further its interdisciplinary studies.

LSRM was absorbed by the Rockefeller Foundation in 1928, but Ruml's lasting contribution was summed up by John M. Hutchins, chancellor of the University of Chicago, "The Laura Spelman Rockefeller Memorial in its brief but brilliant career did more than any other agency to promote the social sciences in the United States."[20] However, the story was just beginning. The work of the Memorial was continued within a new division of the Rockefeller Foundation, the Social Science Division. Its first director, Edmond Day, followed Ruml's policies closely in the early years. The Foundation also created a new fund called the Spelman Fund and endowed it with $10 million. This fund, under the direction of the ubiquitous Ruml and political science professors Charles E. Merriam and Guy Moffett, created on the University of Chicago campus the Public Administration Clearing House (PACH). Affectionately called "1313" (its address on Chicago's campus), PACH became a center for the professional development of public administrators. It provided centralized information services and training for government officials, particularly on state and city levels. Some of those executives, as their careers advanced, assumed important positions in the federal government during the New Deal years. Thus, 1313 made a major contribution to the growing professional self-awareness of management in public administration.

LSRM had no less an effect on business management. Its first major act was to grant Elton Mayo $3,500. Mayo, an Australian, was a visiting scholar at the Wharton School of the University of Pennsylvania. But without continued financial aid from Wharton in view, Mayo contemplated his return to Australia, a prospect that did not thrill him. Fortunately for Mayo, Wallace B. Donham, impressed by his work in industrial psychology, urged him to apply to the Memorial for a grant that would allow him to stay in America at Harvard for another year. Mayo did so, received $3,500, and moved to the Harvard Graduate School of Business in 1926.[21]

Almost immediately, Mayo established a close relationship with the famous Harvard biochemist, Lawrence J. Henderson, who also had been enticed into Donham's fold. Henderson and Mayo led the founding of the Laboratory of Industrial Physiology. The Fatigue Lab, as it was later called, received a substantial LSRM grant in 1927 to establish a research program that soon led to its participation in the illumination studies underway at the Western Electric Company. This research, which came to be known as the Hawthorne studies, had a great and lasting effect on the management field, probably more than any other conducted in the social sciences.

When the Hawthorne findings were finally reported in 1938, management's knowledge of the "human factor" had expanded greatly with new data, perspectives, and applied techniques.[22] But most importantly the Hawthorne studies demonstrated that management could enter the realm of the employees' subconscious and influence their attitudes toward their jobs. Before these studies, the subconscious had been explored systematically only by Freud, Jung, and their followers in clinical cases of psychoses and neuroses. The Hawthorne studies found that "normal" people had natural, but unmet, subconscious needs on the job that shaped their attitudes and influenced their performance. Management, it was hypothesized, could improve employee motivation and productivity by discovering those unmet needs, which then could be either satisfied or altered.

The transformation of management's professional awareness was not limited to the theories and research findings of psychologists and social-psychologists, however. Functionalists and the organization theorists also made significant contributions to management thinking during this period.

The Functionalists' Approach to Management

The functionalists tried to find the universal elements of management activity. Their approach was straightforward. They observed managers in every imaginable situation and created task inventories of those jobs. Their object was to reach a consensus in identifying those functions of all managers in any type of organization or on any level.

The French industrial engineer, Henri Fayol, compiled the best-known early list of such functions. According to him, the universal management functions were planning, organizing, commanding, coordinating, and controlling. He published this conclusion in 1916 in *General and Industrial Administration*, the first small English edition of which appeared thirteen years later. Fayol's contribution was more widely acknowledged in 1949, with the publication of a new edition in English with a foreword by the well-known English management consultant, Lyndall Urwick.[23]

Urwick's comments were illuminating and helped to dispel a number of misconceptions about Fayol's aims. Actually Fayol wanted to improve management's efficiency in dealing with people in the organization, and his listing of functions was secondary to this objective. Fayol's and Taylor's works were complementary, Urwick argued, since "they both realized that the problem of personnel and its management *at all levels* is the 'key' to industrial success. Both applied scientific methods to this problem."[24] Fayol's influence on European management, Urwick claimed, was equal to that of Taylor on management in the United States.

Urwick's analysis of Fayol's contribution was never really appreciated here, and Fayol is remembered for his list of functions. Nevertheless, Americans were also searching for universal functions, led by Ralph C. Davis, an Ohio State University management professor. In his 1929 book, *Industrial Organization and Management*, Davis identified the primary functions of management as planning, organizing, and controlling.[25] This inventory was expanded in later editions to include motivating—an acknowledgment of the growing influence of the behavioral sciences on management. The field of public administration was not outdone in adopting a functional approach. Stemming directly from the Brownlow report, POSDCORB was brought into the world. At least two generations of public administration students learned that public executives plan, organize, staff, direct, coordinate, report, and budget.

The functionalists are not in favor now. Their approach to management is maligned as prescriptive, passive, and superficial. But this judgment underestimates the importance of the functionalists' contribution during a time when the contours of the new field of management were being established. Attempts at taxonomy helped management define itself in terms of work specialization, and by so doing facilitated, as Mary Parker Follett argued, the delegation of authority and responsibility to functions within an organization.[26] Thus, the functions that management performed, together with their associated skills, became the primary basis of expertise upon which the legitimacy of management rested. Organization function, not hierarchical position, provided the grounds that justified management's leadership. Barnard strongly endorsed this argument and made it a central element in his theory of cooperation. As the rudimentary management paradigm, the functional approach survives today, and many modern management textbooks introduce beginning students to the subject using its framework.

The Structuralists' Approach to Organization

Management's classical theory of organization structure developed in the 1930s, simultaneously with the field's functional and behavioral sides. But even before then the German sociologist Max Weber made a significant structural contribution with his theory of bureaucracy. However, like Fayol, the full importance of his ideas was not appreciated until after World War II. Language was a barrier to the dissemination of his views.

Nevertheless some American authors in the 1930s were virtually duplicating Weber's work because they were observing organizations that had the same structural contingencies—they were large and employed many semiskilled and unskilled workers in jobs that were routinized by advanced process technologies. The assembly line, the division of labor, and centralization of authority were hugely influential on the patterns of organizational structure that were analyzed by the classical theorists.

Similar to Weber, Mooney and Reiley proposed a theory of structural dynamics in *Onward Industry.*[27] They believed that there were two major forces in organization that determined structure, centralization of authority and the division of labor. The latter tended to fragment organizations, and it had to be offset by a centralized authority that provided coordination. Management's primary organizing task, as they saw it, was to maintain an equilibrium between these forces, because too much of one and not enough of the other reduced organizational efficiency.

Mooney and Reiley stated that coordination was the "mother principle" of organization: from it all the other principles of organization could be derived. This observation led them to stress organizational hierarchy and the scalar principle. This principle, buttressed by the dictums of unity of command and determinate hierarchy,[28] vested the authority to take coordinating actions in a centralized management chain of command. Mooney and Reiley also recognized that support organizations called "staffs" introduced a special class of organizational problems. They believed that the staff specialists, such as quality-control experts, threatened to violate the unity of command and thus frustrate management's ability to coordinate. Staff groups, accordingly, must always serve in an advisory capacity, and their actions should be subject to review and approval by "line" management. They held that staff should never have command authority over the line. Many of the lessons that Mooney and Reiley taught were learned from the military experiences of World War I. They communicated these experiences to management in less than 100 pages of their book. By doing so, they codified the principles of classical organization theory for business management.

Of equal importance in public administration was the book edited by Luther Gulick and Lyndall Urwick, *Papers on the Science of Administration.*[29] Gulick's ideas conformed with Mooney's and Reiley's, but he put them in terms applicable to public administration that stated the theoretical grounds for the federal government's reorganization. Urwick was no less enthusiastic about the advanced state of organization theory. He believed that all principles of organization had been discovered and that the chief management problem was their technical application.

There are principles which can be arrived at inductively from the study of human experience of organization, which should govern arrangements for human association of any kind. These principles can be studied as a technical question, irrespective of the purpose of the enterprise, the personnel composing it, or any constitutional, political or social theory underlying its creation. They are concerned with the method of subdividing and allocating to individuals all the various activities, duties and responsibilities essential to the purpose contemplated, the correlation of these activities and the continuous control of the work of individuals so as to secure the most economical and most effective realization of purpose.[30]

Such was the general optimism in management about validity of classical organization theory.

These remarkable books of the 1930s demonstrated that the management discipline had a firmer grasp on the theory and practical outcomes of the organizing process than it had on the functional or behavioral sides of professional practice. Classical organization theory was a fully integrated and useful model before 1938. It contributed more to management's disciplinary self-awareness during this time than did all of the other aspects of the field. Its legacy was the metaphor of the organization as a machine, and its principles were used for the structuring of the managerial state in those days.

The professional parameters of the management discipline were sketched in broad outline before 1938. They included the legacy of Progressive values, the scientific management movement, the application of the social sciences to management's human problems, the functional approach to management, and classical organization theory. All of this had considerable impact on Barnard's thought, but he was also sensitive to other forces at work in management. The most important of these was an increasing managerial class consciousness: a growing subjective awareness of a "we feeling" among managers, especially those in the highest reaches of organizational power.

HEIGHTENED CLASS AWARENESS

Management's sense of classness was based on more than a common occupation and a shared set of concepts in a professional discipline. It was deeply influenced by American culture and values, because what was important to Americans was exactly what management promised to deliver. Material progress and social consensus were widely accepted by managers as worthy aims of their professional practice in organizations. But the material prosperity that organizations enjoyed as the result of excellence in management had a moral aspect, namely the Progressive belief in "morally better" and "morally worse" economic results. The former were those that came from service to the customer and the expansion of mass production–consumption technology. "Profits made through such operations [were] of greater merit and of more social value than profits made by other means,"[31] such as greed-driven financial skulduggery and exploitation of labor.

These popular views were translated into the concepts and practices of management's professional discipline, and in astonishingly short order, mostly during the depression when the reputation of American businessmen languished. Consequently, the rapid progress of the management revolution must be accounted for in terms other than simply economic conditions.

Shared Experiences and Class Awareness

Business leadership is one thing and management leadership is something else, which may partially explain why management did not receive the brunt of criticism for the depression while the traditional business person did. Managers were, after all, employees like everybody else. Many of them, of whom Barnard and Gifford were magnificent examples, came from modest, small-town backgrounds. They were men of the people, attuned to the values, the driving forces, and the needs of the times. They perfectly embodied what Vilfredo Pareto described as the "circulation of the elite." Most of these new men brought to their jobs skills and commitments acquired by experience in management. However, their frame of mind was what really distinguished them from the business leaders of the past. They believed that competency, professionalism, rationality, and integrity gave them the right to be the guardians of American organizations.

The managerial state created a new organizational venue for management practice and with it the sense among managers that they had a status, role, and function in society far different than the business leaders of the old order. Although the existence of a managerial elite class is among the more highly contested assumptions in social theory,[32] one might argue that if people came from similar socioeconomic backgrounds, are of the same race and gender, profess similar religious beliefs and political preferences, have like employment experiences, read many of the same books and magazines, and attend the same type of university, then it could be expected that their points of view and behavior will have a certain homogeneity. Conspiracies and cabals need not be invoked in order to demonstrate managerial class consciousness.

Surveys of corporate CEOs over many years, such as those done by Mabel Newcomer, show persistent tendencies. For example, CEOs of major corporations are predominantly white, Protestant males from the middle to lower middle classes. Since the end of World War II the majority have been educated in business or engineering schools, and many now receive MBA degrees regardless of their undergraduate majors. A disproportionately large number of these CEOs have MBA certification from Ivy League schools. Most spend the vast majority of their working years in one corporation. They are over fifty years old when they reach the top of the corporate ladder. Most vote Republican but often nowadays endorse "politically correct" liberal causes in the attempt to appear socially responsible. These similarities in background, attitudes, and values have prompted scholars such as Michael Useem to write about the elite inner circle.[33] Such are the minimum pre-conditions for class awareness.

Also, the sense of classness was reinforced by the specialized knowledge of professional practice, created by managers themselves and by scholars working in the field. Much of this knowledge, upon which managers based their expertise, was public in the sense that it could be gained by study or by experience in organizations. However, this learning was actually available only to a favored few, those who managed, researched, or taught about complex organizations. Taylor, as we saw in his assessment of the mental capacity of the pig-iron handler, emphasized the exclusiveness of this knowledge, and Barnard later capitalized on it in his argument of why management could not be accountable to others for what it did. This myth of exclusiveness is still reinforced by business schools and schools of public administration when they certify students to enter the lower rungs on the ladder of the managerial class.

Finally, the managerial class read a specialized literature and acquired a common language. Much of this literature was technical, but more than a little of it dealt with those normative issues that reinforce the class awareness. The immense popularity of the book *In Search of Excellence*,[34] written by management consultants, can only be explained by its appeal to managers as a class of people pursuing a goal that no other social class could accomplish.

In addition to these experiences, this elite, at the highest levels, moves in the same social circles: on boards of directors of companies, as trustees of universities and charitable institutions, and as directors of philanthropies, social clubs, museums, and so on. They are also found frequently in local, state, and national government. With respect to their own organizations, they control information networks and are the focal point of communication systems. If they choose, they also can use the mass media to promulgate their ideas and to convince the public to accept their programs.

Therefore power, knowledge, values, and experience enable the managerial class to think of itself as apart from, and in some respects superior to, other people in America. Few writers have captured the implications of this aspect of guardianship as well as Barnard did in his description of the informal executive organization. Pondering why some people fit in this organization and why some do not, Barnard wrote, "This question of 'fitness' involves such matters as education, experience, age, sex, personal distinctions, prestige, race, nationality, faith, politics, sectional antecedent."[35] This description covered all the bases, and Barnard was emphatic that an individual's expertise alone would not qualify him or her for elite status. Beyond formal competence were some elusive personal qualities that made an individual the "right sort." One either had it or not, and only other members of the same class were able to make the necessary discriminations that would permit a person to pass into their all-important realm of organizational power.

The Corporation and Class Awareness

No circumstance was more important to management's class awareness than the rise of American corporations. They radically changed the concept of private property, and in doing so, altered managers' conceptions of themselves and their place in the firmament of the American power structure. Their professional skill and trustworthiness outweighed old-time property rights and hierarchical position on the scale of legitimacy.

The corporation allowed managers to control property that they did not own, a situation that gave them great economic power, as well as new obligations that few understood. But one thing was clear. They were supposed to manage in the interests of others. These others, at first, were thought to be the absentee owners of corporate equity shares. The courts held that management had a fiduciary responsibility to exercise "prudent business judgment" in "their" corporations, thereby maximizing stockholder returns.

But strange things happened in management's interpretation of prudent business judgment. For example, ATT's management had from the early 1920s regarded their common stock dividends to be an operating expense payable annually at the rate of $9.00 per share, producing a yield of approximately 8.5 percent. The price of a share of ATT stayed level at a little over $100 during this decade. Just one year after the 1929 market crash, ATT was selling for $103. From the stockholders' point of view, ATT may have represented managerialism at its finest. However, as ATT's corporate biographer Horace Coon observed about its dividend policy, "You may have innocently supposed that dividends are always profits; to consider dividends as part of costs may seem to you the neatest trick of the week. But that is how it is done."[36]

ATT's management was extraordinarily circumspect under Walter Gifford's conservative leadership in the 1920s and 1930s. Bonded indebtedness ran only at about 17 percent of total assets. About one-third of the costs of expansion and modernization was financed through retained earnings, and much of the rest came from the sale of stock-purchase rights to ATT stockholders.

ATT investors had every right to be confident in management's judgment, since their capital stayed intact and returns remained level even during the worst of times. On the other hand, investors in other corporations, such as those run by Samuel Insull, had far less cause for jubilation. Such speculative, pyramided corporate empires collapsed during the depression. Regardless of the investors' financial outcomes, the fact is that corporations gave managers considerable economic discretion and much latitude in which to exercise it. This new status brought with it the opportunity for managers to gain a disproportionate share of benefits from the corporate income stream.

Burnham called this opportunity exploitation, and wrote, "All class economies are exploiting; feudal and capitalist economies are exploiting; and the managerial society will be exploiting."[37] Exploitation, however, did not have quite the pejorative connotation for Burnham as it had for Karl Marx. Burnham thought that it was a kind of managerial rent and would be far less severe in a managerial society than in other class societies. Berle and Means had explored this idea before Burnham, and they observed that managerial power "is virtually new in the common law" and as such entails "the power of confiscation of part of the profit stream and even of the underlying corporate assets by means of purely private processes."[38] Although Burnham credited Berle and Means for pioneering the way, he pointed out that they did not recognize the sociological fact that those who had received preferential treatment in the distribution of property in the past had been losing access to control of property, whereas those who lacked preferential treatment in distribution (e.g., managers) were gaining access to the control of property. Burnham thought that control over access was decisive since it would ultimately determine preferential treatment in distribution, and *this* was the "mechanism of the managerial revolution."[39]

Burnham's criticism might seem a bit picky, especially since Berle and Means were closer to the mark about the overall consequences of management's rise to power. In a famous passage, they wrote: "It is conceivable—indeed it seems almost essential if the corporate system is to survive—that the control of the great corporations develop into a purely neutral technocracy, balancing the claims by various groups in the community and assigning to each a portion of the income stream on the basis of public policy rather than private cupidity."[40]

Had the management revolution been merely a matter of heightened professional awareness of the field as an objective discipline, as Professor Waldo claimed, then it is conceivable that technical experts could manage corporations as "purely neutral technocracies." This vision would have appealed to the staunchest Progressive of earlier years. However, the managerial revolution brought with it a heightened class consciousness among managers, and along with it the realization that they were also stakeholders who were well positioned organizationally to enjoy greater privileges of money and power relative to other stakeholders.

Burnham did not dream of the extraordinary lengths to which managerial exploitation might be carried. Berle and Means did! Their foreboding about private cupidity was justified in the 1980s when corporate management, driven by an ethic of personal advantage, demonstrated that its exploitive power could result in an unparalleled frequency of morally questionable, if not downright corrupt, practices that were contrary to their organizations' interests. However, the present darkness should not envelope our historical perspective. Generally, the significant people in business, government, and academe in the 1920s and 1930s had bright expectations of the benefits that America would reap from the new managerial order. Few argued more ardently in its behalf than those in the Harvard Circle.

3

Barnard's Harvard Circle

Reminiscing about Harvard University in the 1920s and 1930s, the sociologist George C. Homans commented in his autobiography, "Harvard was the best then in a way it will never be again."[1] Harvard's greatness in those days was due partly to the eminent scholars on its faculty and partly to its farsighted administrative leadership. But there was also an ineffable factor, a human chemistry, through which a happy, and perhaps accidental, combination of talents created an intellectual environment of challenge, innovation, and excellence. This may have triggered Homan's memory as he recalled those best of times, when universities were relatively small and less specialized.

Chester I. Barnard moved in Harvard's affairs then, serving on universitywide committees, giving lectures, and keeping close ties with members of the Graduate School of Business. Barnard gave Harvard his experience, judgment, and skill as a top executive, and Harvard provided the intellectual support of people who encouraged him to record his management theories in writing. He acknowledged them in the preface of *The Functions of the Executive*:[2] Wallace B. Donham, dean of the Harvard Graduate School of Business; Richard Cabot, the founder of the social ethics department, the forerunner of Harvard's sociology department; Lawrence J. Henderson, a highly regarded biochemist associated with the business school; Elton Mayo, a pioneer industrial psychologist and the éminence grise of the Hawthorne studies of human relations in industry; Alfred North Whitehead, the famous philosopher of science; and Harvard's president A. Lawrence Lowell, who sponsored the lecture series in which Barnard presented those ideas about management that ultimately became the substance of his book.

As notable and influential as these individuals were, they were few in number compared to the extraordinary circle of people that composed Barnard's Harvard associates in the years that preceded the 1938 publication of his landmark book. Those others included many young scholars, most of whose reputations would not be established until after World War II. A partial list includes Talcott Parsons,

Robert Merton, Lloyd Warner, William F. Whyte, George C. Homans, B. F. Skinner, and Fritz Roethlisberger.

This impressive assembly was due in part to the financial commitments made by the President and Fellows of Harvard College in an effort to raise the university's prestige in scholarship and research. Before World War I Harvard had a reputation as a finishing school for the wealthy sons of the Eastern gentry. When Franklin D. Roosevelt graduated from Harvard, he told his family that, although he was not at the top of his class, he was at least the first among the gentlemen. Regardless of how deserved Harvard's reputation was in those days, the university underwent major changes between the two world wars. Its transformation, begun by President Lowell, continued with his successor, James B. Conant. They made it possible for the faculty to hire great scholars, to reform and add academic programs, and generally to create a congenial atmosphere where research and theory building flourished.

And flourish it did in a world shattered by the social, political, and economic dislocations caused by the first war. These events upended the most cherished beliefs and values of the old order, and many within the Harvard Circle believed that those responsible for the affairs of a modern nation needed to think anew their leadership premises. The Harvard Circle dedicated itself to the advancement of this new thinking.

THE CIRCLE AND ITS SEGMENTS

The group of scholars that we call the Harvard Circle constituted an intellectual community dedicated to scholarly excellence. There were, of course, dominant personalities in the circle and frequent disagreements among them. Nevertheless, the chemistry seemed to work, because its members had similar views about what it would take to modernize America in ways that were consistent with its management revolution and managerial state.

The central figure in the Harvard Circle was Lawrence J. Henderson. He towered in this group, not just because of his impressive physical stature but because of his intellectual influence on all who joined his company.[3] For example, he converted a number of his students and faculty colleagues to the social theories of the Italian sociologist Vilfredo Pareto. The significance of this Paretan connection to the future development of the management field cannot be stressed too strongly.

Henderson's conservatism was legendary. Homans and Bailey observed, "Henderson's beard was red but his politics were vigorously conservative."[4] Ideologically, Henderson had the "right stuff" to appeal to Donham and Barnard, and he also had a certain charming naïveté about world affairs. Just prior to the fall of France to the Nazis in 1940, Henderson wrote Barnard that the United States should rescue the French army officers "of all ranks and branches of service" so that they could advise us in our efforts to build a modern army.[5] What an extraordinary idea! However, it is easily understood since Henderson was a rabid Francophile. But, above all else Henderson was a scientist and philosopher who did not suffer fools gladly. He often displayed the subtlety of a pile driver, a trait he shared with Barnard. Homans and Bailey informed us, "His passion was hottest when his logic was coldest."[6] This formidable man's character and authority were felt throughout the Harvard Circle's diverse academic, social, and intellectual undertakings.

As something of a cabal within the university, the circle was composed of like-minded people who moved easily among four groups imperfectly described as segments of the Harvard Circle. They were the Society of Fellows, the Paretan Scholars, the Harvard Graduate School of Business Administration, and the Laboratory of Industrial Physiology. So intermixed was their membership that it is impossible to determine where the interests of one group left off and where the interests of another began. In spite of the somewhat artificial division, it is a useful device for describing the affairs of the Harvard Circle when Barnard sojourned in its midst.

THE SOCIETY OF FELLOWS

One of the focal points of Harvard's intellectual life was an elitist group called the Society of Fellows, founded in 1933.[7] Arising from a dissatisfaction with conventional doctoral programs, the Society stressed the development of interdisciplinary non-Ph.D. studies. To this end it supported a number of junior fellows with financing provided during the Society's early years by President Lowell from his personal fortune. Of the six junior fellows appointed in 1933, B. F. Skinner was the most celebrated later in his career.

Five senior fellows ran the Society, administering its funds and selecting and guiding the junior fellows in their studies. In 1933 the senior fellows included Henderson as chairman, Whitehead, President Lowell, Charles P. Curtis, Jr., a member of the Harvard Corporation and an attorney with the Boston law firm of Choate, Hall, and Stewart, and John L. Lowes, a professor of English selected to represent the humanities in the Society.

Homans was appointed a junior fellow in the Society in 1934. Faithful to the Society's mandate, Homans did not pursue a Ph.D. degree. Under Henderson's direction he followed an independent path of scholarship tutoring with Elton Mayo and others. His research took him to England in the 1930s, where he studied the sociology of medieval rural English communities. The book he eventually published on the subject, *The English Villagers of the Thirteenth Century*, is regarded as a classic in historical sociology, and some feel that it is Homans's most important work.[8] His analysis of English rural life is rich in detail and sociological meaning. But his last chapter is particularly relevant, because in it

Homans provided a conceptual framework for interpreting his research findings and analysis.[9] Homans acknowledged that he owed most to Barnard and Pareto for this scheme, although the influence of Henderson is also clearly present in this chapter. From Henderson and Pareto, Homans drew the concepts of systems and equilibrium, and he relied on Barnard for the theory of formal organizations.[10] All of these authors stressed the critical idea of interdependence among all parts of a social system.

Homans became a major figure in American sociology without having a doctorate. It was possible to do such things in those days, and Lloyd Warner in anthropology also managed it. Warner, briefly associated with the Harvard Circle, participated in the Hawthorne studies, which are described later in this chapter, designing the "bank wiring room" experiment that investigated the effect of small group behavior on work norms and output. This research was the empirical foundation for the concepts of the informal organization and group culture in management theory.[11] Warner went to even greater accomplishments as leader of the Yankee City studies, the first research of its kind in urban-industrial anthropology, recruiting Conrad Arensburg, a 1934 junior fellow, to participate in their project. In return, Arensburg persuaded William F. Whyte, Jr., also a member of the Society of Fellows, to abandon economics for sociology.[12]

Homans's status as a junior fellow lasted until 1939, when he was appointed a faculty instructor in the sociology department, chaired by Pitirim Sorokin, the irascible Russian sociologist. This department, although it was new, had attracted some extraordinary faculty members and graduate students. Among them were Florence Kluckhohn, Robert K. Merton, and Talcott Parsons. According to Homans, President Lowell may not have trusted Sorokin's administrative judgment and therefore appointed an oversight committee of people with interests in sociology to review the affairs of the department.[13] This committee was chaired by the ever-present Lawrence Henderson, and Elton Mayo was a member.

Thus, the Society of Fellows and the sociology department were rallying points for people who either directly or indirectly oriented management theory and research toward the social sciences.[14] Their interests were broadly intellectual and concerned with building theories of human behavior in modern industrial societies, a perspective exemplified by the loose association of Paretan Scholars active at Harvard from the late 1920s and throughout the 1930s.

PARETO'S LEGACY AND THE PARETAN SCHOLARS

Pareto was the most unlikely European to have dazzled a group of American intellectuals, yet his ideas profoundly influenced the Harvard Circle. Pareto's life and work were reactions to his father's political views. The elder Pareto, an Italian nobleman from Genoa, was connected with the revolutionary Mazzini political party. This party espoused national Italian unity, based on rather fuzzy ideals about democracy, humanitarianism, rationality, progress, the perfectibility of human nature, and Puritanical sexual morality. Pareto's family was forced to flee Italy and take up residence in Paris because of his father's political views.

Garibaldi and his Red Shirts succeeded in unifying Italy in 1860, and in 1862 raised King Victor Emmanuel II to the throne. The ensuing governments did not attend to the constitutional ideals that were dear to the Mazzinists, consequently their disillusionment was deep. Instead "of a heaven on earth" that the Mazzinists thought Italy should have, it received a "not too well ordered, weak, and somewhat corrupted national state."[15]

Although the new governments failed to live up to the all-too-noble Mazzinist expectations, they did use the romantic symbols of the movement to capture popular support. These symbols "provided the more realistic makers of Italian unity with indispensable emotional forces without which their aim would never have been achieved."[16] This cynical use of the emotions to secure mass backing for the leadership colored the monumental book that Pareto wrote at the end of his life.

Pareto was born in Paris in 1848 during his father's exile. Ten years later the family returned to Italy, where he received his formal education. He graduated from the University of Turin, specializing in science and technology. Pareto came of age during the time when the Mazzinists were smarting from their sense of betrayal. After his graduation, he pursued a technical career, working for the Italian railroad system. For twenty years he was both a practicing engineer and a political activist. He threw himself into issues of free trade and the liberation of Italian economic institutions. He finally gave all of this up in 1893 for a lectureship in economics at Lausanne University. One year later he took the economics chair at that university that had been vacated by Anton Walras when he retired.

Pareto hated his father's ideals and the political movement of which his father was a part.[17] This contempt, which he nurtured throughout his life, finally boiled over when he was in his seventies. He vented his frustrations in his *Trattato di Sociologia Generale*, the book that captured the imagination of the Harvard Paretan scholars. In it Pareto held that society could not be understood in Mazzinist terms, that it was not rational, not necessarily progressive, nor democratically inclined. Furthermore, people did not have a bent toward perfectibility, nor was the practice of self-denial, sexual and otherwise, necessarily natural or desirable. Rather, the foundations of human behavior were more likely found in primitive emotions, urges, needs, and drives that were essentially irrational and nonlogical.

The irony is that Pareto is not remembered now for his sociology. His name is associated with a rational concept that is common currency among economists and agency theorists, Paretan optimality. Had Pareto been aware that events would take this turn he would have been appalled. He had concluded that rational analysis was only appropriate to a very narrow domain of logical human conduct that included just economics and the natural sciences. This left the rest of behavior unaccounted for by any theoretical framework. And it was precisely to fill this chasm that Pareto wrote his general sociology. As it turned out, Pareto's sociology became the theoretical hook upon which the Harvard Circle hung its interpretation of the Hawthorne studies, their assessment of national events, and their ideas about the reform of business education.

At first glance, Pareto's sociology seems to be a classification scheme. He chose five major concepts that were central to his analysis of social phenomena: the social system, equilibrium, residues and derivations, nonlogical language and behavior (closely associated with residues and derivations), and the circulation of the elite. But in Paretan analysis there is a dynamic component just beneath the surface of this taxonomy. It avers that a society is an aggregation of interrelated and interdependent parts that are systemically connected and balanced in a state of dynamic equilibrium. Residues and derivations, nonlogical and irrational human sentiments, emotions, and motives, are critical components of the system. They either secure and maintain social equilibrium or cause its disruption. Since language is the symbolic expression of emotional states, its use is crucial to the maintenance or destruction of social equilibrium.

The elite, in Pareto's analysis, are either the conservators, or the destroyers, or the restorers of social equilibrium. They maintain the equilibrium when their leadership expresses the inchoate sentiments of the masses and fulfills their needs. However, in the natural order of things, an established elite eventually detaches itself from the public's values. When the elite become degenerate in this respect, instability is introduced into the social system and disequilibrium ensues. The restoration of equilibrium is achieved by a circulation out of power and influence of the old elite, a process that brings forth from the grass roots of society a new elite more in tune with social values. Pareto derived from this process his famous dictum: "History is the graveyard of aristocracies."

Pareto's concept of the circulation of the elite had something for everyone: a biological justification for domination, a social justification for differentiation, and an economic justification for free-trade capitalists in the sense that free trade is the Darwinistic mechanism that ensures that the fit will rule. In any of its forms Pareto's theory of the elite was intended to prove the "everlasting necessity of class and domination."[18] Pareto did in fact appeal to the more repressive regimes of the day. Henderson acknowledged that Pareto had been called the "Karl Marx of the bourgeoisie."[19] This observation came close to the mark, but Henderson would have none of it, saying that allegations of fascism against Pareto were dangerous "derivations."

The story of the Paretan scholars demonstrates the cross-disciplinary interests at Harvard University. As with so many other enterprises within the Harvard Circle, Lawrence Henderson dominated this group, but Paretan scholarship did not begin with him. Henderson's instincts and intellectual commitments were completely bound up with the natural sciences, and he had an elemental scorn for the social sciences, until William Morton Wheeler, a distinguished entomologist, encouraged him to read the *Trattato*.[20] Almost immediately Henderson became a convert to Pareto's thinking.

Henderson was uniquely qualified to appreciate the full importance of Pareto's views. His own research on blood chemistry was an application of the work of Claude Bernard, who Henderson admired for his extensions to biology of the ideas of the physical chemist, J. Willard Gibbs. These ideas, traceable from Gibbs to Bernard to Henderson, emphasized the importance of systems and equilibrium for understanding many biological processes, including blood chemistry. Pareto's theoretical models of society and individual behavior also used these concepts, and they were analogous to Bernard's application of them to physiology. Pareto's methodology for understanding the social order excited Henderson in a way that other sociologists of the period could not. Talcott Parsons wrote in a letter to Chester I. Barnard that Henderson may have been more interested in Pareto's methodology than he was in his social theory.[21] Henderson's book about Pareto would certainly affirm that assumption.[22] As Bernard Barber observed, "If Pareto had truly joined the social sciences to the natural sciences, an achievement Henderson very much wanted to see, it is only to be expected that he would put Pareto in the great company of Gibbs, Bernard, and even Newton."[23]

Encountering Pareto when he did (he was about fifty when Wheeler suggested he read Pareto) resulted in something like a religious conversion for Henderson. Homans recalled, "Henderson could not refrain from bringing Pareto into every conversation, and thus made a great bore of himself."[24] He was not able to transcend Pareto's sociology, "He never threw Pareto and a lot of other good work in sociology into the pot and tried to boil something new out of it all."[25] Despite this criticism, Henderson had found a theoretical perspective on social phenomena that used those concepts he cherished from the natural sciences. Pareto apparently did not enlighten Henderson, but he did validate his belief in the vast generality and utility of natural science concepts, especially systems and equilibrium. As Holmes once described Watson, Pareto was not a source of illumination for Henderson, but he was a conductor of light.

Henderson, as a product of an age devoted to positivism and rationalism, stressed the importance of reason in human affairs. However, as he aged, other things began to offset the strength of his positivistic views. Freudian analysis, cultural anthropology, and the course of world events, such as the rise of Communism, Fascism, and Nazism, demonstrated that the most important aspects of human behavior could not be understood in terms of positive science.[26] Questions of values and emotions weighed heavily on Henderson's mind, and these were exactly what attracted him to Pareto's ideas about residues and derivations. Henderson believed that by studying them in the Paretan framework, the word "science" in social science could be written in large letters. This opinion was shared by the members of the Harvard Circle, especially Mayo, Roethlisberger, Homans, and Dickson, who were searching for a theory to explain the "facts" that were flowing from the Hawthorne studies.

Because of his stature in the Harvard Circle, Henderson could preach effectively for Pareto's ideas. In 1932, he organized an informal seminar on Pareto that attracted scholars who were, or would soon become, famous: Joseph Schumpeter, Fritz Roethlisberger, Elton Mayo, Robert K. Merton, Talcott Parsons,[27] T. N. Whitehead (the son of the philosopher A. North Whitehead), Hans Zinsser (professor of bacteriology and historian of epidemiology), Bernard De Voto (professor of English), and George Homans and Charles P. Curtis, with whom Homans coauthored a book that was a general introduction to Pareto's thought.[28]

Because he turned out to be its public voice, De Voto played a unique role with the Paretan scholars. Excited by the ideas discussed in Henderson's seminar, he became a vigorous polemicist for Pareto's theories. And while his interest in Pareto eventually waned, according to Wallace Stegner his biographer,[29] De Voto wrote popular articles about Paretan theory during the flush of his initial enthusiasm. His first article in the *Saturday Review* was not well received by liberal readers, since he had the temerity to suggest that Pareto superceded Marx in his description of society.[30] Kingsley Davis, in a letter to the editor, said that De Voto's article was "characterized by presumptuousness, misrepresentation, and inaccuracy."[31] Stung by these criticisms, De Voto wrote a longer and more careful statement of Pareto's ideas, and it was published in *Harper's* magazine.[32] Both articles reflected the conservative leanings of the Harvard group and were intended to bring the public's attention to an alternative system of ideas that was then being studied by this exclusive assemblage of Harvard academics.

Henderson's seminar evolved into an undergraduate course titled Sociology 23, Concrete Sociology. It was first offered in 1935. This course drew pedagogically from Pareto's "clinical" approach to social phenomena, in which Pareto used innumerable historical examples to demonstrate his theories. Both Henderson and Donham felt that this approach had as much to offer for the teaching of business subjects as it had for the teaching of medicine or law.

Henderson gave three lectures on Pareto to introduce the course. The remaining twenty-five sessions were "clinical" studies delivered to the students by members of the Harvard faculty.[33] Barnard, the only lecturer from business, first presented his "case," the "Riot of the Unemployed at Trenton, N.J., 1935," in 1938.[34] He repeated it five or six times at various Harvard locations, including the Medical School, the Harvard College, and the Business School.

The Paretan scholars did not interpret the *Trattato* uniformly, emphasizing different aspects of this work. For example, Henderson stressed the methodologies of systems and equilibrium because these ideas appealed to his inclination toward natural science and because they had the greatest generality. In his extensive notes, which are appended to his book on Pareto, Henderson wrote, "The interdependence of variables in a system is one of the widest inductions from experience that we possess: or we may regard it as the definition of a system."[35]

Of course, the Paretan scholars, especially those who were Henderson's younger acolytes, did not ignore these concepts. They were important to the theoretical framework of the book by Homans and Curtis. But these authors were more interested in Pareto's ideas about "residues and derivations," which also were central to the theoretical and ideological perspectives held by Mayo, Donham, Roethlisberger, and particularly Barnard.

Thus, the importance of systems and equilibrium notwithstanding, the really significant Paretan ideas pertained to human emotions and sentiments. According to Paretan thought, most conduct was a manifestation of the residues that were permanent, nonlogical, and inexplicable components of behavior. Residues were psychic states rooted in subconscious feelings, inclinations, preconceptions, social taboos, religions, myths, and magic. Pareto had six classes of them, but the Harvard Circle emphasized the two groups he called "the instinct for combinations" and "persistent aggregates." The former category involved all of those sentiments that resulted in transitions and innovations in society, the latter contained sentiments that lent to social stability. Residues were for the most part unchanging, and Pareto went to great lengths to describe through historical examples how they endured across time and cultures. For instance, the residues magic and superstition are present in all cultures. They may differ in practice and substance, but they are still magic and superstition.

Derivations, however, varied considerably, and Donham, Mayo, and Roethlisberger were particularly interested in them. In Paretan thought derivations were explanations, disguised as logical statements, that people gave for their emotional states. Thus, when workers complained about pay, they were *really* disguising a sentiment about some psychological or social condition at work. These feelings most often were subconscious and had little to do with economics. Roethlisberger observed that "one of the most time-consuming pastimes of the human mind is to rationalize and to disguise sentiments as logic."[36] Elton Mayo continually stressed that "an articulate complaint only rarely, if ever, gave any logical clue to the grievance in which it had its origin."[37] Therefore, what people said was not what they felt, and one had to dig beneath the logic of the spoken derivations to get at the residues. They were the emotional causes of behavior. This theory guided the interviewing, counseling, and supervisory training programs at Western Electric, the major action-oriented applications of the Hawthorne research findings.

Mayo made much of Pareto's circulation of the elite and was the only member of the Harvard Circle to do so. He was concerned with the emotional basis of the social order and the overwhelming necessity to integrate human emotionality into a stable social system. He believed that the elite maintained the social equilibrium, and the only way they could be successful in this endeavor was to secure the collaboration of the people. The failure to do so resulted in social instability, upheaval, and chaos.

This prospect dogged Mayo because he saw that urbanization, industrialization, technology, and social mobility were modern destabilizing forces. The "elite of yesterday," as he called them, were unprepared to address these issues and therefore failed to obtain cooperation between leaders and the led.[38] According to Mayo, the management elite, then appearing in modern nations, were circulating into power positions. And if a new social order based on collaboration was to emerge from the ruins of the old, it would have to be the work of this new class. Yet they too were ill prepared for the task, and most of all they needed to be trained and educated in the human relations skills of collaboration. Thus Mayo's views about the management elite, formed by Pareto's concept of circulation, were important links to Donham's vision of management education.

THE HARVARD GRADUATE SCHOOL
OF BUSINESS ADMINISTRATION

Between 1922 and 1936, Wallace B. Donham, dean of Harvard's Graduate School of Business Administration, published four important articles in the *Harvard Business Review* that stated his policies for the school.[39] When Donham became dean in 1919, he was intent upon raising the level of business education at Harvard. He visualized his school as the West Point of capitalism. But by 1933 that vision changed. He recognized that "effective responsibility has passed rapidly from capital to a *new managing class*, the executive heads of great corporations and firms."[40] Donham's acknowledgment of the emergence of a professional managerial class, coupled with his understanding of its function to secure social stability, clearly bore the imprint of the influence of Henderson, Pareto, and Mayo. Donham wrote, "This class is not yet equipped for its task, but it must be. For good or evil it controls powerful social institutions."[41] Equipping some of these new professional managers, intellectually, technically, and ethically, for the jobs that lay ahead of them was exactly the destiny Donham envisioned for the school. It had to become the "Annapolis of managerialism," an elite service school for the corporate leaders of the managerial state.

The main theme that ran through all of Donham's articles was the obligation of business schools to prepare students for leadership roles in American corporations. Professional management education required breadth and depth of knowledge, experience with executive decisionmaking that had an action orientation, the social sciences with special emphasis on the emotional nature of human behavior,[42] and a focus that stressed cooperative policymaking among interconnected organizations in the managerial state. There were subordinate themes in these articles as well, such as moral integrity and ethics, the preservation of the social status quo, and a criticism of political and business leadership. But Donham brought all of these issues back to their implications for business education.

Donham authored the lead article in volume 1, number 1, of the *Harvard Business Review* (HBR).[43] This article, published in 1922, discussed the virtues of the case method for teaching business subjects. In March of the same year, Donham wrote a similar piece for the *American Economic Review*.[44] Writing against the background of the severe business recession that struck the United States after World War I, Donham worried that business theory did not help executives to make more than unsystematic, haphazard decisions. This caused them to repeat those mistakes that led to a repetition of business cycle calamities. Donham's opening sentence in this HBR article declaims:

> Unless we admit that rules of thumb, the limited experience of executives in each individual business, and the general sentiment of the street, are the sole possible guides for executive decisions of major importance, it is pertinent to inquire how the representative practices of business men generally may be made available as a broader foundation for such decisions, and how a proper theory of business is to be obtained.[45]

To create a "broader foundation" for decisionmaking, Donham argued for two basic changes in the approach to business theory. First, he suggested that more data be collected on major economic indicators, a job for statisticians and economists. The distribution of this information to practicing business managers was the responsibility of private commercial publications such as *Moody's Manual*, government agencies such as the Department of Commerce, and the bureaus of business research such as those at Northwestern and Harvard. They provided management with its statistical eyes, as noted by Guy Alchon in the first chapter of this book. Second, he thought that business schools had a special responsibility to develop the decisionmaking capacities of students and that business precedents were needed to achieve this end.

Donham, who had been an attorney with a Boston law firm before coming to Harvard, saw the case system in common law as a model method for the instruction of business subjects. He observed:

> the Harvard Business School has thrown some interesting sidelights on this need. Adopting the general principles of Langdell's case system, by which most of the law schools of the country teach law, we have developed on a large scale similar methods of teaching business, and a constantly increasing percentage of the work of this school is conducted on a true case system. The student obtains his business training by solving executive problems . . . so presented that he deals with conditions similar to those which confronted the executive.[46]

Melvin T. Copeland, professor of marketing, recalled that in the academic year of 1919–1920, Donham asked him to prepare a casebook in marketing.[47] This book was the first of many for students in business policy and the functional management areas. Thus by 1922 the school was well on its way toward institutionalizing the case method, an approach that became widespread throughout American business education after World War II.

The memory of the economic glitch of 1920–1921 was dimmed by the prosperity of the rest of the 1920s. The year 1927 was a high point in the economic exhilaration of the decade, and most economic classes in America, with the glaring exception of the farmers, were doing well. In that year, Donham wrote about an expanded role for management, exhorting private enterprise to meet its social and ethical responsibilities.[48] He argued that since science and technology, the vehicles for material progress, were in the hands of the business group, it was its responsibility, not government's, to use them in socially responsible ways. As Donham insisted, sound social progress depended on business.

Such responsibility placed a special obligation on business schools. They were, in a manner of speaking, the van of the vanguard. They educated " . . . thinking men interested in the orderly evolution of civilization,"[49] and that required the study of general administration, business and economic history, moral philosophy, and the functional aspects of management jobs. All this preparation was necessary in order that students had the knowledge they needed to make top management decisions expertly, ethically, and responsibly. Both Alfred North Whitehead and Lawrence J. Henderson echoed this theme in speeches they gave to the American Association of Collegiate Schools of Business (AACSB) at its annual meeting in May of 1927.[50]

Donham's vision of professional management education was precisely what was needed to heighten management's self-awareness and to improve the effectiveness of organizations. Donham's educational policies at Harvard were great contributions to the management field's struggle to come of age. However, Donham was not sanguine about the future. He was concerned that radicalism (Marxism) was festering beneath the surface of prosperity. More specifically he felt that the labor problem, caused in part by the technological displacement of masses of workers in semi- or unskilled industrial jobs, was unresolved. The labor movement, technological unemployment, and radicalism were connected to the basic human fears of lost jobs, grinding living conditions, and dangers in the workplace that resulted from fatigue and monotony. In this light Donham regarded the social sciences highly for their potential to contribute to the understanding "of the physiological and psychological basis for the actions of men."[51]

Writing to Barnard, Donham recalled a conversation with Henderson where Donham had "expressed the belief that if more realistic work was not done in the social fields . . . the constantly changing conditions which then existed [in 1925] would . . . progress rapidly toward government controls."[52] Donham went on to say, "I was convinced myself that we must know more about what makes people tick and had for a considerable time sought a man who would contribute to this end."[53]

That man was Elton Mayo who, as mentioned in the last chapter, established the Fatigue Lab with Henderson and housed it in the business school.

Donham summarized this history as follows:

Henderson's interest in social problems starts with my talks with him culmi-
nating in the lecture I gave him on the Business School work and aims
[1925]. From there it proceeds to Mayo's coming and to Henderson's finding
him a congenial soul. From there through Morton Wheeler to Pareto, etc.
Mixed up with the whole situation was the fact that after he [Henderson]
moved his headquarters to the school, a new world opened up to him in
conversation with me on a variety of administrative problems.[54]

It is fairly clear that Donham's 1927 article, reflecting his conclusions about
the social sciences, was inspired by conversations with Henderson and Mayo.
These conclusions were translated into academic programs of teaching and research. The management of "human relations" based upon the applied social
sciences thence also became grist for case studies.

As might be expected, the tone of Donham's HBR articles changed during the
Great Depression. His attention during that time was not upon the social significance of business but on the failure of business leadership; not upon business
going it alone in the restructuring of American society but on its cooperation with
government in this project; and not upon radicalism and the labor movement as
latent threats to American stability but on them as undesirable alternatives to the
established management order. However, important elements in Donham's perspective remained constant: his firm position that universities had a preeminent,
but unfulfilled, role to educate a competent and ethical leadership elite; his dedication to the social sciences; and his unshaken belief in the moral authority of the
private sector. Nevertheless, Donham's worldview was altered drastically by the
depression.

Reviewing the changes brought by the depression and trying to make some
sense out of them was no easy thing to do. In his article on the failure of leadership, Donham resorted to a biological analogy that probably reflected Henderson's influence. Donham argued that as with the physiology of individuals, the
health of society depended on the "maintenance of a moving organic equilibrium." The depression was evidence that this equilibrium in America was out of
adjustment. Therefore, "the politician as a social physician must carry out conscious plans for restoration."[55]

However, politicians, as well as corporate executives, were poorly suited for
this task. They were specialists, and their education had not equipped them to
transcend the limits of their specialties. Donham commented that Pareto, seeing
the dangers of specialization, devoted the last years of his life to writing "a larger
synthesis" that would help to overcome the narrowness of perspective afflicting
the interpretation of social phenomena. Donham translated Pareto's larger synthesis into educational terms, believing that the type of management programs that
Harvard offered were a step toward preparing the leadership elite to cope with the

complexities of a modern nation that was out of equilibrium. Melvin T. Copeland commented that, although administration occurs at all levels in a corporate management hierarchy, the weight of responsibility and the criticality of errors compound for those higher up. Therefore, "It has been . . . to these upper levels of administrative responsibility that the school has come principally to address its instruction."[56]

Donham's opinion in this respect had not changed. He held throughout his deanship that Harvard should prepare the future corporate elite of America with a broad, action-oriented management education. However, the details of such education did change in two important instances during the depression. First, the social sciences became more central in instruction and case writing. Second, more attention was given in the curriculum to business-government relationships. The depression made obvious the interconnected nature of American institutions, and programs in the school had to acknowledge this fact.

However, Donham also dwelt upon national problems, always returning to the theme of leadership. He expressed confidence, at least in 1933, in Franklin D. Roosevelt, who had been inaugurated on March 4 of that year. Donham thought then that Roosevelt would give the nation able leadership. However, he was apprehensive about one thing, Roosevelt's fireside chats. Donham wrote, "The greatest variable in our social equation since March 4 is Franklin D. Roosevelt's Sunday evening radio talk."[57] Donham took these famous direct and emotional appeals to the American public for exactly what they were. Roosevelt was using nonlogical language to sell his program for restructuring American society, placing in the executive branch of government an undreamed of amount of concentrated power. Donham saw what the moving hand was writing, "Laissez faire is made impossible."[58] This was a shrewd deduction coming so soon after Roosevelt took office.

But regardless of how clever, adroit, persuasive, and enlightened the new president might be, Donham believed that he had to draw upon the leadership of many organizations and institutions to help him run the nation. He needed advice, support, and management skills from corporate executives, social scientists in universities, and politicians. He required flexible people in a "formal or informal group [that] may formulate a coordinated scheme to restore this nation's general framework, its organic equilibrium."[59] Thus, as Miller and O'Leary pointed out, Donham viewed the governance of America in 1933 as a "cooperative enterprise"[60] shared by a professional elite that included government executives as major players in the managerial state.

Donham's opinion of Roosevelt's leadership in his first term soured by 1936 as his programs for reform took shape. He believed that the president's preference for reform, instead of recovery, posed a real danger since no one could manage effectively the "vast and multifarious changes advanced by the New Deal."[61] The president was being seduced, he thought, by the glamour of utopias and sought to change overnight that which might be more adequately accomplished by a slow, orderly strategy of recovery. In Donham's words, Roosevelt had two options, "on the one hand to join the conservatives in defense of the past, trying to slow down change and strengthen the inherent forces of rehabilitation; or, on the other hand to throw his lot in with the present wild gamble with our future even though he knows that many variables introduced suddenly into a social situation can work out into order and social equilibrium only by an Act of God."[62]

The president seemed to be casting his lot with the latter, using the radio very effectively to market his reforms, even though they were having little apparent effect on solving the economic problems. For this reason, Roosevelt's fireside chats still bothered Donham, and in 1936 he lumped the president with some of the more infamous rabble-rousers and crackpots of the time: Father Coughlin, the late Louisiana senator, Huey Long, and Dr. Townsend.[63] These people, with Roosevelt included, were marvelously adept at using nonlogical language to appeal to public emotions. Although such appeals had little intellectual substance, they traded in an emotional coinage that barely concealed the aim to overturn the social order.

Donham had not missed the fact that the European authoritarians using propaganda had hoodwinked whole nations into accepting their radical programs of reform. Such was the danger that Roosevelt's radio talks posed. Reform based upon mass appeal to nonlogical sentiments and passions, rather than the recovery of social stability based upon intellectual substance and reason, was the unthinkable option that Roosevelt offered to America.

However, Donham realized that the emotions could not be ignored, as they were the primitive foundation of human behavior. So what was to be done about these dangerous and volatile elements? Donham believed that emotions should be controlled in order to "strengthen the thin veneer of rationality"[64] that civilized behavior required. Such controls, short of brute force, were "strong social routines, institutions, habits, traditions and customs,"[65] all of which were residues Pareto had termed "persistent aggregates." But, as he had done so often before, Donham acknowledged that business and political leaders were not adequately educated to manage the mass's emotions. Yet those emotions had to be managed somehow if they were to respond adequately to the radicals, the Marxists, and other lunatics who were so good at tapping into the nonlogical wellsprings of human behavior. Thus, the job of the university was to train circumspect, conservative, and expert leaders to beat the crazies at their own game, and this is where the social sciences came in. They promised a rational, scientific approach to mass control.

Donham felt that social sciences had the potential to provide, on the one hand, a powerful national counterbalance to the radicals who were stirring up trouble in the labor force, and, on the other hand, to equip management with the techniques of social engineering that would enable them to regain the stability of the social order. One suspects that Donham's views on the social sciences were not terribly well formed in the 1920s. But as that decade closed and as the Hawthorne studies advanced during the 1930s, his predilections for them strengthened.

THE LABORATORY OF INDUSTRIAL PHYSIOLOGY

Donham's thought grew from a strong base of the pre-1938 achievements at Harvard in the social sciences. They had benefited from an infusion of new faculty, many of whom were just beginning their academic careers. These young people, working in collaboration with esteemed older colleagues, brought fresh points of view to such fields as sociology, psychology, and anthropology. They modernized the social sciences, which encouraged application of those principles to business. Sociology was a good example.

Harvard's sociology had a tradition of social uplift, since its sociology department was preceded by the social ethics department. The formation of the new department came rather late in the game, in the 1930s, and the old social ethics legacy must have been difficult for a person like Pitirim Sorokin, who chaired the department, to accept. He was dedicated to sociological studies that were unsullied by application or "sentimentality." This point of view may have been behind an acerbic paper that he wrote in which he referred to Henderson's and Mayo's Fatigue Lab as the "Harvard Research Center for Creative Altruism." Barnard commented, "I can just see L. J. [Henderson] frothing at the mouth at that one."[66] But more than the Fatigue Lab bothered Sorokin. A number of the most talented graduate students in the sociology department had fallen under Henderson's spell, and some of them were even working on the Hawthorne research project. Sorokin's irritation with Henderson was reciprocated. Barnard wrote, "Sorokin and Henderson probably gave each other mutual pains in the neck."[67]

To say that the Hawthorne studies were management's most influential social science research is no exaggeration. They provided a theoretical interpretation of job behavior and motivation, offered a philosophy of cooperation and social harmony, demonstrated the usefulness of the applied social sciences, and suggested practical techniques for labor control.[68] Donham and his cohorts saw that the clinical use of research data and interviewing techniques coming from the Hawthorne studies had the payoff of deradicalizing labor, and that in turn helped preserve the social order.

The Hawthorne studies is a generic name given to a series of experiments that began in 1924 and lasted until 1932. Through conventional usage this label has been applied to the classic human relations research and theory popularized by the Harvard researcher Fritz Roethlisberger and William J. Dickson, who headed employee relations research at the Hawthorne plant of Western Electric Company. This research, even now, is closely associated with Harvard.

However, the project was not conceived there. Rather, it was the offspring of the National Research Council's (NRC) Division of Engineering and Research. The first "Hawthorne" experiments were organized by this group in 1924, about two and a half years before Harvard became associated with them. The studies were interdisciplinary and interinstitutional, involving physicists, psychologists, and physiologists from eight universities who conducted experiments at four companies that provided research locations within the electrical industry. Western Electric's Hawthorne plant in Cicero, Illinois, was one of the sites. Other research studies were done at General Electric and Dennison Manufacturing Companies.

Considering the NRC's standing interest in psychology, it was not surprising that it promoted research in this area after the war. Furthermore, it was natural for it to encourage ergonomic studies, as this was the new and exciting branch of industrial psychology. The original studies, designed by the NRC and the electrical industry, dealt with illumination in the workplace and sought to determine the relationship between the quality of lighting and the productivity of the worker.

What followed is an often-told story, and it goes like this. The researchers assumed that productivity would increase as the lighting environment improved. It did. However, productivity also went up when the lighting got worse. This anomaly could not be explained by the standard theory of the times. Mayo posited, "Somehow or other that complex of mutually dependent factors, the human organism, shifted its equilibrium and unintentionally defeated the purpose of this experiment."[69] Undaunted by this "failure," the executives at Western Electric turned their attention to the problems of worker fatigue and monotony, subjects that were squarely within the expertise of the Fatigue Lab's scholars.

This new research direction appealed to Elton Mayo, freshly arrived at Harvard. His earlier research on worker fatigue coupled with Henderson's research skills in the natural sciences was a combination that Western Electric executives could hardly hope to improve upon. Henderson and Mayo contracted in 1927 to pursue, in a different vein, the line of research begun at Western Electric in 1924. However, as sociologist James Mulherin has pointed out, Mayo's immediate interest was not in productivity. He feared that "fatigue, monotony and associated mental states could trigger irrational passions which could burst forth in strife and potentially shake the foundations of functional hierarchies and threaten to overthrow the class structure."[70]

But even with this transfusion of new talent and ideas into the studies, something was lacking. While the researchers continued to produce much data, it was data in search of a theory. Mayo and Henderson were acutely aware of this problem. And eventually, from their deliberations, a theory emerged that was far more important to management than the studies' empirical findings.[71]

From the inception of the illumination experiments in 1924, the researchers took workers into their confidence and treated them as coparticipants in order to forestall their suspicion and to secure their cooperation. This approach had the unanticipated, but happy, outcome of increased worker productivity, within both the experimental and the control groups. The researchers did not know it then, but what they were observing was the so-called "Hawthorne effect."[72] Management at Western Electric had a great deal of interest in these results for instrumental reasons, and therefore wanted the matter studied more. Thus, the "relay assembly room" experiments under Harvard's leadership were designed and put in motion in 1927. They lasted until 1932. More than illumination was varied in these new experiments. The temperature and humidity of the test room was altered, variations in rest periods made, shorter working days and weeks were tried, the monotony and fatigue hypotheses were tested, different wage incentives were used, and on and on. This experiment and others that were conducted cost Western Electric over one million dollars before the depression ended the research program in 1932.

Because of the pre-Harvard discoveries, the Harvard researchers were aware "that light is only one, and apparently a minor, factor among many which affect employee output."[73] Consequently, fundamental to the new research was a plan to hold worker debriefing sessions that encouraged the worker subjects to express their feelings and attitudes. From transcripts of these sessions, Mayo concluded that a deep emotional effect was achieved when workers were allowed to participate, given recognition, and informed about what was going on. It often translated itself into higher productivity, as a way the workers had for thanking the researchers for treating them as human beings. Such emotions as those connected with feelings of self-worth, dignity, and acknowledgment of a job well done were more important motivators of behavior, according to Mayo, than the rational reasons people gave for working, that is, earning money.

These early sessions were the origin of an interviewing program established at Western Electric that served as a labor relations technique for employees to air dissatisfactions, doubts, and complaints. But a therapeutic aspect also underlay this program. It provided a safety valve to vent those worker emotions that, if bottled up, might threaten social stability. Donham wrote, "The basis of all successful efforts to control emotional states and to minimize their evil consequences, from the confessional to the most modern techniques of industrial relations and psychiatry, lies in getting such emotions out into the open where they are talked over freely and voluntarily."[74]

By the summer of 1936, with many lessons learned from Hawthorne, Donham was able to clarify the importance of the social sciences to management. "The most fundamental objects of business education and business management always involve methods . . . to devise and impose controls. Controls are necessary as the basis . . . for all effective efforts toward planned decisions and actions." The problems with the application of the social sciences to management were acute. They arose primarily from the difficulty of translating the theories and abstractions of social scientists into terms that made sense to practicing managers. As Donham put it, a man of action, "almost never understands the aids available to him from the work of the social scientists, and the social scientist is puzzled when such men fail to accept his conclusions as the basis for action."[75] Barnard put this problem succinctly when he reported to the trustees of the Rockefeller Foundation that "a science of concrete behavior would be necessary to support the management of concrete situations."[76] Barnard's conclusion was vintage Donham.

The Hawthorne studies seemed to bridge the gap between theory and practice in a way analogous to medicine's clinical model. Donham was certain of this model's utility, for it demonstrated how specialized theories and research findings could be applied to an action-oriented field of practice. But in order to bridge the gap between theory and practice in management, a "new" science of administration was required that integrated other sciences, such as the physical, the biological, the psychological, and the sociological, into a framework of specialized management logics, techniques, abstractions, and concepts of action.[77] In short, management needed a new epistemology and Barnard's faltering attempts to satisfy this need are discussed in chapter 5.

THE HARVARD CIRCLE'S NATIONAL AGENDA

In its broadest aspects the Harvard Circle reflected Herbert Hoover's political philosophy, the main features of which were collaboration, cooperation, education, and the voluntary commitment of individuals to organizations. Hoover molded his thoughts about the national values of voluntarism, associationism, professionalism, and rationality to his Quaker ideals of ordered freedom and individualism.[78]

Although Hoover was seldom cited in the books and articles written by people in the Harvard Circle, it was evident that they were sympathetic to his ideas. His political formula was congenial with the conclusion they had reached. Social problems were management problems, resolvable by:

- the development of a collaborative spirit that united associated economic and social interests in a way that would bring out the best in individuals and organizations.
- the encouragement of a managerial world-view that interpreted organizations as complex systems of interactions whose health depended upon the maintenance of an equilibrium among all of the forces at work in them.
- the governance of the entire nation as a cooperative enterprise under the dominant moral authority of leaders from the private sector.
- the education of this leadership to take decisive action regulated by professional norms of rationality, trustworthiness, justice, and benevolency.

Thus, the Harvard Circle's national agenda had everything to do with maintaining the moral authority, status, and perquisites of the managerial elite who represented the interests of major business corporations, private universities, and philanthropic foundations. The members of the circle were mostly conservatives, many from the Boston establishment, who wanted to preserve the status quo that had placed power in the hands of the private sector's guardians. This agenda required certain actions.

First, it was imperative to deradicalize labor—not just to wean it from Marxism but also to thwart unionization. This effort applied particularly to the industrial unions that were trying to organize semiskilled and unskilled workers in mass production industries. So while it may have been comforting for the elite to discover that their employees' demands were nonlogical, it was more to the point that they learn there were practical measures that could influence employee attitudes and motives. These measures promised to produce the sort of "right-thinking" employees who resisted the industrial unions' radical blandishments. The Hawthorne studies demonstrated how such influence might be applied by managers in concrete situations.

Second, and probably most important, the status quo could be guaranteed only if the public perceived that corporate management exercised legitimate authority. The minimum requirement of such legitimacy was managerial competence, and for that reason Mayo and Donham constantly emphasized the improvement of management's technical, social, and cooperative skills. They recognized the central importance of expertise in the public's perception of the legitimacy of leadership. However, more was at stake than management's competency. Managers also had to be good stewards—demonstratively ethical, honest, and trustworthy. And here education could lay the foundations for good moral character.

Third, management's skill and character could not be based simply on rules of thumb, homilies, and aphorisms. Good management decisions must derive from hard data that came from scientific research. Those in the Circle believed that management's most pressing research needs were in economics and the behavioral areas. Therefore they turned to the social sciences. Among other things, these sciences promised to help management explain the nonrational rationally. But mere explanation in a scientific sense was not the goal of the applied social sciences. Rather they were the means by which technologies could be created for intervening into the processes of individual attitude development and the formation of the norms of the small group. If intervention was successful, management could guide these processes into avenues that it deemed necessary to maintain worker cooperation. The Hawthorne studies seemed to demonstrate the practicality of the social sciences.

No academic group in the country understood the emerging managerial state better than the Harvard Circle. And no conservative group had a national agenda for modernization that could match the one it devised. On both of these counts Barnard's managerial and political views fitted with those of the Circle. He shared its interests on multiple intellectual, scientific, educational, and practical levels. However, given his full-time commitments as a top executive in the Bell System, he could not have been more than an adjunct member of the group. But an active one he was, giving lectures in courses and public forums, serving on "visiting committees" of the university acting in advisory capacities, and maintaining both correspondence and friendships with individuals. In his interview with Wolf, Barnard acknowledged that his most important connections with Harvard were his personal ones,[79] the sort of associations that counted for so much in Barnard's world of professional management.

The themes that the Harvard Circle pursued are apparent in Barnard's writing, but put in a different voice. They cannot be fathomed without some knowledge of his educational background, management experiences, organizational connections, and personal acquaintances.

4

The "Empirical" Barnard:
A Biographical Sketch

Barnard's birth date of November 7, 1886, fell in the short period of time between the Progressive appeals of Woodrow Wilson and those of Henry Towne for the reform of management practices in government and business organizations.[1] This historical coincidence only seems significant in hindsight, but during the years after that fortuitous juncture and the 1938 publication of Barnard's book, America had modernized. The old order of business and political power had reached its zenith when Barnard was a youngster. But reform was in the air, although its great presidential promoters, Woodrow Wilson and Theodore Roosevelt, did not appreciate the magnitude of what had been set in motion. Few knew as well as Barnard did in the 1930s what modernization meant for those professional managers who were leading the change.

ATT AND THE GIFFORD CONNECTION

Barnard called it an "associational specialization,"[2] the euphemism for an old-boy network that aptly described his connection with Walter S. Gifford. Although a scant twenty-two months older than Barnard, Gifford acted as Barnard's mentor and championed his cause throughout their forty-year tenure together with the Bell System. Gifford, who became ATT's longest-reigning CEO, helped Barnard advance his career within the Bell System and encouraged him to accept key appointments in various government and philanthropic organizations. The parallels in their careers were not coincidental. Gifford led and Barnard followed.

Gifford, born January 10, 1885, grew up in Salem, Massachusetts, ten miles or so from Barnard's birthplace in Malden. The Barnard family then moved to Cliftondale, where Chester attended grammar school. Their families were joined by business interests, and, one might suppose, by friendship. Barnard's future wife, Grace F. Noera, for example, had known Gifford when they were children.

She recalled giving him her pony after she tired of caring for it.[3] So it seemed that the tentacles of these small Massachusetts towns brought the Gifford and Barnard families together and resulted in the enduring Walter and Chester association.

Unlike Walter, Chester could not rely on his father, who was an impecunious sort, to help him financially. He said in his application to Mount Hermon school that he "was obliged when . . . fifteen years of age on graduating from the grammar school to work"[4] as a piano tuner, a trade he learned at the Emerson Piano Company in Boston. Having a good ear and with a natural talent for music, Chester picked up the skill quickly. From Emerson he moved to a job with a piano dealership, the George H. Champlin Company, where he tuned pianos in its warehouse. Chester practiced this trade for a little over two years, from 1902 to 1904. However, he felt that he was slated for better things, and that required more formal education. Therefore, he applied for admission to the Mount Hermon school.

Mount Hermon, founded by the famous evangelist Dwight Lyman Moody, aimed "to furnish a thorough Christian training to young men and boys of earnest purpose but small means."[5] The flagship program at Mount Hermon was its college preparatory curriculum that fitted boys of the deserving poor to enter prestigious private colleges in the East.

The application form that the elder Barnard filled out for his son admonished on the cover sheet, "Lazy boys are not desired."[6] Affirming Chester's industriousness, his father wrote that he was "strong minded, studious, ambitious, quick to learne, moral."[7] He also pointed out that "the candidate" was responsible for tuition, room and board, and all other expenses associated with his education.

In a personal letter that accompanied this application, Chester explained to Henry F. Cutler, the headmaster, why he wanted more education. In a revealing passage of this letter, he wrote that "this dormant thirst for a larger education was awakened by my conversion to the Lord Jesus Christ, when I felt that I had capabilities which needed developing for his use. And that is now my ultimate aim—to be used of Him and to make the most of my life for Him."[8] Barnard was admitted to Mount Hermon for the summer term of 1904.

However, Chester delayed starting his schoolwork until the fall term of that year because he had become ill in the spring and the doctor advised him to postpone studying for awhile. So Chester asked Cutler for a job on the school's farm for the summer months. Fortunately, such employment was possible, and Barnard recollected that he worked on the farm for twenty-three dollars a month plus food. He fondly recalled, in his interview with Wolf, that he got up at five o'clock in the morning to groom the horses, pitch hay, and plow. He remarked that he particularly liked plowing because he had "a nice team of horses that followed orders."[9]

Although Chester did not tell Cutler what was wrong with him, he admitted to Wolf that he contracted what was known in those days as "nervous fever." This stress-induced illness resulted from hard work at the Champlin Company as well as intense study in preparation for the Mount Hermon entrance examinations. Barnard confessed to being "pretty sick" for two or three weeks.[10] But rest and outdoor farm life speeded his recovery, and he began classes in the fall term.

The requirements at Mount Hermon suited Chester's religious conversion. Bible study courses were required of students in each of the terms in which they were in residence. Chester took six Bible courses and received either an E (excellent) or a G (good) in them. His other subjects were English, singing, elocution, penmanship, spelling, Latin, Greek, algebra, geometry, geography, elementary science, and history. He did well in all of them except algebra, and that may have reflected his interest in the classics over mathematics and science.[11]

Chester's extracurricular duties at school included that of janitor of the chapel and vestry, monitor of chapel attendance, substitute organist, and ringer of the bell that called students to worship. Much later, Barnard remembered that once some pranksters muffled the bell's clapper, and when he braced himself for a mighty peal nothing happened but continued silence.[12] Chester was not amused by practical jokes.

Although he applied for the diploma program, Chester left Mount Hermon in 1906 without graduating. He had already been accepted at Harvard, and that was his aim all along. He regretted that he had spent only two years at the school, but they had a lasting effect on his character and attitudes. In a letter that he wrote from Cambridge to his former headmaster when he was about to finish at Harvard, he said, "On the whole, I think I got as much or more good from two years at Hermon than from my three years at college."[13]

The school's nondenominational Christian orientation reinforced his Yankee deism and his suspicion of organized religions with their elaborate theologies. Barnard's faith was a very private affair, and he seldom discussed his personal religious views even with family members.[14] Regardless, his attitudes about sectarianism must have come into play as president of the Rockefeller Foundation during the period when it debated the place of moral philosophy in its programs and policies. Barnard adamantly opposed the Foundation's embroilment in interdenominational squabbles (the Rockefeller saga is treated in Chapter 9).

Walter Gifford preceded Chester to Harvard. He entered college at the age of sixteen and finished the four-year course in three, graduating cum laude with his class of 1905. With his degree work complete in 1904, Gifford applied for a job with the Western Electric Company, the manufacturing subsidiary of ATT. Gifford acknowledged on his application that he had no special qualifications but wanted office work.[15] A Harvard education was probably enough to impress the management at Western Electric because Gifford was hired. Gifford's contribution to ATT in later years certainly vindicated this decision.

Barnard entered Harvard in 1906, a member of the large and storied class of 1910 that included T. S. Eliot and Walter Lippmann. He too left college after three years, but without a degree since he lacked a science requirement.[16] That did not bother Chester, especially since he had an attractive alternative. Barnard and

Gifford had been in touch in January of 1909 and had discussed the possibility of Chester working for ATT in the statistics department that Walter had just established in Boston. Barnard showed interest, as did Gifford, who asked the headmaster at Mount Hermon to write a letter of recommendation for his former pupil. Barnard apologized to Cutler for not warning him that this request was coming. He believed that Gifford would not bother to look him up. Nevertheless what Gifford learned from Barnard's references satisfied him. Chester was offered a position that he described to Cutler as "full of great opportunity."[17]

Chester took the occasion of this letter to thank his headmaster for the opportunity to advance his education and for the inspirational sermons at chapel when Cutler encouraged the boys to go to college. Barnard said that he would not have gotten the job with ATT without a college education.

Barnard started as a clerk, directly responsible to Gifford in the statistics department. The position, as Barnard sketched it, required "considerable technical knowledge of accounting and a good reading knowledge of several foreign languages."[18] Chester saw a promising future for himself at ATT. The company was undergoing a major reorganization and expansion when Barnard joined it. These corporate events led to the election, for a second time, of Theodore N. Vail as president of the company.

Vail served his first term as president from 1885 to 1887, when he laid the foundations for the long-distance telephone network. Vail left the company because of a disagreement with the Boston financiers over the best strategy to monopolize the industry in order to maintain control after the telephone patents expired. But expansion at the turn of the century required new capital, and again the backing of Eastern financiers was solicited. These outsiders were not pleased with the current management, and they induced the board of directors to appoint Vail as a director, a position from which he returned as president of ATT.

Vail was one of the great American business imperialists who created the modern telephone company that dominated the industry until the divestiture of 1984. Vail was no friend of competition, believing that more than one telephone company in America was one more too many. He argued that telephone service was a natural monopoly and imagined that the public held the same opinion. However, he felt that this monopoly had to be regulated by government, much as were other public utilities. "Private management and ownership, subordinate to public interest and under rational control and regulation by national, state, and municipal bodies is the best possible system," he stated.[19]

That the public actually saw things this way was not altogether evident when Vail's massive campaign to absorb independent telephone companies was underway. Populist sentiment then opposed the monopolization of the telephone system. The postmasters general fed on this opposition, and most of them endorsed the nationalization of telephone and telegraph services under the auspices of the U.S. Post Office, following the pattern of a number of European countries. Vail perceived such public sentiments and the ambitions of government officials as dangerous impediments to his plans for the Bell System.

The Statistics Department

One of Vail's measures to deal with these threats was the establishment of a statistics department in the corporation, one of the first of its kind in American business, with Gifford as chief statistician. The department had a broadly defined information-gathering mission that included the collection of data about the cost, quality, and distribution of ATT services compared to independent American companies and foreign systems that were government owned and operated. Barnard had a talent for foreign languages, so his first assignment was to conduct a survey of telephone rates and services in Europe. He concluded from this research that state ownership resulted in higher rates, poorer quality equipment, and restricted distribution of telephone facilities. These facts were quickly brought to the attention of politicians and the public.

The statistics department also obtained intelligence on domestic competition that helped management decide what independent companies to acquire. Much of Barnard's work in the early days pertained to analyzing and distributing this type of information.[20] The department also provided the operating companies with staff reports that assisted them with their rate cases before the courts and state public service commissions.

Finally the statistics department prepared public relations material to counter charges that the telephone monopoly was making excessive profits. Since such allegations were often made by those seeking government seizure of the telephone system, Barnard monitored the government ownership movement, which he reported to be losing steam in 1914. He wrote Harry B. Thayer[21] that the movement seemed dormant because public attention was distracted by affairs on the Mexican border. Nevertheless he recommended that ATT continue its program of public education because speeches by corporate executives, informational pamphlets, press releases to newspapers, and lobbying Congress were the first lines of defense against government takeovers.[22]

Thus, as a corporate clearinghouse for information, Gifford made his department a hub of company affairs and a good place for Barnard to begin his career. There he dealt with one of the main financial matters of the company, telephone rates. His reports on these issues and others, such as public relations, put his name in front of upper-level corporate executives. Hard work, loyalty, and intelligence paid off for Barnard, and he was promoted to commercial engineer. In that capacity he served as an advisor to a number of the associated companies that were the regional operating divisions of the Bell System. Barnard's most notable success came before the Colorado Public Service Commission in 1918, where he argued for a rate increase for Mountain States Telephone and Telegraph Company. He admitted to N. C. Kingsbury, a vice president in corporate headquarters,[23] that he did not expect his proposed highly favorable rate schedule to be accepted. But it was, and Barnard got another feather in his corporate cap. He was by every measure an outstanding staff member. Four years after the Colorado hearings, and continued exemplary work, Barnard received a promotion to his first line job, vice president and general manager of the Pennsylvania Bell Telephone Company. He was on his way up the corporate ladder.

So was Gifford. Immediately after World War I, as corporate comptroller and vice president, he devised a financial scheme to capitalize yet another round of company expansion. This plan, brilliant as it was simple, broadened the base of ATT ownership and at the same time avoided the onerous prospect of depending upon the investment of bankers and financiers, who would also interfere with management. The idea was to sell stock in the company to the multitudes.

Gifford reasoned that millions of "little people" had hundreds of millions of dollars earning paltry returns in savings accounts. These now fabled "widows and orphans" wanted a secure haven and a predictable return on their modest savings. Gifford was prepared to give it to them in the form of a fixed dividend on their shares, one that yielded around 8.5 percent per annum, a far better rate of return than the small investor could get in a savings bank.

However, the uniqueness of this stratagem did not lie so much in the fixed-dividend policy. Rather, it was in the method of stock distribution. Gifford conceived the idea of selling stock through the associated companies' commercial offices, enlisting all employees as salespersons. Furthermore, these salespeople would not be paid commissions for the shares they sold. They would sell, Gifford argued, because they were part of the ATT family, and what benefited it would benefit them in the long run.

So with one stroke Gifford cut out underwriters, brokerage houses, and other odious middlemen. The progress of this program was discussed at a commercial conference of the presidents of the associated Bell System companies in 1924. The president of Illinois Bell, one Mr. Bone, told his colleagues that initially his employees resisted selling stock without getting paid. But they got on the band-wagon when he explained to them that "salesmanship is not necessary in the sale of stock and that they are not expected to go out and try to sell stock to strangers, but rather to talk it over amongst their relatives, friends and acquaintances."[24] This argument, according to Bone, quelled employee dissent and they exceeded the 1923 Illinois Bell quota of selling 30,000 shares to 8,000 purchasers by selling 32,744 shares to 8,277 purchasers. Although a model program, Illinois Bell illustrated the operation of Gifford's plan very well. In recognition for his financial wizardry, Gifford was promoted to president of ATT in 1925.

Two years after Gifford's accession to CEO, Barnard was promoted from Pennsylvania to the presidency of New Jersey Bell, a newly created associated company. Formed from the merger of the New Jersey properties of the New York Telephone Company and the Delaware and Atlantic Telegraph and Telephone

Company, New Jersey Bell was to be Barnard's corporate home for twenty-one years until he retired.

Years and Years at New Jersey Bell

Barnard once commented that the fortunes of a telephone company mirrored national events, and the twenty-one years he spent as president of New Jersey Bell Telephone (NJBT) attested to this fact. From the formation of NJBT until Barnard retired, the country went from a dizzy prosperity through an awful depression, a terrible world war, and a wrenching postwar period of readjustment that included serious labor disputes. In its own way, NJBT was a microcosm of the times.

"On October 1, 1927, the Delaware and Atlantic Telephone and Telegraph Company purchased the properties of the New York Telephone Company in northern and central New Jersey, and at the same time changed its corporate name to New Jersey Bell Telephone Company."[25] So begins the new company's first annual report for 1927. The company was formed to exploit the financial opportunities that lay in providing improved service to an economically expanding state.

Barnard's first message to the employees after he became president dwelt on the industrial development of major New Jersey cities, the expansion of recreational facilities on the Jersey shore, and the strong agricultural base of the interior of the state. Management had to provide excellent telephone service to each of these segments of New Jersey's diversified economic base.[26] And the design of such a system had also to take into account the substantial population growth occurring in the metropolitan areas of the northern part of the state. The acceleration of this growth was partly the result of the tunneling and bridging of the rivers that separated New Jersey from the populous adjacent areas of New York, Delaware and Pennsylvania. All of this activity foreordained more telephone installations and a rise in the volume of originating telephone calls. It seemed clear to Barnard in 1927 that NJBT had to make major new investments in plant and equipment in order to cope with the increased demand for telephone services that the prosperity of the times seemed to portend.

Barnard called his employees' attention to another problem that was not unusual to companies formed from a merger: the integration of the operations and the cultures of two distinct organizations. He warned the employees not to think of NJBT as an isolated entity but as a part of the Bell System. As such the Bell culture would provide the integrating force for the new company that served nearly 4 million people, or 98 percent of the state population. It had 570,000 telephones in service and rated eleventh among the Bell associated companies for telephones in use.

Thus, NJBT was born during the halcyon years of the Roaring Twenties. And, despite the management problems of amalgamating two organizations, it prospered, reporting an 8 percent return on investment (ROI) for 1928 and 1929.

Approximately 70,000 new telephones were installed between 1927 and 1929. These and other indexes, such as substantial increases in the volume of originating calls and long-distance calls, pointed to vibrant company health.[27]

The 1929 annual report raised an issue that then seemed to be well in hand—the conversion of the state to dial service. Optimistically, management forecasted that by 1935 "more than half of New Jersey's telephones will be served by dial equipment."[28] When Barnard retired in 1947 just a little more than 40 percent were converted, and he was criticized for his failure to pursue the "dial program" more aggressively. The problem of dial conversion plagued Barnard during most of his tenure as president.

Promising as these beginnings were, they did not last. In 1932, Barnard told employees in the company magazine, "we began on an up-swing of prosperity and ended it at the depths of a depression which has produced a new experience of actually losing business."[29] NJBT was suffering, but less so than most other American businesses. As early as 1930, when the effects of the depression were just beginning to be felt, NJBT reported adverse trends. Many telephones were disconnected, and the net number of new connections was an anemic 18,000. ROI dropped dramatically, the company showing a 5.4 percent return for 1930. Throughout the early 1930s ROI declined, reaching a depression low of 3.29 percent in 1933. Not only did telephone disconnections exceed connections, but also, and worse, the overall volume of local and long-distance calls dropped substantially.

Amid the insecurity and unrest caused by the worsening depression, Barnard decided to address NJBT employee and management representatives in August 1933.[30] Barnard dealt first with economic issues and then told employees a good-news-bad-news story. The good news was that no one would be laid off at NJBT, pension and benefit plans would continue, and paid vacations would not be suspended. The bad news was that hours would be reduced by a work-sharing plan and that some early retirements would be required. Reduced hours would, of course, result in reduced annual income, but Barnard emphasized that because of a decline in the cost of living most employees would be in as good a position financially as they were in 1929.

Apparently receiving some employee criticism about management salaries and dividends to stockholders (ATT, the parent company, owned an overwhelming percentage of the outstanding shares), Barnard observed that management's earnings were reduced and that the shareholders' dividends declined substantially. That managerial earnings dropped some 10 percent, as against 15 percent for employees, was accounted for by the fact that "management are supposed to work harder, they are supposed to work for the benefit of all employees."[31] Pointing out that not a great many people want supervisory jobs and that competent supervision was the only way to develop an organization, fairness seemed to dictate that the managers should be penalized less. Furthermore, even if the salaries of all management personnel were cut in half, the paycheck of each worker would increase only fifty cents a month. Barnard concluded that NJBT employees were not in such bad shape, and they should be happy that they still had their jobs.

Moving on from the issues of wages, hours, and job security, Barnard turned to the new NRA codes and unionization.[32] NJBT supported the objectives of the NIRA, and it was anxious to cooperate with the federal government to bring about economic recovery. So the company signed the code agreement that covered its industry. However, because the policies of NJBT were so generous, it far exceeded the minimum standards set by the industry code for important matters such as total weekly hours of work, wages per hour, and the employment of juveniles. Consequently, these aspects of the NRA code were not a problem for the company.

However, Section 7(a) of the act was. This provision required that management bargain collectively with unions, a matter that had been unthinkable in times past. Barnard stated, "The question of union labor is something we have not been accustomed to talk about to our people."[33] Barnard obliquely described company policy in this respect, "We have no rules about it [unions] and yet we all know and certainly would expect that people who belong to outside unions would not be welcome in this organization."[34]

Yet, NJBT signed the code, and had to abide by Section 7(a). This created a dilemma for the company. Barnard observed that the decision to sign the code did not suggest that the company was changing its policy on unions and collective bargaining; what it did suggest was that employees could no longer be protected by the company if they did not want union representation. Alternatively, the company could not fire any employee who joined a union. And at this point Barnard launched into his philosophy of unions, one of the few times he made a public statement on this subject.

Barnard acknowledged his respect for union leaders. They were, he thought, for the most part honest, able, and true to their beliefs. Unions by and large were not rackets, nor were their leaders corrupt. But "the union method of dealing with employment has never gained anything" for workers except those in highly competitive markets.[35] Therefore, they were not helpful for furthering the welfare of NJBT employees.

Our business is not subject to chiseling by competitors who, by bad treatment of their employees, force unreasonable standards on really fine employers in order that they may compete with the others, and the good employer is helpless, except as some union organization may be able to hold the situation. Our aim has always been stabilization of reasonable results to investors in the business as well as reasonable wages and working conditions for our people, permanency of relationship as far as the employees wanted it, and there are none of the conditions or motives in our business which may justify the adoption of the so-called union method in other businesses.[36]

The alternative to outside unions was the ATT Plan of Employee Representation. Denying allegations that it was a company union, Barnard argued that the plan permitted bargaining if the employees wanted it. However, the plan served a more important purpose of facilitating employee cooperation with management on issues of mutual importance including terms of employment as well as more general aspects of the business. Barnard felt that the plan did more to establish harmonious relations in the company. Collective bargaining, however, presumed an adversarial relationship between the parties, and this attitude was inimical to the spirit of cooperation.

Consequently, he warned his audience about being seduced by the promises of outsiders—labor organizers—who promised things that they could not deliver. Instead, Barnard adjured the employees to trust management because it gave them the opportunity to do a job "that had some interest in it, that could enlist their loyalty, that could make them feel they really belong somewhere in the world and were tied up to an institution that really deserved their support and their continued loyalty."[37] He summarized this exhortation by saying that the company wanted "to maintain . . . a spirit and condition of cooperation on the part of employees, a cooperative frame of mind on the part of the management so that neither side is trying to chisel something out of the other."[38]

Barnard's speech represented the corporate (ATT) position on government regulations and unionization. Nevertheless he personally believed in the values of cooperation and voluntarism, holding a philosophical position on these matters that was similar to Herbert Hoover's. Since Barnard stood for the interests of the managerial class that controlled corporations, government and labor represented a challenge to those interests. If they were successful in pressing their claims, management discretion would be reduced. This prospect of sharing power with labor was no more palatable to management in 1933 than the prospect of doing so with women and minorities is today.

The depression's nadir, in 1933, was also NJBT's worst year until 1947. However, the economy improved slightly in 1934, and with it NJBT's fortunes. The trend begun that year lasted throughout the rest of the 1930s. At 6.25 percent, ROI in 1939 was almost back to 1930 and 1931 levels, although it was not close to its 1929 level of over 8 percent.[39]

The year 1939 also marked the start of America's war preparedness program. NJBT prospered from the economic fallout induced by government spending. Significant growth in the volume of telephone calls, net new telephone installations, and long-distance service testified to the fact that business was improving. And it easily met the increased demand for services because it had retained an able work force, thanks to Barnard's no-layoff policy, and it had a vastly underutilized capacity. With the fall of Paris in 1940, it seemed inevitable, at least to Barnard, that the United States would sooner or later be involved in the war in Europe. Consequently, he felt it was his duty to inform the men and women of the telephone industry of the difficult times ahead. The occasion was the annual meeting of the Telephone Pioneers of America; the time was October 1940, and the place was the Ambassador Hotel in New York City. Barnard apologized for the somber tone of his address.[40]

His speech began in a peculiar way. Barnard made note of the isolationist attitudes in the Midwest and far Western regions of the nation and thought that the internationalist point of view found in the Northeast was by far the most enlightened. He hoped that the rest of the country would take the situation in Europe as seriously and prepare itself for the great demands of war.

Acknowledging that ATT's communication system lay at the logistical core of the war effort, Barnard told the Pioneers about the necessity of personal loyalty and sacrifice for the cause, as they were the ingredients for successfully meeting the tests to come. The future requirements of telephone service in the impending national emergency would require that employees work more hours and receive a relative increase in pay. The prospect of more work and more money increased pressure on the supply of goods and services. Shortages would ensue, and they would force the government to ration, unless people curtailed their buying. In the same breath Barnard warned of the inflationary threat of full employment. Encouraging his listeners to defeat it, he recommended self-denial. "We must go without things,"[41] he intoned, reiterating the theme of asceticism that he seldom tired of mentioning.

After December 7, 1941, an America at war indeed had shortages, rationing, higher taxes, rising prices, and personal dislocations created by war work and military service. As Barnard had predicted, Americans had to sacrifice for the sake of the war effort. The demands on NJBT were particularly severe; its facilities were stretched to the limits, and beyond, by the rapid expansion of war-related activities in the state. The annual reports for the period between 1941 and 1945 documented the company's attempts to meet these emergency demands and still deliver reasonable civilian and business services. However, ROI stayed steady during the war years at a rather lackluster 4.5 percent, "a sufficient indication," so said the 1944 annual report, "that the company was not profiting from its wartime operations."[42]

The explosion of atom bombs over Hiroshima and Nagasaki forced the Japanese to surrender in early September 1945. World War II was over, and the use of atomic weapons spurred the United Nations to establish its Atomic Energy Commission, to which Barnard served as a consultant in 1949. However, that was in the future, and he had his plate full at NJBT during his two remaining postwar years with the company.

NJBT emerged from the war with a depleted physical plant and obsolete equipment; remedying those conditions required a major infusion of capital. Contributing to the problem of raising money were two unfavorable events in 1947. First, the New Jersey Board of Public Utility Commissioners ruled on a rate increase that would yield an additional $10 million a year, $6 million short of what NJBT asked for. Second, a six-week nationwide telephone company strike, called by the

National Federation of Telephone Workers, greatly reduced revenues. As a result, NJBT's 1947 net income compared to 1946 dropped over $5.5 million—a staggering decrease of 84.8 percent.[43] Return on investment during this same year registered a bare 1 percent. NJBT's financial results were bad, and Barnard seemed to be under the gun. Criticism prompted him to write and distribute to his management group an extraordinary memorandum, a few months short of his retirement. In it he tried to justify his decision to go slow on converting NJBT to a dial system. Herein lay the story of what may have been Barnard's most important strategic decision in his twenty-one years as CEO.

Some of Barnard's fellow executives at NJBT and at ATT headquarters apparently had attributed the terrible performance in 1947 to Barnard's go-slow policy toward statewide conversion to the dial system. The 1947 annual report mentioned, for example, that the dial exchanges in the state were unaffected by the strike in that year,[44] with the clear implication that had conversion been more extensive, total revenues would have been higher than the meager 5 percent increase reported. Further, the operating efficiencies of the dial system had the potential to compensate for the unfavorable rate rulings of the public utility commission. Table 4.1 shows the dial phones in service as a percentage of the total number of telephones throughout NJBT's territory during Barnard's years as president compared to the percentage for the Bell System nationwide.

Barnard's memorandum, titled "The History and Economics of the Dial Program of the New Jersey Bell Telephone Company" (later privately reprinted by Barnard as a pamphlet), justified his conservative stance on conversion.[45] In it he traced the development of dial technology that was in use as early as 1922 in the large metropolitan areas of the state. He argued that while practical in high-density markets, this technology was not economical in New Jersey's small towns and rural areas. A wholesale conversion throughout the state, Barnard argued, was a financially unwarranted substitution of capital for labor.

Even though he acknowledged the company's serious financial condition, Barnard nevertheless concluded his memorandum with the observation that "what was done from 1928 on was substantially correct."[46] He indicated that had he decided otherwise and pushed for a more rapid conversion, the financial difficulties the company was experiencing at the time would have been even worse than they were.[47] In retrospect, this assessment seems doubtful. Even at the time, however, Barnard must have known that other operating companies were converting to dial technology far more aggressively than NJBT. By 1937 nearly one-half of the telephones in the Bell system were dial.

Between 1928 and 1932, NJBT had been on a fairly rapid conversion course and in five years increased the number of dial phones in the state by some 24 percent (see Table 4.1), with dial service available to approximately one-third of its subscribers. From 1932 through the depression, conversion slowed, showing a slight spurt in 1940. As Table 4.1 indicates, nearly 60 percent of the phones in New Jersey were still manual when Barnard retired from the company in 1947,

Table 4.1. Dial Telephones as a Percentage of Total Telephones in Service in New Jersey and in the Bell System Nationwide, 1928–1947

Year	NJBT Percent	Bell System Percent
1928	8	22.3
1929	12	26.6
1930	20	31.8
1931	22	37.2
1932	32	42.5
1933	33	45.8
1934	35	47.1
1935	35	48.0
1936	35	48.6
1937	35	49.8
1938	34	52.4
1939	34	55.7
1940	40	59.9
1941	43	63.3
1942	42	65.1
1943	42	65.0
1944	NA[a]	64.9
1945	NA[a]	64.6
1946	NA[a]	64.3
1947	41	65.6

[a] It is reasonable to assume that owing to wartime shortages of materials, the percentage of dial telephones remained at around 40 during these years.
Source: NJBT annual reports for all years except 1947; 1947 percentage is calculated from figures given by Barnard in his twentieth-anniversary message to employees (Chester I. Barnard, "Starting Our Third Decade," New Jersey Bell, October 1947, p. 3, NJBTR); Bell System Statistical Manual: 1920–1962, Business Research Division, American Telephone and Telegraph Co., March 1963, ATTA, B175 11 01, p. 3.

whereas just slightly more than 34 percent were manual throughout the Bell system.

Barnard's conservative philosophy resulted in unsurprising policies. For example, he pointed out that "making a large investment [in dial equipment] much in advance of the period of its efficient use is rarely warranted," a philosophy that apparently was not shared by the presidents of other associated companies.[48] While this was probably sound policy during the depression for a public utility not confronting an emergency situation, it was also a serious miscalculation, as the war crisis proved. Because equipment was unavailable during the war, conversion stalled, and with expanded demand and the shortage of trained personnel, NJBT was severely strained to carry the loads placed on its system. The situation quickly reversed after the war, but labor strife, high operating expenses, and an unfriendly public utility commission cancelled out any advantages that a "peace bonus" might have brought to the company. So Barnard summed up by stating that since the depression, World War II, and the strike were beyond his control, he could not be held wholly to blame for NJBT's troubles.

Barnard's twenty-one years of stewardship at NJBT were not perceived as a disaster by those at corporate headquarters; otherwise he would not have been kept at its helm for so long a time. But neither were these years a brilliant success, and more is said about this at the end of the chapter. However, it is poignant that Barnard felt it necessary to justify his stewardship. Barnard's later career with the Bell System seemed under a cloud, and it says a lot for his character to take the unprecedented step of writing, and publicly distributing, a document that presented his point of view on such a technical and controversial management decision. But what did he have to lose? He was to be off soon to head the Rockefeller Foundation where he would spend all of his time in public service, a role he enjoyed but could only partially indulge as a phone company employee.

Barnard's Other Life of Public Service

As most public utilities, ATT took its social responsibilities seriously and encouraged its executives to participate in all sorts of service activities in the local community, government, education, health care, theater, the fine arts, and philanthropy. Barnard's excursions into public life started soon after he joined ATT, and for many years he followed Gifford's lead in choosing assignments.

Gifford, just thirty-one years old, was given a leave of absence in 1917 from the company to become the director of the Council of National Defense and the Advisory Commission of the Council. These organizations were restructured under his leadership to form a new "general staff of industry," otherwise known as the War Industries Board.[49] In recognition of his organizational skills, Bernard Baruch made Gifford his deputy chief, and he served in this capacity for eight months until the war ended and the emergency agencies disbanded. Barnard was also a member of the WIB, and worked for the war effort as a technical advisor to the rate commission of the U.S. Telephone Administration. Gifford probably encouraged Barnard to accept this assignment and to use his knowledge of languages and telephone rates in the national interest.

Like others in the WIB, Gifford and Barnard learned many lessons from their experiences with government about the advantages of centralized coordination of industry and the indisputable value of cooperation among industrial leaders during emergencies. This knowledge of crisis management proved valuable when they were next asked to help the nation in another major calamity, the Great Depression. On August 19, 1931, Gifford accepted Herbert Hoover's appointment "to create and direct an organization that shall coordinate and reinforce unemployment relief activities throughout the United States."[50] Gifford moved to Washington, D.C., to head the National Unemployment Commission and there worked in close proximity to his old acquaintance, the president.

Hoover's and Gifford's paths had crossed during the first war, but they were more frequently in touch when Hoover was secretary of commerce. In those early days of radio, the secretary assigned broadcast frequencies, a function that brought him into regular contact with ATT management anxious to reserve certain dedicated frequency bands for radiotelephony.[51]

On a widely publicized occasion in 1927, Gifford in New York interviewed Hoover in Washington over the first-ever long-distance television transmission.[52] Hoover, therefore, was no stranger to ATT's affairs, and in addition he and Gifford had much in common philosophically. Consequently, Gifford's nomination to the unemployment commission was a natural extension of a longstanding personal connection. For Hoover, this appointment was particularly sensitive since Gifford's performance in the job would have a direct bearing on his political future.

Following Gifford's example in the federal government, Barnard took command of the New Jersey Emergency Relief Administration in October of 1931, just two months after his chief's assignment to Washington. His work with the New Jersey agency was apparently laudable since the New Jersey Exchange Club awarded him its medal of service for his exemplary contribution to the state's relief program. Proud of these achievements, Barnard wrote up the "riot" incident that occurred during his tenure and used it as a case study in good management for class presentations at Harvard. Barnard's work with the state relief program led to his appointment, in 1934, by the U.S. Chamber of Commerce to its committee that studied relief expenditures and related activities in America. But by 1935, feeling that he had done all that he could for the unemployed, Barnard ended his services to these voluntary programs. Of course, by that time the New Deal was in full swing. Barnard disapproved of many of the reform measures taken by the administration, especially its "make-work" schemes. As Hoover's cherished voluntarism disappeared in the wake of massive government intervention in the economy, Barnard disappeared with it insofar as his work for the unemployed was concerned.

The values that informed Barnard's position toward the unemployment question did not deviate greatly from Hoover's or Gifford's. In his opinion, as well as in theirs, economic recovery depended on voluntary national coordination and industrial cooperation inspired by the moral authority of leaders in private enterprise. These WIB tenets, modified to suit the private interests of corporate management, were well understood by these men. Hoover in particular believed that needed reforms could be had by appealing to peoples' better natures, an approach he had developed during his involvement with Belgian Relief and with food conservation and production during the war. Hoover did not approve of draconian social experiments, such as the syndicalization and cartelization of industry. That had to wait until Franklin Roosevelt's presidency. When it came, the Barnards and the Giffords of America were appalled. Voluntary cooperation and coordination were jeopardized by centralized state planning.

As Hoover, Barnard held subsidiarity-type principles of community self-help and local government action, believing them to be most desirable for solving the problem of unemployment and distributing relief for the intractably jobless. Clearly the New Deal's national employment programs such as the Civilian Conservation Corps (CCC) and the Work Projects Administration (WPA) violated Barnard's ideals of local self-determination (and drove up labor costs in the bargain). At the most fundamental level of human motivation, Barnard reasoned that people wanted to work, that they did not want charity, and that relief should be given to those only in the most extreme cases of need. He sent this message to the Trenton rioters who he portrayed as confused, misinformed, and poorly led. However, he admitted that the six cents per meal per person food dole was probably not enough to survive on. However, the angst of the depression years was dispelled by a new national emergency brought on by the war in Europe. As the American economy geared up for military preparedness and to supply its allies with war materials, unemployment and underutilized industrial capacity vanished like a bad dream. The war, not the New Deal, ended the depression. But different imperatives and problems replaced the old, and many American managers took on new roles.

As early as July 1940, Barnard had been courted by Washington to help the government with war preparations. He declined these initial overtures, saying that his duty was "with himself, his industry, and his family." However, once it became evident to him that his primary duty lay with his country above all else, "there will be no debate."[53] Barnard reached that critical point in October 1941, when he accepted the invitation of Secretary of the Treasury Henry Morgenthau, Jr., to serve as an assistant to the secretary. Barnard joined the growing numbers of corporate executives who were on loan from their companies to the government, working as "dollar-a-year men" for the nation. Barnard's duties at NJBT were temporarily assigned to his vice president and general manager, G. W. McRae, who had run the company for years on a day-to-day operating basis.

McRae did not have to fill in for very long because Barnard left Washington and government immediately after the Japanese attack on Pearl Harbor. He returned to his old stand in Newark before the New Year of 1942. His first Washington tour lasted nine weeks, and he recounted it as an unpleasant experience.[54] Several things made it so. First, Barnard felt that government was in the hands of the Communists and that they made life miserable for the dollar-a-year-men from industry. Second, although Morgenthau promised Barnard he would not have to work on taxation policies, that was what he spent most of his time doing. Third, he was put off by Morgenthau's personality, work habits, and most of all, by his administrative incapacity.

In a revealing estimate of Morgenthau, Barnard wrote, "His mind is of the intuitive type, involving shrewd judgements of men and propositions . . . ordinarily associated with the Hebrew mind . . . in other aspects it was highly feminine—rather disorganized and disorderly."[55] Even though Barnard found Morgenthau to be courageous, conscientious, and a persistent hard driver, he thought that "these qualities lead him to be a superior-chief clerk rather than an executive."[56] All in all, Morgenthau's limitations seemed due to a "lack of practical experience, and to a lack of reading and study, thence to a greatly inadequate intellectual equipment."[57] Nothing pleased Barnard more than when he found the opportunity to bow out gracefully from the Treasury Department, and he noted wryly that seven weeks after resigning he received a Treasury check of eighteen cents, his prorated dollar-a-year salary.[58]

The second time Barnard left NJBT was in the spring of 1942 to assume the presidency of the United Service Organizations (USO), a nonprofit corporation that provided recreational and welfare services for the armed forces. Upon releasing Barnard for this assignment, the NJBT board of directors again named the long-suffering McRae acting president,[59] where he stayed for over a year. Barnard got the USO off the ground by the end of 1943, when he returned to active duty at NJBT. He remained USO president until 1945, and he received the Medal of Merit awarded by Harry S. Truman for exemplary service in its behalf. Three years after the USO, Barnard captured the plum assignment in the management of nonprofit organizations. He became president of the Rockefeller Foundation.

The Rockefeller Foundation

Walter Gifford, who had been a member of the RF's board of trustees since 1936, may have had a hand in Barnard's appointment to it in 1940. Although this is not certain, it is clear that Gifford and Walter W. Stewart, the chairman of the board, championed Barnard's candidacy for president of the Foundation eight years later, when Raymond B. Fosdick planned to retire.

Gifford told the board members that Barnard would do a "brilliant job" and that "he spoke well and had a good reputation" with acquaintances outside the business world. Admitting Barnard's writing was "hard to understand," Gifford emphasized that he "would lean toward the social sciences."[60] The board responded positively to that strength because they were the cause of a protracted, contentious debate between Fosdick and the head of the RF social science division, Joseph Willits. These disagreements were basic to decisions about the type of research that the RF would fund. Fosdick wanted to support applied research because he believed that it was consistent with the goals of the Foundation, whereas Willits supported pure research and theory building.

Barnard tilted in Fosdick's direction on this issue, which gained him some support among the officers of the Foundation. Nevertheless, the board would choose the next president, and Gifford summed up Barnard's case by stating that he "could run ATT well if [he] could have jumped to the top."[61] This was an odd statement for Gifford to make; nevertheless, with the two Walters, Gifford and Stewart, behind him, Barnard prevailed over the other candidates and was elected RF president in 1948, at the age of sixty-one.

Fosdick was pleased and delighted when he learned about the board's decision. In a letter to John D. Rockefeller, Jr., who had been less than thrilled by Barnard's candidacy, he wrote that, although he was "a little rough," Barnard was "a mature and seasoned leader of outstanding ability" and just the right person to help the Foundation through the dangerous years after World War II.[62] Fosdick reminded Rockefeller of Barnard's great loyalty and personal affection for him. He also noted that Barnard had done a wonderful job with the USO, an organization in which Rockefeller had a great interest, paralleling his father's in a similar organization that served the troops in World War I. Despite his virtues, Rockefeller was not keen on Barnard. He thought he was too old for the job and that not much planning or program development would occur during the short time slated for Barnard to be in office.[63]

Although he had always been on the board's short list, Barnard was not number one. The board had at least nine other serious candidates. So while Fosdick was pleased by Barnard's appointment, he was also surprised, since he expected to be followed by a much younger man: a man such as Dean Rusk.[64] John Foster Dulles, also a member of the board, led the campaign in favor of Rusk. Rusk and Dulles had become acquainted when they served at the United Nations. However, the other board members felt that at forty-five Rusk was too young for the job and needed a few more years to mature. Since it was understood that Barnard would retire from the Foundation in less than four years, Rusk would have time to season.

Meanwhile, under Barnard's steady administrative guidance, the Foundation could be expected to ease itself into the postwar period. By some accounts, therefore, Barnard's presidency was considered as an interregnum.[65] Stewart, however, wrote to Rockefeller that "we believe he will provide a brilliant leadership and make a distinctive contribution."[66] While Barnard's performance certainly could not be compared to, say, Pope John XXIII (who, it may be recalled, was considered another interim leader), he was not inert. He helped heal the rancor over the Social Science Division, and he supported a notable grant to Ohio State's Carroll L. Shartle to continue his leadership studies.[67]

But more importantly, as the head of a philanthropy that had diverse and extensive disciplinary and global interests, Barnard addressed himself to policy questions that were of broad consequence. Specifically he recommended the strategies that the Foundation ought to pursue in the postwar years and outlined them in a summary of his first year in office.[68] Barnard advocated a shift in RF emphasis from research to education, arguing that the educational systems in the United States and Europe were in disarray partly as a result of the war but mainly because of what he called a "false idea of democracy" that placed too much emphasis on mass education rather than on the quality of education delivered. This trend threatened educational standards at home and abroad when they could least afford to be compromised. But the democratization movement had a more insidious side. It shortchanged students who were the most competent and the best qualified intellectually to cope with technological and social changes. While warning against elitist snobbery in education, Barnard pointed to the even greater danger of giving higher education to people with third- or fourth-rate minds.

Barnard also observed that science had been given lavish support by the government during the war and was in a sound position. Private philanthropy could not compete with government in the support of science, and so while not abandoning its commitments to scientific fields, education should be elevated among the RF's priorities.

Turning from science and education, Barnard raised another question that was to consume much of his time as president. It concerned the "world's moral deficit." In the eyes of John D. Rockefeller, Jr., and some prominent board members, namely Dulles and Henry Van Dusen, head of the Union Theological Seminary, the decline of Christian values in the West had been of concern for years. The war had simply brought it to a head. Thus, moral philosophy and theology were much on their minds, and they wanted the Foundation to move assertively into these areas. To their chagrin, Barnard did not share their enthusiasm, and this may have been another reason for Rockefeller's coolness toward him when he retired.[69] Given the present interest with "business ethics," this whole episode is instructive and discussed at greater length in chapter 9.

Unlike Pope John, Barnard did not bring an equivalent of Vatican II to the Foundation. He opened the window a crack, but not enough to bring gusts of fresh air to Foundation policies in either education or moral philosophy. In this sense Rockefeller's predictions were confirmed. However, Barnard's regime was not a failure. He gave the Foundation good transitional leadership at the minimum. Conservative and forthright in his policies, he was, like Fosdick, a professional manager who applied his commitment and skills to the unique endeavors of a philanthropic organization.

That dedication was gravely tested by the death of his only child in June 1951, midway in his Foundation presidency. His daughter Frances, thirty-two, was pregnant for the fourth time and expecting twin girls when she developed severe abdominal pains. Her condition was misdiagnosed in the hospital as premature labor. She had actually developed a strangulated hernia from which she died. Barnard and his wife never recovered from this tragic loss,[70] but he completed his work at the Foundation and continued as chairman of the National Science Board.

The National Science Board

Concerned about the condition of American science in competition with the Soviet Union, President Harry S. Truman signed into law a bill that created the National Science Foundation (NSF) on May 10, 1950. This bill committed the nation to the promotion of pure science and for the first time dedicated the resources of the government to basic research. The NSF was responsible for the day-to-day assessment and selection of grant proposals for funding and the allocation of money to four areas specified by, but not limited to, the act: medical research; mathematical, physical, and engineering sciences; biological sciences; and scientific personnel and education.[71]

The act also required the establishment of a governing body that would make policy and oversee the operations of the NSF. This body, known as the National Science Board (NSB), was composed of twenty-four part-time members, all appointed by and reporting to the president of the United States. By November 1950 Truman completed his appointments to the board, and James B. Conant, president of Harvard University, served as its first chairman. Barnard also was a charter member.

Finding a director for the NSF was the first task undertaken by the board. Truman's choice from the start was Alan T. Waterman, who he nominated for the position. However, the board was not pleased with the prospects of a "political" appointment, and Conant set up a committee within the board to conduct an independent selection of candidates. Barnard, who chaired this committee, set it to the task of deciding upon the personal characteristics that a director should ideally possess. In true Barnardian fashion the list of characteristics that resulted named "three 'desirable' and two 'indispensable' qualifications."[72] Ten individuals who met these standards were rank ordered on the board's short list. Alan T. Waterman was seventh. For a number of reasons, all of those ahead of Waterman either dropped out of the race or were nixed by the president as unsuitable.[73] In the end Waterman received the nod and was awarded the directorship, much to Truman's satisfaction. His appointment turned out to be a good one, and he served for twelve years in the post.

With this major task completed, Conant resigned as chairman because his duties with the NSB distracted too much from his considerable responsibilities at Harvard. Barnard, while still president of the Rockefeller Foundation, became the new chairman in 1951. He served concurrently in both capacities for over six months and was head of the board until 1955. The NSB during Barnard's chairmanship faced three major policy questions: defining the territory of each scientific field, establishing scientific accountability, and deciding what to do about the social sciences. The position that the board took on these matters was critical during the NSF's formative years, and it is of interest that Barnard's opinions on each were almost diametrically opposite to the views he held at the Rockefeller Foundation, an example of disinterested professional neutrality that many thought should characterize the managerial class.

Barnard did not have much choice about his stand on the definitional issues. Even though other government agencies, such as the Office of the Navy and the Office of Scientific Research and Development, pressured the NSF to undertake certain functions more appropriate to applied research, the congressional mandate was clear. Pure research was NSF territory and that was that. Nevertheless, in the early days, the board had to both delineate and defend this territory against the depredations of other agencies that threatened to dissipate its resources. However, the defense of pure research, against attacks by those who favored the applied, was certainly a major departure from the stand Barnard took at the Rockefeller Foundation.

The second policy area, scientific accountability, was murky, and it involved two issues. The first issue pertained to scientific quid pro quo. Barnard elaborated that unlike expenditures in business and government, the NSF should not be expected to hold its grant recipients responsible for producing specific results of any particular kind. However desirable that "concrete and practical results were secured by the grants," Barnard averred, "we do not adopt in connection with any grants for research the idea that we are buying something more or less specific which the grantee is obligated to produce for us."[74] Thus, NSB policy did not hold grant recipients accountable for the outcomes of their research. Summing up, Barnard wrote to the other members of the NSB, "to depart from this fundamental policy would . . . force us into the position of being an operating agency, which in my opinion would be fatal to the fundamental purposes for which we were established."[75] Again the differences between NSB and RF policies, especially under Fosdick's administration, were dramatic, and the way Barnard quickly and handily shifted gears between these two organizations was a remarkable technocratic achievement.

The second issue of scientific accountability pertained to the administration by universities of the grants that the NSF made to faculty members. What seemed to be at stake, on the surface, was the autonomy of the universities versus the desire by the government to enlist their scientific resources for national purposes. The issue appeared at first to be philosophical: how much scientific freedom was compatible with the achievement of the country's scientific goals? With the urging of Vannevar Bush, the founding father of the NSF, a committee composed of university representatives and members of the NSB was established in late 1953 to try to sort out the thorny matters of mutual responsibilities. Bush browbeat Barnard into accepting the chairmanship of this committee.

Barnard reluctantly entered the dicey terrain of government-university relationships because he knew that committee service of this type would most likely be an unpleasant and unproductive experience. Nevertheless, after he was subjected to "an almost indecent amount of heat" from his colleagues on the board, he accepted the assignment.[76]

The real issue being contended soon became apparent. It had to do with the amount of overhead that the universities charged the government for the administration of grants. Bringing the full board up to date on the work of the committee between 1953 and 1955, Barnard discussed this matter under the general rubric of indirect costs. The most controversial part of university practices, from the point of view of the NSB, appeared to be charges made for grants to individual scientists doing basic research. Barnard did not seem to have similar reservations about overhead charges for contracts that were negotiated with universities for specific projects by other agencies.

He complained that the university members of his committee viewed the distinction between grants and contracts as merely an accounting procedure. Barnard argued otherwise. The differences were not technical but philosophical. Grants to individual scientists were made to further their personal development, to advance their field of research, and generally to improve the quality of the pool of scientific talent in the United States. On the other hand, contracts for applied research were awarded by many government agencies to universities. In this case, administrative overhead charges were justifiable, whereas in the former instance they were much less defensible because universities should be conducting basic research anyway, with or without government funding.

Everyone on the board, including Barnard, understood that the problems between the universities and the NSF were neither philosophical nor procedural. They objected to an unwarranted skimming of government funds by the universities to cover administrative expenses that at best were just tangentially connected to research. As Paul Klopsteg, Waterman's assistant director and head of the mathematical, physical, and engineering sciences division, put it, "University presidents [were] acting like moneygrubbers rather than intellectual custodians."[77] To date, this issue is still a point of contention, especially in view of the uproar in 1990 and 1991 over university administrative charges billed to the government.

As Barnard predicted, his committee accomplished little, other than to heighten the antagonism between its academic and board members. Many of them lost interest in carrying on, and toward the end of the committee's life, after Bush retired from government, Barnard could not muster a majority for the meetings. However, despite his advancing age and failing health, he stayed with the committee, even after retiring from the NSB.

Given that the financial resources available to support research and fellowship programs in the hard sciences were meager, the NSF at first avoided the social sciences. However, responding to certain political and administrative pressures to do something with the social sciences, Harry Alpert, a sociologist from the old Office of War Information, came to the NSF and immediately began a campaign for it to assume a role in these areas. Looking for allies, Alpert started with Barnard in 1953, who, as he knew, favored social science research.

Alpert, reporting upon a discussion with Barnard, informed Waterman that Barnard "placed major emphasis on the scientific aspects of social science research . . . drawing a sharp distinction between the application of scientific methods in the social sciences, and the essentially political, ethical, and welfare activities which frequently pass as social science."[78] Barnard stressed in their conversation the importance of the "hard core science" aspects of the social sciences and urged Alpert to prepare a staff paper highlighting these aspects in his presentation of a program to the board.

Barnard outlined topics that such a paper might cover. They included the present support of social science research in government, industry, and philanthropy, a review of the status of various social science disciplines that assessed their achievements and needs, and an interdisciplinary vision of the social sciences as they intersected the natural sciences. Relative to the latter point, Barnard underscored in his remarks a unified interdisciplinary approach that wedded the social sciences to the life sciences, "provided that the life science concept could be sufficiently delimited to avoid some of its vague, global connotations."[79]

Alpert's conversation with Barnard demonstrated that his position on empirical social science research had altered from his RF days, although he continued to push for an interdisciplinary social science epistemology. Both of these subjects are discussed at greater length in the next chapter. It should suffice to say that Barnard's epistemological vision seemed at odds with his sudden conversion to orthodox positive science methods at the NSB.

Alpert submitted his staff paper to the NSB one year after his conversation with Barnard.[80] Politically alert, Alpert cleverly linked his recommendations to Barnard's philosophy of the social sciences that he expressed in his 1942 memorandum to the RF board of trustees. Alpert suggested that his recommendations for funding were in the same spirit: to encourage scholarly research in such areas as economic history, to be of value to men of affairs, and to study matter-of-fact scientific knowledge. The NSB passed favorably on the report, and at a subsequent meeting in August 1954 authorized limited funding through 1956 of $250,000 per year for the social sciences.

In 1956, after serving six years with the NSB, four as chairman, Barnard retired yet again, this time permanently from all major service assignments. He died five years later on June 7, 1961, a few months short of his seventy-fifth birthday and almost exactly ten years after the death of his daughter.

CAN A PHILOSOPHER BE A GOOD KING?

Barnard spent most of his career as president of NJBT, and one might wonder why his friend Gifford did not call him to the Valhalla of ATT's corporate headquarters in Manhattan just across the river from Newark. Apart from Gifford's curious remark about Barnard's qualifications to run ATT well, there were other prestigious jobs at corporate headquarters besides that of CEO. In the ATT hierarchy, corporate-level vice presidents and executive vice president were more highly regarded, and often paid better, than the presidents of the twenty territories from coast to coast. Regardless, further promotions for Barnard were not to be, and we are left to wonder why.

One obvious reason is that New Jersey suited Barnard and he preferred to stay there. Since McRae had been delegated the company's operating responsibilities, Barnard had the freedom to pursue his extensive commitments to public service, which he enjoyed. Unlike other associated company presidents, he was able to split his time between his corporate duties and his service organizations. On the other hand, it is reasonable to think that Barnard would want his devotion and contributions to the company recognized by a promotion to headquarters, and management lore holds that Barnard was disappointed by not receiving such promotions.

The second speculation is that personality may have had something to do with Barnard getting passed over, and on this matter there are at least two points of view. At one extreme, Barnard was revered as a great, humane man. For example, a former NJBT executive, H. Roy Hershey, who was with the company for most of Barnard's years, recalls that "he owed his job to Mr. Barnard during the depression."[81] Hershey observed that while other operating companies throughout the Bell System were laying employees off, such was not the case at NJBT. Its non-layoff, reduced-hours policy was Barnard's doing. Furthermore, Barnard already is a folk hero in the present NJBT corporate culture. His larger-than-life reputation persists among a number of people who worked with him or who followed him in the organizations with which he was connected. This point of view is consistent with the esteem in which Barnard is held by most management scholars. Many of them agree that Barnard was great because he humanized management.

But on the other extreme, there is a Jekyll-and-Hyde aspect to Barnard's personality. While Barnard's associates respected his knowledge, intellect, experience, and command presence, they also found him aloof and daunting. James M. Mitchell, Alan Waterman's deputy chief at the National Science Foundation, was intimidated by Barnard; and William B. Wolf, one of Barnard's most ardent admirers, called him a loner.[82]

The most candid opinions about Barnard are in his personnel file at the Rockefeller Center Archives. Written in longhand by members of the board of trustees are certain preliminary impressions of him recorded during the board's deliberations about who would succeed Fosdick as president. Fosdick himself noted that Barnard had well-defined opinions but was not a patient person, another way of saying that he did not have much tolerance for those who disagreed with him. One anonymous trustee believed that Barnard would not be a satisfactory president. He was too forceful, not diplomatic, a "bull in a China shop." This trustee noted that Barnard had a "difficult personality problem, doesn't give time to people, and had a big fight at the USO, a fight to the last ditch, his was not a tranquil and happy administration."[83] Another trustee, similarly unnamed, thought Barnard was an able administrator and organizer but tended toward brusqueness, and "overly ready to pick up his marbles and go home." However, this trustee felt that Barnard had done a good job with the USO.[84] Arriving at work in a company-supplied, chauffeur-driven car, always surrounded by lackeys when inspecting the premises of district telephone offices, and seldom acknowledging that he knew his subordinates when they passed each other in town or ate in the same restaurants, Barnard projected an imperial image.[85]

Without venturing into the dubious territory of psychohistory, what can be concluded about this side of Barnard's character and how it may have affected his career? Perhaps Barnard himself can answer this question, since for whatever the reason he was not part of the in-group at ATT. Writing about the informal executive organization, Barnard noted that belonging to it was a "question of fitness." Acceptance depended on such intangible things as "very specific personal traits [such] as manners, speech, personal appearance, etc."[86] Because of his remoteness and his difficult, often acid, personality, the corporate powers might have concluded he did not fit. He lacked the right stuff for headquarters. So he stayed in New Jersey.

The performance of NJBT under Barnard's leadership was less than spectacular, perhaps the most significant reason that Barnard was not promoted. But even it is clouded because ATT did not give the management of its subsidiary companies much latitude in making basic policy decisions. For example, even if Barnard had wanted to suboptimize NJBT operations in order to turn in more impressive performance figures, he could not and continue to stay president of that company. ATT was interested in maximizing corporate performance, which often required imposing investment policies that were detrimental to the performance of its associated companies.

ATT was highly centralized in those days, and its headquarters had a short-run perspective insofar as its performance expectations of operating companies were concerned. Performance was measured in such terms as net telephone installations, toll charges, total volume of calls, records of customer service, return on investment—"this year compared to last." What is more, the associated companies competed with each other statistically, and those that were awarded the kudos were the winners of the annual statistics contest. This policy of internal competition created an atmosphere in which management, from the highest corporate level down to the lowest supervisor in a district office, set impossibly high goals for their subordinates. But as is often the case in protected monopolies, no one really cared whether those goals were met. In other words, few lost their jobs or were demoted because yearly performance objectives were not achieved. Therefore, NJBT's performance record may have had more to do with the constraints of the corporate environment than with Barnard's personal limitations.

The financial record must speak for itself, as best it can, and an analysis of NJBT annual reports from 1928 to 1947 indicates an erosion of the company's financial strength.[87] Figure 4.1 summarizes return on investment (ROI), a conventional measure of financial health. The downward trend in NJBT's fortunes were probably produced by four causes: the depression, apparent inefficiencies in controlling expenses, an inadequate rate structure for sustaining growth, and a relatively inflexible dividend policy imposed by ATT on its associated companies. In this instance, the corporation required its pound of flesh extracted in the form of a relatively level dividend. Barnard often mentioned 6 percent as the target return for operating companies. NJBT met this objective just six times in his twenty years as president. Dividends were paid to the parent corporation by the associated companies from their retained earnings during times of business downturns.

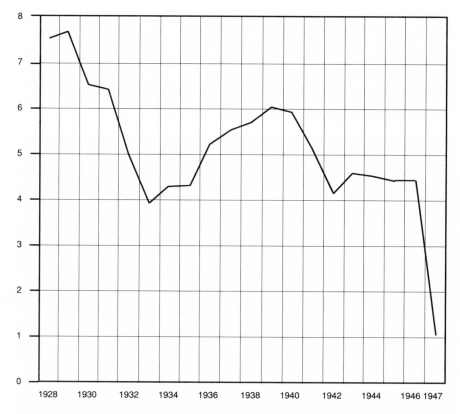

Figure 4.1. Return on invested capital in percent for New Jersey Bell Telephone Company, 1928-1947. (Source: *Twentieth Annual Report of the New Jersey Bell Telephone Company, 1947,* p. 11)

That limited NJBT's ability to invest its earnings in modernization programs, slowing down its conversion to the dial system. Thus, the unfavorable ruling by the New Jersey public utility commission in 1946 and the strike of 1947 magnified what was, from 1929, a declining performance picture for Barnard's company.

But in fairness, the operating results for certain other selected associated companies (Illinois Bell, Southern Bell, and New York Telephone), in addition to ATT itself, followed similar patterns during this twenty-year period. The difference was that NJBT performance overall compared unfavorably with these other companies, regardless of whether they were experiencing increases or decreases. For example, in 1947 the ROIs were as follows: ATT, 4.4 percent; New York Telephone, 6.1 percent; Illinois Bell, 1.4 percent, and Southern Bell, 2.6 percent. We can conclude that NJBT simply was not a top-performing company in the Bell

System. Barnard's results in the statistics game were lackluster, and that may have had a negative effect on his promotion to corporate headquarters.

Although inadequate as explanations go, these speculations about Barnard's career suggest answers to the question of whether or not a philosopher can be a good king. Granted that Barnard probably was a better manager than the king of Syracuse, he still had serious limitations. The assessments of his leadership of the USO, the Rockefeller Foundation, New Jersey Bell, and the National Science Board were equivocal. His intolerant, but often vague, genius was unappealing to his peers, and his imperiousness alienated some of his subordinates. His paternalistic attitude toward employees must have been particularly galling and in the end did not forestall the company from being unionized. Finally, some might argue, less than charitably, that Barnard could not have risen, either inside or outside of the Bell System, had it not been for Walter Gifford's influence. Although there is some truth in this observation, Barnard's achievements also depended upon his strong character and powerful mind. Furthermore, he owed Gifford nothing insofar as his intellectual pursuits were concerned, and his accomplishments in the realm of management theory are what should impress us now, not his inadequacies as a manager. The following six chapters consider Barnard's contributions to the paradigm of modern management practice and values.

5

Barnard's Intellectual Debts and His Epistemology of the Social Sciences

The relativity of knowledge and the nature of truth, determined by organizational needs, were the ideas that shaped much of twentieth-century thought. Albert Einstein promulgated the first, Max Weber the second. Due to the work of these two men, the presuppositions of truth and knowledge were changed in modern times.[1]

The special theory of relativity, based on a paper published by Einstein in 1905, raised doubts that certain knowledge could be had about the physical universe. These doubts were quickly extended to the social and moral universes. As all was relative in nature, so must it also be in human affairs. The despairing liberal, Max Weber, taught that the spontaneity and affectivity of community had given way in mass industrial societies to the impersonal, instrumental, and systemic norms of organization that defined truth as bureaucratic rules. People, imprisoned in the organizational cages of this rationality, had one primary obligation—obedience. Weber gloomily admonished in a 1919 lecture, "The honor of the civil servant is vested in his ability to execute conscientiously the orders of superior authorities."[2]

Relativity and bureaucracy dominated the thought of Barnard's generation and he harnessed them to his management epistemology. Holding that all organizational events are contingent upon the concrete situations in which they occur, absolute principles were useless for making management decisions. Realizing also that grudging worker conformity to formal bureaucratic rules would not yield satisfactory organizational performance, Barnard altered Weber's dictum of obedience in order to emphasize willing employee cooperation with management, of course on management's terms. Barnard did not support the elimination of bureaucracy, rather he recommended changes in management practices that took the workers' nonlogical attitudes into account. These changes were expected to improve the performance of established bureaucracies rather than to replace them with a different organizational form. But implementation of these ideas had to await Barnard's maturity as an intellectual and as a corporate executive in the Bell System.

American modernization of the 1920s created a need for new thinking about economic organization, the social class system, and the political philosophy required for changing times. Herbert Hoover set the tone by his vision of America as an associated state characterized by integration, stabilization, and cooperation. Barnard, inspired by the same ideals, tried to demonstrate that corporate management was the legitimate leadership organ of this state, the social institution that must lead America's surge into world prominence after the war.

For its legitimacy to be realized, management had to create the material and psychological conditions for national well-being without undue violation of democratic principles—a daunting, but critical, enterprise. To help management succeed with this project, Barnard proposed a worldly, and he hoped, practical philosophy, much of which he incorporated in his book.

But, in the final analysis, legitimacy had to emerge from the public's perception that management's interests were congruent with its own. This situation would not be automatically forthcoming. Management had to evince it in a number of ways: by becoming evermore competent in practice, by putting theory and practice on scientific foundations, by eliminating the causes of social destabilization, and by demonstrating heightened moral and ethical behavior in practice.

Most of this behavior would necessitate improved management skills, since expertise was the bedrock of management legitimacy in modern nations. By Barnard's time, Weber had already taught this in his theory of bureaucracy. Barnard, familiar with Weber's ideas, wrote extensively about the technical, social, and cooperative skills that management had to have in order to merit the people's trust and their consent to its leadership. These skills were acquired, according to Barnard, from education, experience, and science.

Although Barnard was a tireless campaigner for the special type of elite education that Wallace B. Donham was pioneering at Harvard, he also stressed the importance of management experience for developing a person's intuitive understanding of complex organizations and cooperative systems. However, the management skills that Barnard identified were not equal. Technical skills improved almost as a function of rote learning and repetitive application, but proficiency in the social and cooperative skills required expertise of a higher order. Here science could serve executives by replacing rule-of-thumb management with reliable concepts from which rational guidelines for practice could be extracted.

The control of human behavior in the workplace was the most pressing management need at the time. Therefore, the use of the social sciences for purposes of social engineering had a high priority. They promised to give managers new technologies for behavioral control. Managers could, if properly informed by the social sciences, intervene in the ways that employees thought, implanting in their minds pleasing views of their work situations, and this would help to reduce worker antagonisms toward jobs and employers.

However, the scientists themselves had to reorient their thinking toward the concrete, applied, and practical problems of management, something that hard-core empiricists and abstract theory builders were loath to do. Their detachment from the problems of application worried Barnard, because he was deeply committed to enhancing the usefulness of the social sciences to "men of affairs." Moreover, if the scientists went along with management, they might help it succeed in its struggle with the radical forces of destabilization that seemed to threaten the social order's equilibrium.

Members of management were considered by those in the Harvard Circle to be the protectors of social stability. Buttressed by the social sciences, management might wean labor from Bolshevism and thwart the union movement. Labor warfare in the 1930s was management's clearest example of the dire consequences of militant unionism. Labor radicalism and Communism went hand in hand, or so it seemed to the conservative leaders of the Eastern establishment.[3] Social scientists claimed they could deliver quiescent workers, and Barnard and Donham were receptive to their arguments. Particularly appealing was the brand of applied social science that Elton Mayo promoted as an antidote to all forms of social disorganization brought on by the industrialization and urbanization of the working classes.

While hardly a friend of the labor movement, Barnard did not preach virulent antiunionism. He preferred a less antagonistic attack on the labor problem in particular and Bolshevists in general. For him good management was the best way to achieve deradicalization. Managers had to work on the problem daily by persuading and propagandizing employees to prefer cooperation to confrontation. And even though the cards were stacked in management's favor, they had to be played effectively through an incentive system that rewarded employees, financially and psychologically, for choosing the cooperative alternative. Barnard placed the burden for stabilizing the social order on management's shoulders, and his solutions to radicalism were very similar to those of his Harvard confreres.

Imposing as these management obligations were, for Barnard responsibility as the moral aspect of executive character and action was more important than any of the others. It meant honor, duty, and faithfulness in the manner that managers acquitted their responsibilities. It was shaped by the virtues of asceticism, humility, dependability, determination, conscientiousness, honesty, courage, conviction, and moral character. "Organizations endure . . . in proportion to the breadth of morality by which they are governed."[4] But more to the point, "A low morality will not sustain leadership long, its influence quickly vanishes, it cannot produce its own succession."[5] These prophetic words made the point that ethical practice determined corporate management's moral authority and the capability of one generation of managers to pass their power on to the next.

If management did not solve the problems of competency, science, social stability, and morality, it could not become a significant force for progress in American life. In this regard, some have interpreted Barnard's contribution to management thought as guidelines to help managers improve their performance.[6] However, to evaluate Barnard's book merely as a manual of practice seriously understates its significance. He created a new paradigm based upon Progressive ideals for judging management's legitimacy. But in the process he accumulated many intellectual debts to the leading thinkers of his day, and it is to those people who influenced his thoughts we now turn.

INTELLECTUAL DEBTS

Barnard was not a single-variable man. He was obsessed by the need to convey in his work, as precisely as the language allowed, the complexities and interdependencies in organizational life, treating them as systems, as forms of mutual causation.   Being a voracious reader and an eclectic thinker, Barnard explored all the major branches of the social sciences: psychology, sociology, social psychology, economics, anthropology, law, political theory, and philosophy of science. Although he paid attention to the theory building and research findings in these fields, he was more interested in integrative constructs that made logical and empirical sense and that also accorded with his observations and experiences as an executive. Barnard acknowledged many obligations to others for ideas, theories, insights, and data.

Table 5.1 lists twelve key Barnardian ideas. The constructs of systems, cooperation, and responsibility would have to be the most significant concepts in such an inventory. Less certain, of course, were the sources from whom Barnard drew his ideas, and it is often impossible to decide where one scholar left off and where Barnard began. For example, he cited Follett, Mayo, and Roethlisberger in connection with the informal organization, but he also presented a unique analysis of it that pertained to the informal executive organization.

With these caveats in mind, Table 5.1 shows the main theoretical components of Barnard's book and relates them to the scholars who stimulated his thinking. Where no citations appear, it has to be assumed that the concept was generated by Barnard alone or was part of the intellectual atmosphere at the time.

The dozen concepts mentioned in Table 5.1 and their interrelationships reappear throughout the next five chapters of this book. It is helpful to have in mind some description of those constructs before embarking upon a more detailed consideration of them.

1. Open systems theory. Barnard based his concept of systems on the works of Pareto, Henderson, and Whitehead. Paretan sociology interpreted society as a cluster of interdependent but variable units in a desirable state of equilibrium or in an undesirable state of disequilibrium. The interactive processes among these units were part of Pareto's theoretical framework.[7] Henderson drew from Pareto to observe that "the interdependence of variables in a system is one of the widest inductions from experience we possess; or we may alternatively regard it as the

Table 5.1. Major Constructs and Their Origins in Barnard's Management Theory

The Constructs[a]	The Origins[b]
1. Open systems theory; organizations as organic systems FOE, 46–50, 77–80, 240–44	Pareto, *The Mind and Society;* Henderson, *Pareto's General Sociology;* Whitehead, *Process and Reality*
2. Cooperation FOE, 3–7, 23–31, 40–41, 45, 232–53	Koffka, *Gestalt Psychology;* Mayo, *The Human Problems of an Industrial Civilization;* Hoover, No specific reference but his ideas about cooperation permeated the atmosphere at Harvard and at ATT
3. Responsibility, moral codes FOE, chapter 17	No acknowledgments or citations

4. Decision theory—individual, organizational
  A. Exchange theory
  B. Theory of opportunism
FOE, chapters 11, 13, and 14
	Commons, *Institutional Economics*

5. Structural-functional analysis
  A. Structure
FOE, part 2 and chapters 10, 11, 12
  B. Functionalism
FOE, part 4, and chapters 13, 14
	Parsons, *The Structure of Social Action*

6. Equilibrium DC, 11–12, 15; FOE, x, 163–65, 171–72, 173–74, 182–83	Pareto, *The Mind and Society;* Henderson, *Pareto's General Sociology*
7. Consent theory of authority DC, 14–15; FOE, 163–65, 171–72, 173–74, 182–83	Ehrlich, *Fundamental Principles of the Sociology of Law;* Michels, "Authority," *Encyclopedia of the Social Sciences*
8. Limited choice, restriction of action (bounded rationality) DC, 5–8; FOE, chapter 2	No acknowledgment or citations; indirectly, Commons, *Institutional Economics*
9. Theory of formal organization FOE, chapters 6, 7, 8	Parsons, *The Structure of Social Action;* Weber, *Theory of Social and Economic Organization;* Pareto, *The Mind and Society*
A. Span of control FOE, 109–10	A. Graicunas, "Relationships in Organization," in *Papers in the Science of Administration*
B. Communication FOE, 89–91, 175–81, 217–26	B. Pareto, *The Mind and Society;* Roethlisberger and Dickson, *Management and the Worker*

10. Informal organization FOE, chapter 9	Follett, "The Process of Control," in *Papers in the Science of Administration;* Roethlisberger and Dickson, *Management and the Worker;* Mayo, *The Human Problems of an Industrial Civilization;* Whitehead, *The Industrial Worker*
11. Logical and non logical mental processes DC, 15; FOE, appendix, 301–22	Pareto, *The Mind and Society;* Mayo, *The Human Problems of an Industrial Civilization;* Roethlisberger and Dickson, *Management and the Worker*
12. Social science methodology DC, 15; FOE, 287–91	Brown, *Psychology and the Social Order*

[a]FOE—*The Functions of the Executive;* DC—Draft copy, chapter 1, FOE, BL, Case 1
[b]These sources are either cited or acknowledged by Barnard in FOE and DC. Full documentation of the original sources appears in the notes.

definition of a system."[8] Henderson went further, introducing the idea that social systems were open, organic, and indeterminate. This interpretation, probably rooted in his medical education and biochemical research, was central to Barnard's conceptualization of organizations as organic, self-sustaining collectivities of mutually dependent functions, processes, and ideals. As Barnard wrote, "I regard systems of cooperation . . . 'alive.' "[9] But to give some highly generalized cosmological and ideological significance to this view, Barnard relied on Alfred North Whitehead.[10] He wrote, in reference to *Process and Reality,* that this "profound work in speculative philosophy and metaphysics . . . presents a fundamental organized philosophy of the universe."[11]

The ideological spin that Barnard, via Whitehead and Henderson, gave to system analysis is much too provocative to ignore when we recall that organicism was a peculiarly seductive geopolitical point of view during the first forty years of this century. Its operational principles of autarchy and lebensraum gave "living" organizations, such as nation states, corporations and the like, the right to grow and to be self-sufficient by acquiring resources at the expense of other, weaker systems. There is no need to dwell here on the mischief that the doctrine caused in the twentieth century. But it is important to understand that its notion of organizational sovereignty characterized the intellectual climate of the times in many countries, regardless of their economic and political system.

2. Cooperation. Mayo concluded his book *The Human Problems of an Industrial Civilization* by stating that the deterioration of human collaboration was the most pressing issue of the day, and he mentioned Herbert Hoover as an authority who supported his view.[12] Mayo found the solution to the problem of collaboration in a management elite that dedicated its administrative efforts to the task of securing cooperation from people.

From Barnard's perspective, cooperation constituted the most desirable characteristic of social action, because it produced outcomes that were always greater than the sum of individual contributions. From the gestalt created by cooperative efforts, "surpluses" were forthcoming; and when those surpluses were distributed, they produced the material and psychological satisfactions necessary to induce people to contribute to the effective and efficient performance of organizations. Barnard, as Mayo, believed that management was the fulminator of cooperative processes.

Barnard regarded Kurt Koffka's, *Principles of Gestalt Psychology*[13] as an "organismic" theory of the utmost importance because it reenforced the notion of cooperation as a management ideal. His debt to Koffka for the intellectual and theoretical justifications of cooperation was immense.

3. Responsibility. As Barnard defined it, responsibility "is the power of a particular private code of morals to control the conduct of the individual in the presence of strong contrary desires or impulses."[14] It pertained to individual integrity when conducting transactions with either an organization or with other individuals.

Barnard's discussion of moral attitudes and actions reduced mainly to a classification scheme, and is not especially interesting or important. It is his portrayal of management's moral philosophy that is significant, because here he considered the complexities of responsibility. Managers confronted many moral codes in their work, and the higher the executive position in an organization, the more involved those moral conflicts became. This imposed on executives certain moral imperatives that entailed a high capacity for personal responsibility governed by moral codes and by a determination to solve, creatively, clashing moral demands. This required managers to inculcate their moral codes in others, helping them to adjust their personal codes to the codes of the organization. Thus, moral action compelled managers "to bind the wills of men to the accomplishment of purposes beyond their immediate ends, beyond their times.[15]

Barnard did not recognize any sources for this philosophy, probably since it was not a subject to which the management field, then, gave much attention.

4. Decision theory—individual, organizational. One of Barnard's most influential contributions, his twofold theory of decisionmaking, is traceable directly to John R. Commons's labyrinthian book *Institutional Economics.*[16] This book had a curious effect on Barnard. On the one hand, he was impressed with Commons's idea of the firm as a nexus of transactions and that the transaction itself must be treated as the primary unit of economic analysis. Barnard acknowledged that this view of the economic world corresponded with his own experience.[17] However, transaction theory did not surface in Barnard's book in so many words. Rather, it became transmuted into a psychological explanation of individual decisionmaking, exchange theory. On the other hand, Barnard made extensive use of Commons's notion of "strategic and limiting" factors in organizational decisionmaking. He based his theory of opportunism on them.

Exchange theory is a description of the psychological process by which individuals decide whether or not to participate in and produce for an organization in the light of those inducements and contributions that management offers and expects. Commons treated this activity of giving benefits in exchange for the costs of participation as a "managerial transaction" between two persons in an inferior–superior relationship. This relationship contrasted with the "bargaining transaction" between equals. The psychology implicit in the former is the use of persuasion or coercion to induce the inferior party to be obedient to the commands of the superior party. However, Commons observed that in modern "managing," something that seemed like bargaining among equals was coming to the fore. As an example, he quoted an eminent manager as saying "we never give an order; we sell the idea to those who must carry it out."[18] Although Commons detected some irony in this comment, Barnard would have certainly approved of it in spirit. Such psychological managing of transactions between superiors and subordinates was the subject matter for his chapter 11, "The Economy of Incentives."

The theory of opportunism describes the process by which managers make organizational decisions. This theory depends heavily on the economic notion of efficiency. It suggests that since executives are not informed about every variable that goes into the creation of a utility, they have to find the limiting or strategic factor that gives them the greatest leverage over the efficient production of a good or service.

Commons made much ado about the difference between a strategic factor and a limiting factor. The former was "subjective" and more or less selected upon the will or volition of a decisionmaker, whereas the latter was an "objective" condition upon which all rational decisionmakers could agree.[19] Barnard preferred the concept of strategic factors because it better conveyed the complexities of organizational decisionmaking.[20]

Both Commons and Barnard illustrated their arguments with the same example. They described a farmer applying a potash fertilizer to a field. Potash, generally known as a source of nitrogen, promoted the growth of crops and was therefore an objective variable in the farmer's decision process. But how much to use, the method of application, the machines for spreading it, and the time and labor to be expended in putting it down were all subjective, volitional decisions that the farmer made in an attempt to maximize the profit from his yield.

Generalizing from all of this, Barnard opined that regardless of whether one called them strategic or limiting factors, they were always the controlling conditions in whatever operations one described, "business transactions, political transactions, mechanical operations, chemical combinations, scientific experimentation, or whatever relates to accomplishment of intention."[21]

5. *Structural-functional analysis.* Barnard followed the Parsonian method of structural-functional analysis in his book, although he did not credit Parsons for this framework.[22] Chapters 5 through 11 categorized in considerable detail different formal and informal structures. Based on these structures, Barnard derived the functions of decisionmaking and communication, discussing these aspects of functionalism in chapters 13 through 16.

But by far more important than either methodology or framework was the quality that Parsons imputed to functionalism as the dynamics of social action. He held that it was the chief medium through which social systems achieved integration and effectiveness. Functionalism provided an explanation of critical states within systems of interdependency and showed how alterations in these states were both a consequence of and an accommodation to change.

Given Barnard's system theory orientation, Parsons's mode of analysis must have appealed, but it cannot be said confidently that he had a direct influence on Barnard's method of inquiry or presentation of subject matter. Nevertheless, both authors wrote that functionalism was key to understanding the behavior of systems, and, as evidence of its importance to Barnard, consider the title of his book.

6. *Equilibrium.* This concept had a special place in Barnard's galaxy of constructs. He defined it as the capacity of a cooperative system to preserve a balance between the demands it placed on people for their contributions with the satisfactions it provided to them for their participation.[23] Equilibrium consequently was the operational construct central to Barnard's notions of the efficiency and effectiveness of organizations. These terms pertained respectively to the ability of a cooperative system to meet the goals of the people in them as well as its own goals. Cooperative systems worked best if there was a balance between the two, generating an ever-upward spiral of improved employee satisfaction and organizational performance.

Barnard relied on Pareto for the idea of equilibrium.[24] Pareto defined it as "the state of X is such a state that if it is artificially subjected to some modification different from the modification it undergoes normally, a reaction at once takes place to restore it to its real, its normal state."[25] Of course, this definition covers all kinds of systems. But Pareto used it in specific reference to human organizations through his notion of "residues." These human attitudes and sentiments were the equilibrating mechanisms of social systems because they restored the "normal" balance if it was disrupted, provided that such attitudes were properly conditioned by a leadership elite.

Roethlisberger and Dickson, following Henderson and Pareto, noted that social equilibrium was "an interaction of sentiments and interests in a relation of mutual dependence, resulting in a state of equilibrium such that if that state is altered, forces tending to reestablish it come into play."[26] These ideas were rather airy, so they brought them to earth by using the concept of equilibrium to explain many of the findings of the Hawthorne studies.[27]

Equilibrium was, it seems, the intellectual property of the Harvard Circle, not just because it had analytical power but also because it projected an ideologically desired condition. It connoted a social system on an even keel, one that permitted cooperation and mutuality of interests to thrive.

7. *The consent theory of authority.* Barnard pondered over the nature and origin of authority in society, feeling that it was not adequately accounted for by traditional legal and political scholarship. He stated in his preface that all this scholar-

ship succeeded in doing was to create an intellectual impasse since it failed completely "to explain the most elemental experience of organized effort."[28] The result was a dilemma he described in this way, "The doctrine of states as sources and bases of formal organizations . . . is inconsistent with the theory that all states are based on organizations."[29]

A reading of Ehrlich's *Fundamental Principles of the Sociology of Law* suggested how this dilemma could be resolved. Ehrlich gave a one-sentence summary of his thesis in the 1912 foreword to his book. He said, "At the present as well as at any other time, the center of gravity of legal development lies not in legislation, nor in juristic science, nor in judicial decision, but in society itself."[30] The basis of law, therefore, must be sought in associations, Ehrlich's equivalent of organizations, of which the family was the most elementary social unit. Consequently, since the law came from subsidiary social units, then it was clear that authority must also be based upon those customs and norms that bubbled up, as it were, from below. Not mincing words, Ehrlich wrote, "To attempt to imprison the law of a time or of a people within sections of a code is about as reasonable as to attempt to confine a stream within a pond."[31] The result was a stagnant pool, not a living current.

Ehrlich's argument appealed to the sociologist in Barnard because he believed that the universals of organization lay in customary and contemporary social usages, the "current phenomenon of living human affairs."[32] So Barnard concluded that authority came from the people, not from the higher level of the state. If this was true for the state, then, by extension, it would also be true for the formal structures of authority in the organizations that composed the state. Therefore, armies, corporations, government agencies, universities, and so on merely appeared to be authoritarian structures, while actually the right to exercise command came from those who were led.

This was reinforced by Roberto Michels's entry, "Authority," in the 1930 edition of the *Encyclopaedia of the Social Sciences.*[33] The passage that struck Barnard as particularly cogent went as follows: "Whether authority is of personal or institutional origin it is created and maintained by public opinion, which in its turn is conditioned by sentiment, affection, reverence, or fatalism. Even when authority rests on mere physical coercion it is accepted by those ruled, although the acceptance may be due to a fear of force."[34]

Ehrlich and Michels gave intellectual firepower to Barnard's position that since all authority was based on consent, it had to be "democratic" in nature. People submitted to authority because they wanted to, and this was an extremely positive idea. However, Michels was not so positive in his assessment of how people submit to authority. Immediately following the above passage, he wrote, "It [submission to authority] may result either from a deliberate recognition of it as a good or from an acquiescence in it as inevitable, to be endured permanently or temporarily with skepticism, indifference or scorn, with fists clenched but in the pockets."[35] Although he did not quote this passage, Barnard was well aware that employees did not always accept the orders of their superiors with wild enthusiasm. Consequently, he introduced to his theory of authority a notion that pertained to the degrees of submission in employee behavior—the zones of indifference, neutrality, and unacceptability within which people evaluate the orders given to them.

Michels was too good a political scientist to miss the point that authority and legitimacy were inextricably connected. Barnard had a clear sense of this connection as well, which is the reason that the zone of indifference figures so largely in his management theory. It is the zone where employees willingly accept and submit to the orders or communications they receive. Management had to work to widen the zone of acceptable orders, because the positive employee behaviors forthcoming from it would establish management legitimacy. Barnard knew that most workers "kept their fists clenched in their pockets," and this response was dysfunctional when harmony and cooperation were the desirable conditions for a content and productive organizational ship.

8. Limited choice, restrictions to action. Herbert Simon received credit for labeling this construct "bounded rationality," which more accurately described an idea that Barnard named "limited choice."[36] However, the concept does seem to be a Barnardian invention and refers to a human condition wherein physical, psychological, social, informational, and environmental circumstances prevent people from maximizing their utilities. Barnard carried this notion further and rested his case for cooperation on it. Cooperation always extended the capacity of a single person to accomplish things that would otherwise be beyond reach.

Some such consideration as this must have been on Barnard's mind for a long time. He emphasized restricted choice in his Lowell Lectures and dwelt upon it at length in the draft version of the first chapter to his book. The concept appears in full bloom in chapters 3, 4, and 5 of the book as it was published. There, he considered why limited choice was a fact of organizational life and expanded upon its various aspects. Significantly, his construct of cooperation followed immediately the chapters on limitations.

9. The theory of formal organization. Barnard's statements concerning the formal organization were less than innovative, perhaps because he considered it to be merely a segment of a larger, organic network of relationships. He conceived of the formal organization, in its own right, as a structure of conscious rational design whose purpose was to reconcile the opposing forces of specialization and coordination by such commonplace bureaucratic devices as record keeping, rules and policies, and the standardization of personnel practices. These techniques were intended to achieve uniformity of organizational practices.

Barnard treated the formal organization in the classical vein, and he owed considerable debts to Max Weber, as well as to Parsons, Durkheim, and Pareto.[37] One notable source on this subject missing from Barnard's acknowledgments was *Onward Industry,* by Mooney and Reiley.[38] Oddly, there is no evidence of Barnard's awareness of this influential management book, the definitive text for the classical theory of organization.

Barnard seemed smitten by Graicunas's concept of *span of control*.[39] It pertained to the size of an administrative unit, measured by numbers of subordinates, that optimized leadership effectiveness. Span of control was the factor, according to Barnard, that lay behind the growth of levels in an organization hierarchy. Barnard seemed wedded to the classical notion that employees needed close supervision, and therefore, management had to design an organization with a narrow span that permitted detailed supervision of what employees did. The organizational geometry of this works out so that narrow spans result in tall organizations with many levels of authority.[40]

Communication was the vehicle for transmitting management's rational orders concerning organizational activities as well as the means by which people expressed their nonlogical personal interests, attitudes, and aspirations. Both aspects of communication were essential in organizational life, and Barnard highlighted them in his book.[41] As a result, communication became one of the concepts in management for which Barnard is best known.

However, he was not alone in recognizing the importance of the subject. Pareto and Roethlisberger and Dickson stressed communication's formal and informal aspects.[42] They all believed that formal communication required a structure for sending orders that minimized ambiguity. But management had also to "listen in" on the informal communications of the employees, because such exchanges were a barometer of organizational morale.[43]

10. Informal organization. Those spontaneous groupings and associations of people that arose in formal organizations were referred to as informal organization. Barnard defined it as "the aggregate of the personal contacts and interactions and the associated groupings of people."[44] He thought that informal organizations were natural to and necessary for formal organizations. Although Barnard's treatment of this construct was the least satisfying in his theoretical scheme, it was insightful in a number of respects. For example, he observed that formal organizations grew from informal associations and that they legitimized management authority, an idea that probably is traceable to Ehrlich's work.

The management implications of the informal organization were evident. As managers had to gain access to the individual's psyche in order to shape attitudes, it also had to manipulate group culture and norms in order to make them compatible with organizational values. However, the social sciences then had not produced the theoretical equipment or the research data to provide managers with a particularly firm foundation for influencing the informal organization. Consequently Barnard floundered around, relying on Mary Parker Follett's quiet homilies for some of his ideas.[45]

But he was also aware of the opinions in the Harvard Circle about the informal organization, and he paid attention to the reports on the bank-wiring room experiments coming from the Hawthorne studies. These experiments were the first attempt to apply anthropology and social psychology to informal groups in a manufacturing plant,[46] although their implications had not been thoroughly digested when Barnard was writing his book. However, his description of the informal behavior of executives, based on his experiences at ATT, was the best ever written.[47]

11. Logical and nonlogical mental processes. Barnard used logical and nonlogical mental processes as a construct to contrast the conscious effort of reason with human feelings, attitudes, and sentiments. The former led to rational behaviors such as those managers displayed in organizational decisionmaking, whereas the latter led to nonrational behavior of the sort often shown in individual decisionmaking. Barnard held that most human behavior was of the nonlogical variety, and he made it abundantly clear that it posed special problems for management.

Pareto was the source for this rich construct, and, in tribute to his imagination, the key figures in the Harvard Circle elevated it to a high place in their theoretical scheme. Pareto used the term "logical mental processes," to describe the conjoining of means to ends, not only from the standpoint of the person engaged in it but also from the objective, outside perspective of other persons who had more extensive knowledge.[48] Nonlogical mental processes depended upon the "residues," or those culturally derived norms, standards, beliefs, or superstitions that could not be assessed by an outside authority as true or false, good or bad. Residues were often made to seem logical by elaborate rationalizations that Pareto called "derivations."[49]

One of the problems that the researchers had at Hawthorne was to understand derivations, in order to separate the facts about a human situation from the attitudes of an individual toward it. For example, when a person said that he or she was unhappy because they "weren't paid enough" (a logical expression), he or she was often disguising some other complaint—"my boss picks on me," or some such.

The interview program at Hawthorne was intended to penetrate these clouds of rationalization so management could take steps to "adjust" employee attitudes. What the applied social sciences could do for management was to make nonrational behavior rational to people who supervised it. If this was achieved, then management would possess a valuable scientific tool for engineering social controls.

12. Social science methodology. Positive science, as the social sciences' epistemology of choice, was inadequate, Barnard thought, to the task of discovering truths about the nature of complex organizations. Following the imperatives of their empirical methods, social scientists devoted themselves to the rigorous solution of trivial problems, leaving unexamined and untended the larger and more important questions about systems of human interdependency. Not only did this orientation limit the ability of the social sciences to add to the store of human knowledge, it also prevented them from being relevant to management. The social sciences badly needed a new epistemology, but where was it to be discovered?

Barnard found great potential in Kurt Lewin's field theory, a psychological theory based on the assumption of mutual causality in human systems. Field theory, with its force-field dynamics, seemed to be just what the social sciences needed for a fresh approach. However, Barnard never mentioned Lewin. He was put on to his ideas by the social psychologist, Junius F. Brown, one of Lewin's main disciples and chief advocates in the United States.[50]

Brown, who had been Lewin's student at the University of Berlin, may have been a more ardent field theorist than the master himself. Brown declaimed the scientific virtues of field theory on virtually every page of his book and was a bit too much of the true believer for Barnard's taste.[51] Barnard wrote that while Brown "cried science" throughout his book, his assumptions and generalizations about social psychology depended for support on the shakiest foundations of theory and fact.[52]

Nevertheless, Brown's overall explanation of field theory was attractive, and Barnard even fell into using its terminology.[53] It appealed to him for a number of reasons. First, its analogies with modern physics and mathematics were compelling. They seemed to make it an up-to-date method for looking at the relativity of complex behavioral phenomena. Second, field theory was directly translatable into systems theory because both dealt with interdependent social variables or forces. Third, the "field" concept provided a way of thinking wholistically about individuals, groups, and formal organizations that was entirely consistent with Barnard's point of view. He often had urged the social sciences to develop an epistemology that was appropriate for conceptualizing in this manner.

TOWARD A NEW SOCIAL SCIENCE EPISTEMOLOGY

Two years after being named a trustee of the Rockefeller Foundation, Barnard circulated a paper to board members titled "Memorandum on the Nature of the Social Sciences."[54] This paper joined Barnard to the ongoing debate between Raymond B. Fosdick and Joseph H. Willits. Fosdick, who literally interpreted the Foundation's mandate "to benefit all mankind," believed in the support of research that promised tangible outcomes to improve human well-being. RF grants in medicine, public health, education, and the natural sciences were models of sound policy from Fosdick's point of view. However, Willits had a much different idea. He held that since the social sciences were not advanced, and since the needs they addressed were poorly defined, support of basic social sciences research (theory building, data collection, and construct validation) was more appropriate. Simply put, the disagreement between Fosdick and Willits was over funding pure versus applied research.

Growing in intensity over the years, this controversy continued until Fosdick retired. For example, Fosdick recorded in his diary that he wrote to Willits, "research by itself just isn't enough. Unless we do something with research, we aren't getting anywhere." Fosdick feared that the social science division did not "understand this fundamental Foundation policy."[55]

Given Barnard's views on the social sciences, it is not surprising that his memorandum favored Fosdick's position. He thought the social sciences' commitment to positive science orthodoxy stood in their way of being helpful, in an applied sense, to management. He reasoned that the social sciences bootlegged its epistemology from the natural sciences, so their methodologies of research were distorted and the development of techniques was limited by applying the "criteria of the epistemology of abstract physical science where it cannot apply."[56] He argued that while the natural sciences dealt with two dimensions of "knowing," sense data and constructed theories and topologies, the social sciences were concerned with at least three dimensions. Crucial data in the social sciences were human beings themselves, who, unlike the objects of study in the natural sciences, had the capacity for "proprioception" or self-awareness of their subjective states. According to Barnard, a proper epistemology had to take subjectivism into consideration, although scientists often rejected it as not verifiable. Thus, social scientists frequently ignored those facts about behavior that possibly were the most useful in practical management situations: people's states of mind, attitudes, intuitions, purposes, interactions, thoughts, and so on.

Collaterally, the Fosdick-Willits debate was also over issue-driven versus theory-driven research, with Fosdick favoring the former and Willits the latter. Barnard was not silent on this subject either, and in his memorandum he wrote about it as a problem in "the level of concreteness." The problem, as he framed it, was easily understood since it referred to the old metaphysical axiom that the greater the comprehension, the less the extension, or, as Barnard put it, "The more the aspects of the concrete are taken into account, the more one approaches the uniqueness of a thing or event; the less widely it is possible to generalize; and the less it is possible rigorously to prove the validity or define the limits of any generalization."[57]

In modern terms, this is expressed as internal and external validity. Internal validity verifies causal relationships, whereas external validity establishes the generalizability of scientific findings. As Barnard noted, in order to obtain internal validity, an event under study had to be isolated to a point of almost pure abstraction wherein most reality was removed from the experiment. Consequently, generalizability (external validity) was severely limited. Conversely, in order to increase external validity, so many variables had to be introduced into an experiment that the determination of causal paths (internal validity) was greatly hindered.

But lack of internal validity was a small price to pay, since the real world of organizations and management was enormously complex and uncertain, with so many variables that it was hopeless to try to sort them out by conventional scientific means. Notwithstanding all of this, orthodox social scientists, marching to the drum of positivism, opted for internal validity, and this was exactly why Barnard thought that their contributions to management would be minimal. "Their [social scientists'] aim is not to produce specific events, effects, or situations but explanations we call knowledge."[58]

Barnard's message to the trustees thus stated in considerable detail the faults of positive science, but he was less than clear about an alternative to it. Granted that he did make an attempt to draw, in broad outline, a new epistemology for the social sciences, one in which subjective facts were taken as objects of scientific inquiry. To advance on this tack, he believed that the social sciences must first borrow from the physical sciences the measurement of sense data and their approach to theory building. However, second, they had to add to these elements social subjectivism. Then they had to find a way to know about the relationships between the two.[59] The social sciences were the most deficient in this third requirement.

In this regard, Barnard argued for a concrete science of behavior that supported the efforts of management in concrete situations. Of necessity, this new science had to be integrated, drawing upon history, biosocial facts, and sociology for concepts and data. In short, social science needed an epistemology that led to the knowledge of human systems by way of an integration of all the sciences that addressed behavior.

Barnard's book and the architecture of his thought in general approached organization and management in this way. The next five chapters will give more attention to his efforts at creating an integrated science of behavior based on an alternative way of knowing about social systems. But mostly Barnard's advice went unheeded at the Rockefeller Foundation,[60] and in the social sciences as well. As he predicted, overspecialization in research fragmented them and produced even higher barriers between scientists and those who needed useful knowledge for making practical policy decisions. Issue-driven social science languishes now while empiricism and particularism thrive.

6

The Search for Behavioral Control: The Individual and the Small Group

Successful management depends upon the cooperation of nonmanagers, so the scientific control of worker behavior seemed promising to Barnard and his friends in the Harvard Circle. But much more research and theorizing still had to be done by the social sciences, and managers had to be informed about the lessons already to be learned from them. Barnard chose the role of informing, and he constructed an integrated model of organizational behavior to educate executives. He believed that the social sciences could improve management techniques for controlling employees, so a grasp of what made people work cooperatively was indispensable to management. Therefore, he settled his organization theory upon the foundations of the individual and the small group, the fundamental units of all cooperative systems.

True to this instrumental perspective, Barnard held that knowledge alone was not sufficient, that knowledge had to be useful. He put this view unequivocally in 1946. As chairman of a special committee on policy and program for the Rockefeller Foundation charged with the mission of establishing broad, postwar policy guidelines, Barnard reported, "It is the committee's thought that work in this area [the social sciences] would consist of projects which promise to make a contribution to, or lay the necessary foundation for, an increased understanding of the factors which modify or control human behavior."[1] The influence of Barnard's earlier memorandum on the social sciences was evident in this committee's report.

Barnard's position was that the social sciences ought to develop techniques that management could use to induce workers to cooperate willingly in the accomplishment of organizational goals. Barnard had arrived at this conclusion several years before becoming a Rockefeller Foundation trustee. Impressed by the results of the Hawthorne studies and influenced by his associations with Elton Mayo and Lawrence Henderson, Barnard wrote, "Persons [may be regarded] as *objects* to be *manipulated* by changing the factors affecting them or as *subjects* to be *satis-*

fied."[2] Although the difference between people as objects or subjects in this quotation was not immediately apparent, the managerial implication was obvious. Management can and should influence behavior because "organization results from the modification of actions of the individual through control . . . or influence. Deliberate conscious and specialized control [of behavior] is the essence of executive function."[3] This implied questions concerning application, and they were addressed by Barnard in terms of incentives and persuasion, subjects that are treated in the next chapter.

Thus, individuals and groups were critical components of organization, and their cooperation with management was vital to the success of any enterprise. Commitment, or lack of it, was caused by individual attitudes and group norms; therefore, management should try to influence and modify them. Barnard encouraged management to search for the means of effective behavioral control within the framework of social engineering, but that required management to make certain assumptions about human behavior and motivation.

HUMAN BEHAVIOR

Free will, internal versus external causes of behavior, reverse causality, and tension reduction were the premises on which Barnard based his theory of human behavior. But before he discussed them, he put an important limitation on his analysis, a distinction between individuals and persons.

Individuals and Persons

Barnard discussed persons and individuals in organizational contexts that he understood to be systems of interactions "unified by a purpose or purposes which constitute . . . immediate objectives."[4] Since people belong to many organizations, only part of their attention, commitment, and activities were claimed by any one of them. Furthermore, over and above all of the organizations with which people were associated was the fact that they spent part of their time in isolation. From this Barnard concluded "The social world consists of organizations *and* individuals, not organizations *of* individuals."[5]

To Barnard, the individual was "a simple, unique, independent, isolated, whole thing, embodying innumerable forces and materials past and present which are physical and biological factors."[6] He saw the individual as having purposes, impulses, or desires that he called motives. Behavior, therefore, was a process based on motives that drove the individual to achieve desired goals or states. He described motives as "ends sought." This interpretation of human behavior was not unique. Similar ones can be traced to Aristotle's notions of the intentional, goal-directed qualities of human action.

The singular aspect of Barnard's theory was that individuals, in their wholeness, were too complex to be managed. What is more, managers, bounded by their own individual limitations, could not control individuals effectively. Still, that part of themselves that individuals brought to an organization could be controlled. Barnard called this part "persons." Persons had certain generalizable work-specific attitudes, motives, goals, and intentions that were fairly uniform, making them susceptible to scientific predictions and management direction. Although individuals could not be controlled, persons could.

However, where persons left off and individuals began was not clear, and any such delineation had to be arbitrary. Nevertheless, this distinction led to Barnard's critical concept of "limited choice,"[7] wherein he suggested that people, especially executives, in organizations are "bounded"[8] in their actions by an enormous number of limitations. These he described in the draft of the first chapter of his book. "At every turn . . . the executive is confronted . . . with requirements, prohibitions, limitations, disabilities, inertia, obstruction, recalcitrance, disintegrating influences, that rule out one after another the possibilities and desirabilities as 'impracticable,' 'not susceptible of accomplishment'; and that restrict the choices of the methods by which only the meagre remainder of 'promising' ideas may be carried out."[9]

Because of these limitations, he perceived managerial power as not absolute and managers as restricted to taking "satisfactory" as opposed to "optimal" actions. Thus, with regard to the human factor, Barnard advised management to concentrate on what it had the best opportunity to control, persons in work situations, rather than individuals in broad social situations. Against this background, he discussed the four behavioral premises—free will, internal versus external causes of behavior, reverse causality, and tension reduction.

Free Will

Persons have free will because of their power of choice and their capacity for self-determination. This assumption, central to Barnard's theory of behavior, derived from those moral and legal doctrines that stress personal responsibility for actions. These doctrines contrast with those that argue for socially conditional behavior. Barnard was not a determinist as it applied to responsible behavior, and his endorsement of the free will doctrine underlay all his notions of management's moral obligations.

Despite Barnard's philosophical predisposition toward free will, he recognized that self-determination and rational choice had limits. He observed that people often say they have used the power of choice (a derivation) when, in fact, they have not. People frequently behave in ways that are dictated more by habits and scripts (residues) than by free choice. Therefore, deliberate choice was often ascribed to persons when actually their behavior may have been the result of a far less clear or logical process. Barnard argued that much of what persons do "is for the most part carried out on the basis of experience and intuition."[10] Constraints on free will were among the more obvious connections between Barnard's views of behavior and those held by members of the Harvard Circle who were in the thrall of Pareto's residues and derivations.

Barnard's insights are relevant to research by contemporary social scientists. For example Nisbett and Wilson, and Langer, observed that in many cases people cannot accurately account for the cognitive processes that led them to take a particular action.[11] Barnard wrote, forty years earlier, that when one inquires about the motives that lead to the selection of certain goals, they are "usually unknown to the person whose action is involved."[12]

Internal versus External Causes of Behavior

The question of causation stems directly from the concept of free will. Does behavior result from internal or external impulses and stimuli? In this regard, Barnard joined the debate between philosophies that "regard the individual as merely responsive" and "deny freedom of choice or will" and those philosophies that "grant freedom of choice and of will" and "that depress the physical and social environment to a secondary and accessory condition." He described the former as theories based on environmental determinism and "behaviorism" and the latter as based on the cognitive notion of "purpose."[13]

This explicit recognition of the controversy between the behaviorists and the cognitivists was the first time the issue was discussed in the management literature. But Barnard's insights go one step further. He resolved the debate by proposing that any theory of cooperative systems and of organization required that both positions play a part. He argued for a contingency approach. "What then is needed for our purposes is to state under what condition, in what connections or for what purposes one or the other of these positions may be adopted usefully and to show how they may be regarded as simultaneously applicable."[14]

Barnard's conclusion about the external versus internal causality debate is a perfect example of his instrumental, middle-of-the-road, and relative solutions of many management problems. Instrumentality does not leave much room for endless academic debates over subjects such as causality that cannot be resolved in any case. The finding of the golden mean between opposite concepts characterized much of Barnard's work.

Reverse Causality

Barnard noticed that the causal direction between thought and behavior is a two-way street—thought influences action and vice versa. Not only did Barnard recognize that the environment or simple rules cause behavior, he also realized that many explanations of behavior are "inferred from action, that is, after the fact."[15]

On the one hand, he observed that some choices "will be made on the bases of . . . purposes, desires, impulses . . . and the alternatives available."[16] In other words, people's motives and intentions combined with their evaluations of options precede behavior. On the other hand, he argued that people explain retrospectively their behavior by reflecting on their actions. "But usually what a man wants can be known even to himself only from what he does or tries to do, given an opportunity for selective actions."[17]

Barnard anticipated some of the theories that evolved from reverse causality in the behavioral sciences, specifically dissonance theory and other balance-type models. However, these ideas did not reappear in the management literature until the 1970s. Their revival was due mostly to the contributions of Festinger and Bem in psychology and Weick in organizational behavior.[18]

Tension Reduction

Unfulfilled motives, purposes, and intentions create a dynamic tension in a person that prompts behavior. Barnard discussed behavior in these terms, pointing out that "the activities incited by desires, impulses, wants, motives sometimes result in the attainment of the end sought and a reduction of the tension," created when they were unsatisfied.[19]

Again, Barnard anticipated current research, since tension-reduction models have been the basis for work in areas such as attitude formation and change, job satisfaction, and decisionmaking.[20] Although currently there is debate over an information-processing approach opposed to the tension-reduction model in motivation theory, Barnard integrated the latter notion into his ideas about the basic foundations of human behavior, and it became part of the canon of management theory.

MOTIVATION

Some of Barnard's assumptions about motivation were implicit in his theory of behavior, in that behavior is jointly caused by environment and cognitions and that tension reduction is the dynamic, driving force for a person's actions. However, he went into more detail about behavior in his theories of motivation, anticipating ideas that were the foundation for the major cognitive theories that now dominate the motivational literature in management: goal setting, cost-benefit analysis, contingent rewards, and equity.

Goal Setting

Goal setting played a pivotal part in Barnard's overall view of organizations. He held that a person's actions are directed toward goals or end states, and he carried this analysis into the organizational context, observing that formal systems of cooperation, for example, the formal organization, require objectives, ends, or purposes.[21] "Unless there is such an objective it cannot be known or anticipated what specific efforts will be required of individuals."[22] That there are major differences between the goals of persons or small groups and the objectives of organizations was a point of emphasis in his treatment of this subject. He thought the personal goal was "an internal, personal, subjective thing" while the group goal was "necessarily an external, impersonal, objective thing even though the individual interpretation of it is subjective."[23] This caveat is important. Barnard realized that "subjective interpretations" can be modified or influenced by incentives and persuasion. Regardless, Barnard based his well-known distinction between "efficiency" and "effectiveness" on this matter of goal definition. Efficiency in Barnardian language means the satisfaction of a person's motives, whereas effectiveness is the accomplishment of the cooperative purpose. Clearly there is a potential for conflict between personal and cooperative goals. However, they can also reinforce each other, and when they do, organizations achieve higher performance and persons experience greater work satisfaction. The task of management, as Barnard saw it, is to augment both efficiency and effectiveness, so that the cooperative system becomes a source of personal gratification for those who are in it as well as a potent engine for impersonal goal achievement. The two, interacting and reinforcing each other, would drive the cooperative enterprise into ever greater conditions of harmony and achievement.

Cost-Benefit Analysis

Barnard wrote that the "willingness of people to contribute efforts to the cooperative system is indispensable."[24] Willingness is demonstrated by a person when he or she gives up personal control over some aspect of work-related behavior and submits to superior authority or to rules that regulate behavior. Relative to the willingness to cooperate, Barnard wrote that it "is the expression of the net satisfaction or dissatisfaction experienced or anticipated by each individual in comparison with those experienced or anticipated through alternative opportunities. That is, willingness to cooperate is a net effect, first of the inducements to do so in conjunction with the sacrifices involved, and then in comparison with the practically available net satisfaction afforded by alternatives."[25]

Barnard included as rewards money and physical surroundings and nonmaterialistic inducements such as distinction, prestige, and power. Under other categories of rewards he mentioned "pride of workmanship, sense of adequacy, altruistic service, loyalty to the organization, and the feeling of enlarged participation in the course of events."[26] One can certainly imagine that this list described the personal benefits that Barnard, himself, derived from his work at ATT.

We return to Barnard's cost-benefit analysis in the next chapter, but it is important to note its centrality to concepts of motivation. Persons evaluate overall costs and benefits associated with behavioral choices and then make a choice based upon a comparison with alternative actions. Although these ideas had already been discussed by John R. Commons in relation to economic theory, Barnard introduced them to the literature of management as a major concept of motivation and decisionmaking.

Equity

The action that a rational person takes should lead to higher rewards than any alternative action. However, Barnard realized that persons' evaluations of inducements, including negative inducements, and alternatives are socially conditioned perceptions. He noted that equity in the distribution of rewards (or costs) could be an important factor in the evaluation of alternatives. "There takes place a social dissatisfaction as to some [alternatives], and a satisfaction as to others, because of the equality of the distribution of a product. Thus A, who puts forth more effort than B, thinks he should have a larger share."[27] Barnard analyzed in some detail how perceived equity and inequity arise, how they influence a person's effort, and how they condition the quality of cooperation in an organization. All in all the perception of costs and benefits, as well as the fairness of their distribution, was a critical motivational concept in Barnard's scheme. He pointed out that "an organization can secure the efforts necessary to its existence . . . either by the objective inducements it provides or by changing states of mind."[28] This stance acknowledges that management has the responsibility to manipulate worker attitudes by altering persons' perceptions of equity in order to secure from them greater commitments to the organization.

Motivation and Cooperation

Rounding out the picture of Barnard's theory of motivation, two additional points are worth noting. First, he recognized that individual differences are important, especially as they apply to management's use of incentives. According to Barnard, people are moved by different incentives, at different times, and in different combinations.[29] Thus, the use of incentives is a contingency problem that management must diagnose according to the needs of the concrete organizational situation. Second, Barnard was aware that degree of effort does not necessarily correlate with effectiveness of performance. Such performance is also influenced by the faculties and capacities of the persons, the biological and physical conditions of the work environment, and the social and interpersonal conditions that prevail in the work situation, factors emphasized by Henderson, Mayo, and the rest of the Hawthorne research group. Management can, to a greater or lesser extent, control some of these factors, and the extent to which they are controllable depends on a correct situational diagnosis. This clinical application of the social sciences was regarded by Barnard and the Hawthorne scholars as the major contribution of behavioral research and theory to management practice.

A BEHAVIORAL MODEL OF PERSONS

A summary of the position of current industrial psychology textbooks on the subjects of human behavior and motivation would not significantly differ from the straightforward, instrumental approach taken by Barnard fifty years ago. He held that persons have motives that can be defined as purposes or goals. When motives are not fulfilled, a person seeks to reduce the tension that is caused by this deficiency. If active, thoughtful reflection is involved in decisionmaking, as opposed to reflexive reaction based on rules or scripts, the choice of behavior is a function of the costs versus the benefits of a particular action compared to alternative actions. To some extent this cost-benefit assessment is influenced by how persons perceive the relative distribution (equity) of inducements and contributions for themselves compared to others in similar situations. Whether or not the behavior that results leads to high performance depends on such contingencies as personal ability and the social and technological environment. If all these contingencies of human action are favorable and if management has diagnosed and intervened in the concrete situation correctly, then the probability is increased that employee satisfaction and organizational performance will improve.

The utility of this model of behavior for management is readily apparent. It identifies, with some operational precision, the variables in behavior that are most pertinent to the executive process, a process that is, in the end, aimed at securing better cooperation from employees. Furthermore, the model is practical because it is delimited to the actions of employees at work. As Barnard saw it, management could do something about job attitudes and motives of persons directly under their authority; it could not realistically expect to do much to influence the sentiments and desires of the whole individual.

Thus, Barnard's psychology of persons was deeply pragmatic and consistent with the ideological position of the Harvard Circle and the formal policies of the RF. Elton Mayo had stated the ideology in terms of a cooperative industrial commonwealth led by a managerial elite.[30] Human relations programs, which included employee counseling and interviewing, were the major applied techniques that resulted from this ideological orientation. But when Mayo wrote about this in 1933,[31] the ideology was yet ill formed and the place of the social sciences in it poorly understood.

Barnard stepped into this cauldron of doubt and confusion with a model of behavior that had variables that could be researched and also applied to improve management practice. This model was manipulative and could be used by the powerful, namely managers, to alter employees' perceptions of their work reality *without their awareness*, a reality that management was controlling in an attempt to mold or adjust workers' behavior. But for Barnard such manipulation was merely the means to an end, the achievement of cooperation. Therefore the quest for manipulative techniques, inspired by the ideology of cooperation, could be justifiably funded by the RF because that research promised to result in industrial harmony and higher productivity for the "benefit of all mankind." Barnard focused on those elements of behavior that were the most assessable to science and usable by management, in the hope that by their manipulation employee interests could be aligned with those of the elite. Such was the ideological stuff of cooperation applied to persons on the job.

Allowing Barnard to speak for himself on these issues, he pointed out that managers must influence "the conditions of behavior including a conditioning of the individual by training, the inculcation of attitudes, by the construction of incentives."[32] This, in Barnard's opinion, "constitutes a large part of the executive process."[33] By manipulating behavior, executives could achieve a "modification of the action of the individual through control or influence upon"[34] attitudes, choices, incentives, and alternatives. Barnard was at his strongest when he addressed the psychology of behavior and motivation. Nevertheless, he was keenly aware that persons at work are interdependent. They form groups and they communicate with each other. In this regard, Barnard put his toe into the waters of social psychology, a subject about which mainline management previously had been innocent.[35]

GROUP DYNAMICS

The significance of small group behavior to management was just beginning to be noticed when Barnard was writing his book. Roethlisberger and Dickson brought attention to it in their description of the "social organization of employees."[36] Their remarks about the "informal" organization were based on the bank-wiring-room experiment at Western Electric. Barnard acknowledged this contribution in his book, as well as citing Elton Mayo, T. N. Whitehead, and Mary Parker Follett as sources of theory and research on small-group behavior. What little was known about the informal organization at that time came from studies of factory workers, although Barnard attempted to make a wider application of small-group theory in his aforementioned observations about executive cliques.[37]

Even with the paucity of research on small groups, Barnard knew that they were ubiquitous and essential to formal organizations. But he considered them to be rather like inchoate blobs. He observed that the "informal organization is indefinite and rather structureless, and has no definite subdivision. It may be regarded as a shapeless mass of quite varied densities."[38] Despite this lack of form, he noted the considerable pressure that such groups exert on individuals, referring to this phenomenon as akin to either "mob psychology," "public opinion," or "group consensus." Shapeless though it is, group influence causes persons in work situations to accept or reject the values and goals of the formal organization.

Barnard's diagnosis of the informal organization was half right. He erred, for instance, in his hypotheses that small groups are shapeless masses. Study after study in the postwar years demonstrated that informal organizations have leadership, status structures, and highly articulated value systems. They are far from being mobs. However, he was correct about the impact of groups on behavior and motivation, through the influence of their "culture" on personal attitudes and values. Thanks to Lloyd Warner, Barnard and the Hawthorne researchers were introduced to the idea of culture. And while they did not treat it explicitly in their work, the inferences they drew about social norms and customs were anthropological in nature. The implication was clear; the culture of an informal group could, in effect, support or oppose the culture of a formal organization.

It is fair to conclude that Barnard, and his friends at Harvard, believed that informal cultures of industrial employees were more likely than not to be at odds with management and formal organizations. Something needed to be done about that, because it reduced the quality of cooperation.[39] The cogency of this insight resonated in management at the time, but not much was made of it. Social scientists and management practitioners did not know how to "get at" the informal organization in order to modify its cultural values. Years later, in 1982 to be exact, Peters and Waterman showed the way in their popular book *In Search of Excellence*.[40] They lauded Barnard as one of the three great organization theorists of our age for his recognition that control of culture was critical to the harmonization of all the interests in an organization.

But what did Barnard have to say on the larger subject of group dynamics? To answer this question we need to understand his position, not only on the informal organization but also on group processes and communication.

The Informal System

It is one thing to portray the informal organization as an entity with certain behavioral properties. It is quite another to analyze its relationship to the formal organization. Barnard's framework for this analysis was the relationship between the informal organization and the other elements of the larger organizational system with which it interacts. But first let us examine Barnard's view of the informal organization as a discrete phenomenon.

Group interaction creates a network of values, perceptions, and expectations that are transmitted to group members in the form of expected behaviors through roles, defined by "customs, mores, folklore, institutions, social norms and ideals."[41] Barnard discussed roles in some depth and highlighted the concept of split roles and the fact that employees often have multiple roles to fill. He wrote about the foreman with dual roles as a "member of his gang or shop crew" and as a "member of a distinct management group or shop executive group."[42] He recognized that roles reflect authority and provide the grounds for the acceptance of communication.[43] He called attention to role conflict stating, "Conflicts . . . will increase . . . with increases in the number of [roles]"[44] and that the higher the organization position, the greater the likelihood of role conflict.[45] Although Barnard's observations were couched in terms of the formal role expectations of executives, it did not escape him that the informal organization added to the complexity of role networks.

Barnard discussed norms in detail, treating them as the informal system of expectations that controlled actions within groups. Norms result "in the exercise of an influence on the subject or on the attitude of the individual, that maintains a certain stability."[46] The normative maintenance of behavior was described by Barnard as "organizational opinion," "feeling in the ranks," or "group attitude."[47]

In general, Barnard acknowledged the lack of information about the informal organization, saying that it is "a special technical field that had hardly been recognized."[48] Parenthetically, this is an area in which considerable strides have been conducted during the last fifty years, in terms of role theory and normative influence. But more importantly, Barnard believed that executives must "manage" the informal system by controlling both role prescription and norm development. However, he did not address the implementation of this executive function in detail, and management still knows little about how to influence directly informal groups' norms. Yet since about 1983 great efforts in management have been made to find out, and the management literature has been flooded with "organizational culture" pieces that pertain to the control of group norms, values, and behavior.

Group Process

The systemic character of group processes is the hallmark of Barnard's legacy to the theory of informal organizations.[49] He may have been the first management scholar to notice that formal organizations grow out of informal ones and that they require informal organizations for their maintenance. He was fond of saying that one cannot understand a formal organization by merely looking at its chart of relationships, its charter, its policies, or its regulations. To know who does what and who's who, one must learn about an organization's informal society.

Barnard had a Gestalt view of the informal organization that he described as being "something more or different from the mere sum of the interactions composing it."[50] Considering the optimum size of groups, Barnard thought that it depended on "technological complexity of the tasks involved, the ease or difficulty of communication and the complexity of personal relationships."[51]

Barnard also felt that competition and cooperation are important to the small group's interactions with the larger system. He argued that when people must work together closely, the reward system should distribute inducements fairly equally. But when low interdependence prevails, a reward system that distributes inducements unequally is appropriate. One might guess that this conclusion was based on the observation that when people are isolated from one another, they do not have the chance to engage in much invidious comparison over equity issues.

Nevertheless, it was not until the 1960s that Miller and Hamblin clarified this issue in the sociology literature.[52]

However, cooperation dominated Barnard's attention, and in this regard management played a major role in the control of those informal processes that bear directly on organizational effectiveness.[53] Communication is the chief means that management has for sequencing and controlling group action.

Communication

Barnard received much contemporary recognition for his treatment of communication because he recognized that by it management maintains its authority in organizations. For example, C. I. Hoveland in a memorandum to Willits in 1947 outlined seven communication principles that he found in Barnard's book that he thought were appropriate research subjects for the RF to fund:

- the channels of communication should be well known and defined,
- objective authority requires a definite formal channel of communication to every member of the organization,
- the line of communication must be direct and as short as possible,
- the complete line of communication should be used,
- the competence of persons serving as communication centers must be adequate,
- the line of communication should not be interrupted,
- every communication should be authenticated.[54]

Because employee compliance depends upon clear information and command flows, formal communication must be unambiguous. Thus Barnard saw his communication principles solving "a primary or essential continuing problem of formal organization."[55]

Barnard recognized that informal communication is important too. The intent of a message and of nonverbal acts often reveals more than the formal message itself. He observed, "A very large element in the special experience and training in continuity of individual association is the ability to understand without words not merely the situation or conditions but the *intention*."[56] He went on to describe a number of cases where appropriate action resulted without any verbal communication.

Along with population and cooperation, Barnard ranked communication as one of the three major problems of modern life that must be controlled. He recommended in his first annual report as president of the RF that studies of "what we talk about" should be supported. This covered grant funding in such fields as language, history, social science, cultural anthropology, and art.[57] Barnard had expanded his view of communication from a management tool to an instrument of social control necessary for national cooperation.

MODERNIZING THE SOCIAL SCIENCES FOR MANAGEMENT USE

The psychology of human behavior and motivation at work had a long applied tradition that predated Barnard's book by nearly forty years. In chapter 2 we saw how thoroughly this territory had been staked out by Walter D. Scott, Robert M. Yerkes, Lillian Gilbreth, Hugo Munsterberg, Elton Mayo, the industrial psychologists of the 1920s, and the Harvard researchers of the 1930s. So many of Barnard's strikingly original insights were based upon years of groundwork done by others. Even his central theme, that social engineering could improve management practice, was not original. The uniqueness of his contribution stemmed from placing the concepts of behavior, motivation, and group processes into systems frameworks. This, he thought, gave management a practical way to understand and to control behavior in terms of the larger contexts in which it occurred. This approach guaranteed Barnard a place in management's hall of fame.

But such instrumentality also ensured for Barnard a less flattering interpretation of his views. By his own admission, behavioral control is manipulative, and even in Barnard's time questions were raised about the moral right of people with power to alter the attitudes of others without their awareness. Nevertheless, the applied social sciences, as Barnard assessed them, give management the means to enter the realm of the employee's subconscious in order to inculcate attitudes, motives, and values that are organizationally favorable.

Applied social sciences have supplied many such techniques, and they include participatory management, democratic management, management by objectives (MBO), quality circles, sensitivity training, organizational development (OD), the managerial grid, management initiated grievance systems (MIGS), and a plethora of combinations and repackagings of all the foregoing in the present craze of total quality management (TQM). When properly applied, with a diagnostic eye on the systems and contingencies of practical organizational situations, these techniques promise higher productivity and job satisfaction, more effective goal setting and performance appraisal, smoother organizational change, and better decisions about day-to-day work practices. These results are exactly what Barnard had hoped for because they indicate a healthy cooperative organization with good prospects for long-term survival.

Although the person appeared susceptible to manipulation, such was not the case with the small group when Barnard wrote. It seemed impervious to management control because few methods were available to influence its norms and role prescriptions. But Barnard's insights on organizational culture were the wedge that opened up the possibility for control of the group. Culture, a system of shared symbols woven into elaborate tapestries of images and metaphors, imparted meaning to employees' work roles. More importantly, however, such meanings placed individuals into the larger mythic context of the organization. By doing so, they enriched an individual's understanding of self. From the instrumental standpoint, if management controls the organizational culture, it can also influence the content of the small group's norms. That, in turn, will affect the attitudes and motives of individual employees. Although he did not know how to close this particular circle of manipulation, Barnard appreciated the logic of these relationships. They are, after all, contingent and systemic, and a natural extension of the manipulation of individual behavior. If management intervenes in the choice-making processes of the person's attitudes to increase organizational performance and individual satisfaction, then it should intervene in the meaning-making processes of the group culture for the same reasons.

Current research emphasizes that management is symbolic action, and current theory takes the position that management must manipulate employee attitudes through symbols of the organization's culture. Barnard supplied the groundwork for these modern views, and Peters and Waterman provided the high-voltage inspiration. Since their book was published, cultural manipulation has become the topic of an avalanche of scholarly articles in professional journals and books. Management training programs on the subject abound. And consulting opportunities for "culturalists" are bountiful. In the end, however, Barnard has to be acknowledged for his recognition of culture as the key to unlocking the mysteries of informal organization control.

In a perverse way, Barnard's attitude toward behavior manipulation stood Kant on his head. Barnard thought that people must be used instrumentally, and the reasons for his belief are obvious. Successful manipulation promised to motivate action, reduce disagreement and conflict, increase employee commitment to cooperate with management, and cement management authority by engineering the perception of mutual interests between the leaders and the led. But do these ends justify the means?

Barnard had, most certainly, a justification for manipulation that will be addressed in later chapters. For now it is sufficient to note his two moral premises. First, he assumed, a priori, that the spontaneous decision among people to cooperate is a moral act. Therefore, any managerial efforts that facilitate and extend this primary decision must also be moral. The second premise indirectly relates to the first. People do not really know what is in their own self-interest. As bundles of Paretan residues, shrouded in false derivations, persons are bereft of self-knowledge. Management, with superior knowledge and intuitions about organizations, is in a position to fill these otherwise empty vessels with new meanings and correct derivations. This project, driven by the premise of the innate emptiness of human nature, seemed from Barnard's elitist perspective to be inherently moral and the quintessence of management virtue.

7

Engineering Consent in
Formal Organizations

Management caught the formalization fever from economic development and industrial expansion throughout the industrialized world from the beginning of the twentieth century. Other countries, especially Germany, were similarly exposed, and they too rationalized their organizational practices, a phenomenon that Max Weber captured in his bureaucratic theory. The uniqueness of the American experience came from our people's materialistic aspirations for more golden eggs, and that required rational, efficient, and adaptive organizations for the mass production and distribution of consumer goods.

The consequences for American management were almost immediate. The mega-organizations that arose to satisfy these expectations required increased efficiency, reduced waste, and better control over the huge immigrant work force and new technologies. An Americanized form of bureaucracy emerged in practice to deal with these contingencies, and the theory that accompanied it seemed to describe the best way for accomplishing the management task ahead: the internal coordination of organizations whose complexity had risen to unimagined heights.

Management, therefore, early in this century concentrated its attention on such organizational matters as specialization, standardization, horizontal and vertical integration, centralization and decentralization of decisionmaking, spans of management control, line and staff relations, positional and functional authority, and many other practical, but fairly mechanical, formalization subjects. Classical organization theory, whose development peaked by 1940, provided an acceptable model because it addressed the problems faced by large organizations of this period.

The central problem was the coordination of the specialized routine tasks created by the division of labor. Classical theory solved it through creation of hierarchy, which became management's coordinating method of choice. However, hierarchy, which implied centralized command management, was not absolute, and so there had to be modifications in the theory to account for decentralization and delegation of authority, processes that increased the decisionmaking latitude of subordinates. Consequently, the advocates of hierarchy spent their energies saving what they could of its principles by modifying some of their strictest interpretations. Barnard was one of those who set himself to this task, because he realized that formalization created as many difficulties as it solved.

In Barnard's scheme, formal organizations were a second level of analysis. They linked individuals and groups with management's broader concerns for leadership, governance, and moral responsibility. So the theory of formal organizations was something that Barnard wanted to dispatch quickly. Therefore, he accepted most of the theoretical canon popular with the organizational scholars of the 1930s.[1]

THE COOPERATIVE SYSTEM

Cooperation, together with individualism and voluntarism, was central to the American ethos from the time of the Pilgrims. Barnard deeply believed in its power to bring America into an age of affluence and harmony. This expectation was held by many, whatever their political convictions. Cooperation was efficient, rational, moral, and American.

Barnard put it this way in his speech to the Newark Exchange Club in 1932:

> The cooperation that now and henceforth is necessary to repel the tide of barbarism that is welling up within us means more than mere acquiescence in democracy, more than a mere accommodation to the interferences of the crowd. It means genuine restraint of self in many directions, it means actual service for no reward, it means courage to fight for principles rather than for things, it means genuine subjection of destructive personal interest to social interests.[2]

Throughout this speech, Barnard stressed the larger notion of personal sacrifice for the sake of the collective. Just as this spirit mobilized the country to fight in World War I, Barnard believed it would help it recover the economic prosperity lost during the depression.

But blind faith in cooperation was not enough for Barnard. He had to justify it with the most precise and elaborate arguments he could muster in its behalf. He began with implicit assumptions about what human life would be like in a "state of nature" without cooperation. A priori, such a life would be intolerable, since people would find that their biological and psychological limitations prevented them from doing individually what they could accomplish cooperatively. Therefore, people made a cooperative contract in order to avoid frustration and dispair. Along with Hobbes, Locke, and Rousseau, Barnard was a social contractarian.

He thought that cooperation arose spontaneously from the processes of human interaction, as a social commitment among just a few individuals at first. "The essential need of the individual is association and that requires local activity or immediate interaction between individuals."[3] So people in small, informal associations produced cooperative protocols—norms, values, roles—consistent with the needs and contingencies of the situations that confronted them, and in so doing laid the foundations for formal organizations.

This fact of cooperative life was crucially important because it bore upon what Barnard felt that the persistence of cooperation required.[4] He argued that people continued to cooperate as long as they thought that the costs of personal freedom sacrificed by conformance to group norms were outweighed by the benefits secured through cooperation. He called this outcome "efficiency," and it pertained to the satisfaction of individual goals. Simultaneously, group goals had to be met. This outcome was "effectiveness," and it applied to the accomplishment of collective purposes. Such purposes were more than the sum of the aggregated individual goals,[5] and from them those *surpluses of satisfaction* necessary for efficiency were brought forth.

Consequently, effectiveness and efficiency were interactive. The more people were satisfied, the more they would contribute to the cooperative enterprise; and the more effective the enterprise, the more it would be able to distribute satisfactions to its participants. In persisting cooperative systems, the simultaneity of effectiveness and efficiency had a certain theoretical elegance because an act taken for the sake of effectiveness would produce efficiency and vice versa, mutually enhancing group performance and individual satisfaction.

The longer this dynamic equilibrium between effectiveness and efficiency persisted, the longer a cooperative system lasted.[6] But persistence and long-term survival were not the same thing. Survival depended on the closeness of fit between a cooperative system and its environment, plus the equitable distribution of the system's resources to its participants through an exchange process. The relationships as seen by Barnard among the variables of the cooperative system are shown in Figure 7.1. Management practice, provided that it was of the highest order, produced individual satisfaction and good collective performance, for both the short and long terms of an organization's life.

Despite the rational explanations that cooperative systems should survive, they fail to persist for many reasons. Individuals may decide that their costs of participation outweigh their benefits; the cooperative system may be unable to create adequate satisfactions, monetary or otherwise, to reward participants; the purposes of cooperative systems may be inconsistent with their environment—their "fit" may be wrong; and, finally, the distribution of resources within systems may be unfair. Given all that can go wrong, cooperative failures tended to be more common than successes. As Barnard put it, "Most cooperation fails in the attempt, or dies in infancy, or is shortlived. . . . Failure to cooperate, failure of cooperation . . . are characteristic facts of human history."[7]

Cooperation's most dangerous enemies are formalization and technology. For-

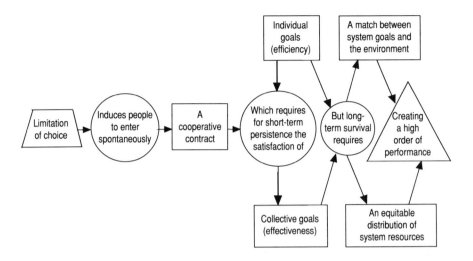

Figure 7.1. Barnard's model of the cooperative system.

malization, Barnard argued, disrupts the fragile internal equilibrium between effectiveness and efficiency. He was aware, on the one hand, that many successful cooperative efforts have been inspired by centralized management authority, such as Wilson's mobilization of the nation demonstrated during World War I. In Barnard's words, "only as there is regimentation [e.g., formalization], that effective cooperation is possible."[8] On the other hand, he believed, as did Herbert Hoover, that regimentation, or imposed formalization, saps individual strength and initiative. This was clearly a dilemma in social progress, as Barnard perceptively called his 1936 commencement address to the graduating class of the Newark College of Engineering.

But formalization is a powerful method for achieving organizational goals, and it easily overwhelms personal motives for work. So as formalization increases in intensity, a fundamental divergence occurs between employee and organizational goals. Most typically, organizational goals are pursued with disregard of those of persons. This all too prevalent organizational condition creates employee dissatisfaction, distrust of management, and the destruction of cooperation. But while the cooperative spirit might die, the formal organization can go on as long as it has an appropriate fit with its economic and market niche. Nevertheless, its performance suffers and its management's legitimacy is compromised by unwilling and untrusting employees.

Barnard described this prevalent state of organizational affairs, "The preponderance of persons in a modern society always lies on the negative side with reference to any particular or potential organization. Thus of the possible contributors only a small minority actually have a positive willingness [to serve in formal organizations]."[9] In this critical passage Barnard captured what he thought was the cause of employee malaise and impaired organizational performance. Most people do not expect their goals to be consistent with those of the organization for which they work. Therefore they assess most potential jobs negatively, and withhold maximum contributions from them once they are employed. Barnard believed that the vitality of modern business depends on reversing this condition.

Although Barnard clearly appreciated the effect of technology on organization structure, he was much more interested in its wider impact on social cooperation. Trying to make sense of the outbreak of war in Europe, Barnard wrote to Henderson in 1940 that while issues of autarky, lebensraum, and national ideology had a part in explaining the course of events, the chief reason for the war was the pressure of technology. The technological civilization was incompatible with both the old absolute governments and the democracies that had evolved in the twentieth century. The new civilization required decisions based upon expert knowledge of specialized technologies. Therefore organizational forms emerged that destroyed traditional institutions of the family, private property, and government. Worse yet, organizations, which were compatible with the technological needs of the time, separated the efforts of individuals at work from any sense of contribution or place in the creation of the final product.

Barnard summed up his gloomy assessment by telling Henderson, "Until a new equilibrium can be reached, general cooperation could be maintained only by force based chiefly upon some dogmatic doctrine supported by some energetic group with a quasi-religious fervor." In the face of things generally falling apart in Europe, Barnard got to the point. "It is not more important that some group should succeed in dominating and organizing the world than that a stalemate should occur. Without some firm formal organization of society, technology seems to me to spell extreme insecurity."[10]

Barnard's letter contained an important statement of his beliefs, formed by World War I, the depression, and the new war just breaking out in Europe. These events represented threats to world stability, and until a new equilibrium was reached, some form of imposed cooperation appeared necessary. Who would do the imposing was an open question, and such groups would be different for the Soviets, Italians, Germans, and Americans. However, the necessity "of some group dominating" for the sake of cooperation in a time of upheaval struck an autocratic chord. But after World War II, Barnard saw the decline of cooperation as a failure of democracy. He noted in his first annual report as president of the Rockefeller Foundation that stability secured by authoritarian methods in formal organizations is an important index of the absence of the peoples' willing cooperation with democratic leaders.[11] Perhaps Barnard, as others all over the world, was fed up by then with all totalitarians. Regardless, Barnard's ambivalence toward the merits of autocratic versus democratic methods of organizational governance ran throughout his lifetime, even though he leaned toward favoring systems of formal organization wherein the authority of the professional management technocrats was undisputed.

THE THEORY OF FORMAL ORGANIZATIONS

Barnard placed formal organization in a social system framework. As he pointed out, the purpose of his book was "to enhance the understanding of the nature of organization, of the social forces that govern it, and of the structure of society in terms of organization."[12] For him, organizations were systems within systems of ever greater magnitude. But he did not limit this view of systems to the inside of an organization looking out. Rather, formal organizations were integrated within rational-legal systems, force fields systems of attraction and repulsion, and systems of human interaction.

Barnard's rational–legal analysis of formal organizations closely followed Max Weber. Weber argued that organizations required a legal mandate in order to exist, and this was exemplified by the corporate charter. This mandate, conferred by society through the state, allowed an organization to pursue certain specialized purposes. "Thus, 'to organize,'" according to Barnard, "means . . . to establish the legal conditions necessary to a particular status of a cooperative system."[13] From this grant of "right" by society, managers and other employees derived their legitimacy to command and to practice those specialized skills that helped the organization fulfill its mandate.

But the law established just the minimum conditions necessary for formal organizations to exist. Barnard noticed that organizations were composed of people who had specialized interactions that caused them to gravitate toward each other. These interactions were held together by a force field of common interests, skills, and attitudes. And so, he wrote in Lewinesque language, "an organization is a 'construct' analogous to 'field of gravity' or 'electromagnetic field' as used in physical science"[14] and "persons are the objective sources of the organization forces which occupy the organization field."[15] These somewhat strained analogies to physical phenomenon did make an important point. Barnard thought that people self-selected themselves into organizational associations and were attracted by the specialized activities derived from the legal and rational purposes of the organization.

Barnard also recognized that when people were involved in a system of interaction, the sum of the specialized components of the system was greater than the elements of the individuals, groups, and functions making it up. This Gestalt consideration was a reminder of the biological metaphor that appeared all through Barnard's book, a metaphor that Henderson might well have inspired. As Barnard wrote, and we repeat, "The systems of cooperation which we call organizations I regard as social creatures, 'alive'."[16] These creatures had certain anatomical features that Barnard discussed in terms of executive functions, complexity and specialization, and structural designs.

Executive Functions: Common Purpose, Doctrine, and Discipline

It followed from the biological metaphor that if organizations are alive, they need a brain for the coordinating agency. In formal organizations the brain is management, and it coordinates by three impersonal processes: communicating orders, engendering a willingness to serve among employees, and creating worthy goals. Although unmentioned by Barnard, Mooney and Reiley identified similar processes. Seven years earlier, in 1931, they had stated that coordination requires a common organizational purpose, doctrine, and discipline.[17] "Common purpose" refers to organizational objectives whose importance in Barnard's thinking was clearly evident. Objectives unify an organization and rally employee contributions to its causes. Barnard's emphasis on communication echoed Mooney's and Reiley's notion of doctrine. Doctrines were in effect organizational policies necessary for achieving its objectives. Barnard extended the point by noting that there is a relationship between how policies are transmitted within an organization and the way formal authority is structured. He wrote that "communication technique shaped the form and internal economy of organization,"[18] a remarkable insight for the time. The modern field of organizational communication gives a considerable amount of attention to the connections between organizational communication channels, both formal and informal, and the official and unofficial structure of relationships within an organization.

Discipline, in Mooney's and Reiley's organization theory, has two forms: self-discipline and imposed discipline. While self-disciplined workers are most desirable, most employees cannot be relied upon to exercise it. Therefore, discipline must be imposed on them through the hierarchy of the organization. Barnard shared this opinion, holding that people in general are not disposed to contribute willingly to an impersonal formal organization. Although this implied the necessity of imposed discipline, Barnard thought that good organization performance and high employee satisfaction could not possibly result from a coercive environment. His solution to this dilemma of discipline involved "engineering" employee compliance by behavioral science techniques.

In general, Barnard treated the executive functions with reasonable straightforwardness. His views ran along these lines. Management establishes organizational purposes and transmits policy doctrines to employees through formal communication channels that correspond to lines of formal authority. It secures employee cooperation with these purposes and policies by discipline. Management practice falters on this last step. Given the conflict between personal and organizational goals, the lack of employee compliance to management authority is a major barrier to cooperation. Barnard introduced his exchange theory within the context of this problem. It follows later in this chapter.

Complexity and Specialization

Barnard explained complexity with a biological metaphor. Each organizational unit (cell) is limited in its activity by communication, effective leadership, complexity of purpose and function, and complexity of personal relationships.[19] Given these unit limitations, the only way an organization can grow is by adding more units, combining them into a complex organization—a cell mass.[20]

Barnard's rather pedestrian conception of structural complexity fits the classical model, because the rules of "cell" aggregation could be reduced to prescriptive "principles" that managers could follow in formalization procedures. Thou shalt not violate the unity of command! Thou shalt subordinate staff to line authority! Thou shalt unambiguously delegate authority! Based on these ideas, Barnard observed that complex formal organizations are divided into functional groups of "working units" and "executive units."[21] The way they are combined in practice turns out to be the classical pyramid of organizational structure so favored by top executives when diagraming their organizations. The brain is always on top.

Barnard's treatment of organizational complexity was conventional even to the point of applying in detail Graicunas's Theorem[22] about the span of control[23] to which he gave a strong hierarchical twist. Nevertheless, span of control geometry did not resolve how executives could get employee compliance without coercive measures in complex organizations. That resolution depended on the management of incentives and persuasion.

The specialization theme that runs through Barnard's organization theory is a subset of complexity. Organizations specialize as to purpose, for example, transportation, retail trade, manufacturing. These organizations are in turn partial systems in networks of other such partial systems that are subordinated to the state.[24] Subordination creates specialization.

Barnard's discussion of specialization is generally uninteresting[25] except for his treatment of technology. He pointed out that varied technological processes require differentiated specialized functions that are, in turn, translated into organizational structures.[26] These observations foreshadowed the work of Woodward, Aldrich, the Aston group,[27] and other contemporary scholars who have researched the relationship between technology and organization structure.

In summary, effectiveness of the organization cannot be had without specialization, that, in turn requires coordination. Barnard clearly recognized the built-in tension between specialization and coordination and the need for executives to find a balance between the two. This conclusion anticipated the studies by Lawrence and Lorsch, from which they drew the same conclusion.[28]

Structural Design

Managers need to do more than merely make organizational design decisions about the division of labor and its coordination. They have also to innovate unique organizational configurations that take into account the special circumstances that management confronts in its environment. This involves strategic considerations in organizational design and Barnard's recognition of them was a contribution of singular importance,[29] one that Alfred D. Chandler expanded upon in his work on strategy and structure.[30]

Of no less importance, especially to Barnard's overall logic, was his treatment of "analysis of purpose." At first glance, this analysis seemed merely to describe how management breaks down goals into priorities—unit goals, intermediate goals, and final goals. Each of the subordinate goals is the means of obtaining the next higher level goal of the organization.

This interpretation of goal hierarchies was conventional, and it is found now in many standard management textbooks. Often overlooked, however, is Barnard's application of this interpretation as a springboard to his exchange theory. He believed that employees in subordinated units cannot understand the higher level goals of a complex organization. However, they have a good idea of detailed unit objectives because they are the nearest to them at work. Therefore, Barnard argued that unit objectives must be clearly communicated by management to the "troops": "into the valley of death rode the six hundred," but never mind the reason why. Knowledge of larger goals only confuses employees because it is outside their ability to comprehend them.

But this does not mean that "larger purposes" dropped out of importance as a factor in motivation and performance. Barnard put it this way: "It is belief in the cause rather than intellectual understanding of the objective which is of chief importance. 'Understanding' by itself is rather a paralyzing and divisive element."[31] If employees accept the virtue of organization purposes on faith, then effective action to achieve the specific objectives of subordinate units follows as the result of their belief in a cause.[32] The problem, of course, is how management stimulated this faith, commitment, belief, and unthinking acceptance of organizational purposes. Barnard solved this problem with the concept of exchange. It became the keystone of his organization theory since it showed how to engineer employee compliance and cooperation.

THE THEORY OF EXCHANGE

Persons serve organizations if they perceive that their rewards are equal to or exceed their sacrifices. This transaction represents an exchange in which benefits are set against the costs of participation in a cooperative system. The amount of difference between these two elements determines the degree to which people commit themselves to organizational life. Such transactions are at the center of what Barnard called the economy of incentives, "the net effects of income and outgo of things resulting from the production of objective incentives and the exercise of persuasion."[33]

Incentives may be material or nonmaterial. But more importantly, they are perceptual, in the sense that persons, subjectively, put different qualitative and quantitative values on them. In other words, the same incentive, or sacrifice, might mean different things to different people. Since they are not fixed in people's minds, they can be influenced by management. As Barnard wrote, people "must be induced to cooperate," and often to induce them it is necessary "to change the state of mind, attitudes, or motives, so that the available objective incentives can become effective."[34]

The management of incentive perceptions requires that material inducements—money, working conditions, fringe benefits, and so on—be supplemented with propaganda that influences people to assign higher values to nonmaterial inducements. The reason to do this is clear. These inducements do not cost as much, thereby permitting an organization to produce surpluses of satisfaction in the exchange process.[35] Barnard understood that securing these favorable perceptions is not an easy undertaking and therefore discussed elements in the process of influence: inducements and contributions, the method of incentives, and the method of persuasion.

Inducements and Contributions

Barnard's notion of motivation included a cost-benefit component, as we discussed in the previous chapter. People weigh their inducements (benefits) against their contributions (costs) and, accordingly, make decisions about their level of participation in an organization. Barnard's understanding of this basic individual decision process did not differ from the utilitarian calculus: people seek pleasure and avoid pain. Barnard wrote, "The net satisfactions which induce a man to contribute his efforts to an organization result from the positive advantages as against the disadvantages which are entailed."[36] This formulation was adopted by Herbert Simon, and he used it as his central premise of decisionmaking. He owed Barnard a large debt for this idea and acknowledged him in his book, *Administrative Behavior.*[37]

However, Barnard claimed that his approach was not strictly utilitarian[38] because such a deterministic doctrine oversimplified the nature of decisionmaking. He observed that a specific adjustment to one side of the equation, such as paying more money or increasing the scope and prestige of a job, would modify both sides of the I and C equation simultaneously. For example, job enlargement could be seen by some as a contribution (a cost) and by others as an inducement (a benefit). What is more, an increase on the I side, say more money, might be negative from an individual's point of view if it also meant increasing the level of job responsibilities. The behavioral consequences from a decision standpoint would be indeterminate.

But notice that Barnard mentioned specific adjustments. When it came to the overall calculus that people use in their decisions, he seemed to rest his case on utilitarian assumptions. Thus, he concluded that people balance their relative advantages (benefits, pleasures, inducements) with their relative disadvantages (costs, pains, contributions) in the process of deciding to participate in and produce for an organization. The one caveat he entered was that a person's calculation is infrequently rational because of his or her residues and limitations of choice. Simon, cognizant of this aspect of Barnard's analysis, was led to his concept of satisficing.[39]

Thus, Barnard saw people motivated in their exchange decisions by most of the same forces that the nineteenth-century classical liberal economists identified. Translated into the language of decision theory, people will participate in an organization if they perceive inducements greater than contributions ($I > C$); they will not participate if $I < C$; and they will search for more information if $I = C$. Similarly, people will produce for an organization at a high level if they perceive $I > C$; they will not produce, that is, they will quit or goldbrick, if $I < C$. However, if people perceive $I = C$, they will limit their production to the minimum necessary to keep their jobs.

The last point was singularly Barnard's. He viewed employee production decisions of the $I = C$ variety as the common state of affairs in industrial nations. Workers, for whatever their individual reasons, limit output because incentives are poorly managed. This observation led him to examine the nature of incentives themselves.

The Method of Incentives

Barnard discussed two classifications of incentives, the material and the nonmaterial. He wrote at length about material inducements and argued, in a way anticipating Herzberg,[40] that they were weak motivators of behavior beyond the level of physiological survival. He stated "that material rewards are ineffective beyond the subsistence level excepting to a very limited proportion of men; that most men neither work harder for more material things, nor can be induced thereby to devote more than a fraction of their possible contribution to organized effort."[41]

Barnard felt that people are attracted by material rewards because they have been influenced by advertising and salesmanship to desire them. Such desires are satisfied relatively easily since science, technology, and commerce make goods available in abundance. All of this has created the "illusion" that material incentives are what spur people to action and that they are effective motivators. Barnard concluded that the result, "has been the creation of sentiments in individuals that they *ought* to want material things."[42]

Barnard did not put much stock in the efficacy of material incentives. He believed that people's desires for "more" (accelerating aspirational levels) would quickly outrun the organization's ability to satisfy them. It could not produce from its internal economy sufficient material incentives to create a surplus of satisfactions from them alone. Furthermore, Barnard, as did the Hawthorne researchers, thought that people intrinsically want nonmaterial rewards, even though they cannot articulate these wishes. Barnard's overall criticism of material incentives stemmed from two sources. The first was his personal belief that people ought not to want an excess of material things. The second was his connection with the Harvard Circle and its interpretation of nonlogical employee attitudes: people are unaware of their motives, they cannot put their attitudes into words, and they are unable to understand what is in their own best interest. This elitist assessment of the limitations of the "common employee" was clearly evident in Barnard's work, leading him to eloquence about nonmaterial incentives, such as distinction, prestige, and the wonderful category, aesthetic and religious in nature, that he called "ideal benefactions." These incentives were suited to "the capacity of organization to satisfy personal ideals"[43] of a nonmaterial nature.

Barnard stressed nonmaterial incentives for sound reasons from management's point of view. They could be given to employees without placing undue strain on the internal economy of the organization. Furthermore, social science research showed them to be powerful motivators. Finally, they were intangible and subjective, and this characteristic was exceptionally well adapted to management's efforts at persuasion.

The Method of Persuasion

Since organizations cannot survive if they provide all the material incentives needed to sate employee desires, management must influence employees to value nonmaterial rewards and "by persuasion so change the desires of enough men that the incentives it [the organization] can offer will be adequate."[44] Considering when this was written, Barnard proposed an extraordinarily modern justification for management's intervention into the ways that people structure their preferences. The question was how to intervene, and the answer was by persuasion.

Management persuasion had three forms: coercion, the rationalization of opportunity, and the inculcation of motives. Coercion, the application of organizational power to exclude or punish reluctant or miscreant employees, required the use of management force in varying degrees. But Barnard rejected it because it aggravated the problem of securing cooperation in organizations.

Rationalization of opportunity promised more, even though it was not an ideal approach to persuasion. It appealed, through propaganda, to the baser human instincts that, at the extreme, stirred people into a frenzy of political or religious fervor. While not as bitterly antagonistic as the propaganda of the totalitarian regimes of the 1920s and 1930s, the rationalization of opportunity was a similar form of influence used by advertising and the cult of science to glorify inventions and to justify the exploitation of natural resources. It made people covet material things.[45] Nevertheless, the rationalization of material opportunity, although it was necessary to a point, was insufficient to bring forth from people a full measure of cooperation.

And this is where the third form of persuasion, inculcation of motives, came in. This approach induced people to prefer nonmaterial incentives, and it was achieved by "deliberate education of the young and propaganda for adults."[46] Barnard thought the inculcation of nonmaterial motives should begin in childhood, doubtless a reflection of Mayo's views about the place of early education in preparing reliable people for citizenship in industrial societies.[47] However, Barnard's idea that adults' work motives could be influenced by propaganda helped define management's role as the chief propagandizers in the managerial state.

The type of propaganda Barnard thought appropriate for them to use was far different than that employed in the rationalization of opportunity. The inculcation of motives did not set people against one another in competition for scarce material resources. Instead, by changing their minds, it welded them into a cooperative whole. The motives that management inculcated would not be competitive, divisive, or acrimonious, and most certainly they would not conflict with organizational values. Rather, this benign managerial propaganda influenced people in ways that were compatible with the mutual interests of all parties in a cooperative system. As Barnard put it, the inculcation of motives "chiefly conditions the motives and emotional response of individuals to incentives."[48] As such it was the axis upon which turned his theory of authority.

THE THEORY OF AUTHORITY

Barnard wrote that "authority is another name for the willingness and capacity of individuals to submit to the necessities of cooperative systems."[49] Implicit in this statement is the consent theory of authority, one of his better-known concepts. Its main point is deceptively simple, authority does not exist unless people agree to comply with the orders they receive through the communication channels of the organization. He quoted, approvingly, Maj. Gen. James G. Harbord's opinion that the army is a democracy because men will not move forward unless the ranks agree with the "motion" to advance.[50] Although Barnard warned against taking this idea of democracy too literally in formal organizations,[51] he observed that even the most autocratic of them depend on consent of those led. But the real democratic experience in formal organization is found in informal groups, according to Barnard.

The Fiction of Superior Authority

Since informal groups create solidarity among their members, one of an executive's important functions is to use them to induce people to comply with formal authority. Barnard did not see this as unnatural because formal organizations grow out of small groups. Thus employee compliance with management orders results from pressure within small groups even though authority appears to emanate from the top.[52] Such was the fiction of superior authority.

Barnard believed that management had to preserve this fiction for two reasons. First, it objectified job responsibilities. Second, it put nonconforming employees on notice that they could not arbitrarily flout the organization, especially since a majority of their comrades had informally agreed on the legitimacy of the orders received from management.[53] Given this argument, it is evident why Barnard thought that the manipulation of group norms was so important. It kept potentially deviant employees in line.

Consent to Authority

Employees withhold their compliance either because they do not see the relevancy of an order to their situation or because they are unable physically, mentally, or morally to consent to it.[54] Putting this in familiar cost-benefit terms, Barnard wrote that when "authority fails [it is] because the individuals in sufficient numbers regard the burden involved in accepting necessary orders as changing the balance of advantage against their interest, and then withdrew or withheld indispensable contributions."[55]

Since effective organizational performance depends on consent, management must "engineer" it by appropriate incentives, persuasion, and communication. Engineering consent, in effect, is the same as impression management. Orders must be expressed so that people perceive them as falling within their "zone of indifference," the zone where orders are unquestionably acceptable. In other words, people receive the orders they expect to receive, and that results in the impression that I will be greater than C if they are complied with.

Naturally, if a zone of indifference exists in people's minds, then there must also be a zone of unacceptable orders, where $I < C$, and a neutral zone where $I = C$. Barnard summarized all of this as follows: "The zone of indifference will be wider or narrower depending upon the degree to which the inducements exceed the burdens. . . . It follows that the range of orders that will be accepted will be very limited among those who are barely induced to contribute to the system."[56] Based upon this reasoning, Barnard tied his theory of authority to his inducement–contribution analysis as shown in Figure 7.2. Management's task is to move employees from conditions A and B to condition C by manipulating their perceptions of inducements and contributions. Thus, if people are influenced to think

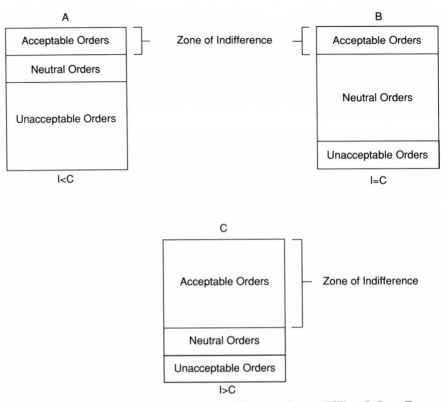

Figure 7.2. Consent to authority and the zone of indifference. (Source: William G. Scott, Terence R. Mitchell, and Philip H. Birnbaum, *Organization Theory*, 4th ed. [Homewood, IL: Richard D. Irwin, 1981], p. 181)

that I > C in their work situation, it is more likely that the orders reaching them will fall within their zones of indifference.

But little is quite as obvious as it first seems in Barnard's thought. Orders are the tangible symbols of management's objective authority.[57] Therefore, as the zone of indifference widens, employee consent to authority increases, thus raising managerial legitimacy. In one masterful stroke, Barnard merged the essential components of his exchange theory and his theory of authority into a legitimacy-enhancing package that reconciled formalization with democracy on terms that were favorable to management's interests and values.

"HUMANIZING" THE FORMAL ORGANIZATION

Barnard's true general theory concerned social hierarchy and the maintenance of order. Barnard's organization and behavioral theories were parts of these wider concerns. His treatment of formal organizations was, to a great extent, his theory of individual behavior and small-group dynamics once removed. And well this should be because these two levels of theory are inseparable. But, to the extent that they are analyzable as distinct components, his organization theory bridged his concepts of individual and group behavior and his overarching views of management's place in society.

The key to understanding this link lay in cooperation. Since the formal organization impedes cooperation, management must instill the cooperative spirit into its enterprises by drastically altered practices. No small task, and it probably would have been thought impossible were it not for the work of Elton Mayo and the rest of the Harvard Circle involved in the Hawthorne studies. This research suggested that people are far more malleable in their attitudes than previously imagined, and therefore they might be influenced in ways that encourage a sense of mutual interests between employees and management.

However, the great institutions of the managerial state could not be transformed into spontaneous cooperative systems. Instead, management had to shape the motives of people and the norms of groups so that they corresponded better with the purposes of centralized command management. That required the development of managers' social and cooperative skills. Barnard did not want to revolutionize organizations as much as to humanize them. So he took the formal organization as a given and showed management how to modify people's attitudes toward it.

But Barnard's humanism did not originate in the milk of human kindness. He recognized that the economic health of formal organizations depended on willing employee compliance to management aims. This could be accomplished by skilled managers who were able to create a sound organizational economy as well as satisfied employees. Thus the twin goals of organizational survival and enhancement of managerial legitimacy were met by the means of employee manipulation. This assessment of Barnard's organization theory is rather Machiavellian, but as Harvey C. Mansfield, Jr., pointed out, if managers took the trouble to read Machiavelli they would understand why they felt an uneasy kinship with him.[58]

8

The Leadership Attributes
of the Management Elite

With the foundations for his managerial ideology established, Barnard turned to the third level of his analysis, where he addressed the larger, more important subjects of leadership, moral responsibility, and national governance in the managerial state. Management and leadership are not the same. The former pertains to skill in practice, the latter concerns moral responsibility. Warren Bennis and Burt Nanus cleverly wrote, long after Barnard, "Managers are people who do things right and leaders are people who do right things."[1] Barnard might have agreed. Doing right things determined organizational survival; doing things right reflected management competence; and together both caused public acceptance of the moral authority of the managerial leadership elite.

However, few of Barnard's ideas were quite so simple. He asserted the importance of management competency as strongly as that of management morality, and it is sometimes difficult to decide if he saw any differences between the two. Doing things right often equated to doing right things. Therefore, an artificial distinction between them could be misleading unless one is alert to the intricacies of Barnard's reasoning. But to not put too fine a point on it, he thought that the attributes of morality and competency jointly determined how much confidence people had in their leadership. Both were ideals toward which all managers should strive. But who were these managers, and why, among all the potential leaders in America, should some few be more capable than others in setting and fulfilling a national agenda? Barnard had unequivocal answers to these questions.

WHO SHOULD RULE AND WHY

As we observed both in the introduction and chapter 1 the leadership contest in Barnard's day was over the location of moral authority. Should it be in the public sector or in the private? That Barnard favored the protection of private corporate power was no revelation, nor was it a surprise that he thought the private sector was the best source of leadership. Nevertheless, Barnard did not oppose government interference in some aspects of private affairs, even though he said on one occasion that government intervention increased the "hostility and intolerance of men and groups, not toward authority or regimentation as such, but toward each other."[2] He accepted government as a major player in the national agenda, but he limited its role to regulation, vehemently opposing centralized planning.

But despite this grand and integrated view of roles in national governance, the leadership peers in the public and private sectors still struggled over who would be first among equals in the managerial state. For corporate management to win this contest, it had to be elevated in social status and public affection. Barnard maintained that if professional managers were educated in the science and rationality of administrative practices and if they were morally cleansed by their heavy obligations, then they could claim the legacy of reputation and legitimacy left by the nineteenth-century business entrepreneurs.

But the wrangle over public or private suzerainty was to Barnard more than a brutish power struggle. He favored the private sector because he truly believed that it was the source of nobler people. He encased this opinion in an extraordinarily complex argument. Barnard observed that the quality of cooperative effort depended on the purposes that an organization pursued. Worthy purposes drew better cooperative behavior from people than less worthy ones. His writings were filled with examples that illustrated this contention.

However, organizational purposes were arrayed along a moral continuum, and most organizations had goals that fell between the extremes of absolute good and evil. Nevertheless, organizations were both the source of and the reflection of individual and collective morality, because they arose from the moral act of cooperation. Since their goals differed, some organizations were more moral than others. Barnard believed that corporations improved the nation's welfare by providing goods and services for a profit. Government merely regulated the use and distribution of this wealth and created nothing to advance the nation's material well-being. Based upon these premises, Barnard reasoned that management leadership in the private sector was worthier to exercise moral authority than were government officials.

Perrow commented that this reasoning was based on deterministic assumptions:[3] organizational functions determine organizational morality. There is without question a large dose of functional morality in Barnard's book. However, Perrow's criticism falls short. It was no more obvious to Barnard than it was to Perrow that the private sector cornered the market on virtue. Who was to say that the regulation of wealth's distribution was morally inferior to its creation? Barnard needed another angle to support his belief in the moral superiority of corporate leaders and found it in a leap of faith.

Barnard's formative years coincided with an intellectual climate strongly influenced by the utilitarianism of Bentham and Mill, the social Darwinism of Spencer, Dewey's pragmatism, and Freud's concept of the subconscious. In one way or another, these ideas were being forged into a philosophical defense for the business aristocrats of the time.[4] Later, especially in Barnard's own work, they were adopted as the bedrock philosophical foundation for American managerialism.[5] One could imagine that Barnard, as a successful middle-aged manager (he was fifty-two when his book was published) would look back on his impoverished youth and attribute his considerable accomplishments to the hard work of personal survival in private enterprise. Barnard may have viewed himself as a product of a system that tested the wit and ingenuity of managers who had to make profits for their companies. Business leaders, subjected to these competitive trials, were eliminated if they were found wanting. Just the fit survived. Public administrators were insulated from this kind of competition.

Barnard wrote Herbert Simon that the selection process in business worked better than in government to winnow out managers whose capacity to make sound judgments was impaired. He said, "I think selection as respects this faculty [judgment] works more accurately in the business world in general than in public administration. As I see it, it works there also but is considerably vitiated by the subtle influence of party politics which . . . considerably interferes with the best selection [of executives] in public administration whereas . . . the competitive factor in business promotes it."[6]

But this intellectualizing could take him only so far, and he realized that behind all managerial success stories was the passion that corporate leaders brought to their jobs, and the best of them made a "declaration of faith" in the power of cooperation. He stressed their "belief in a cause," their "spirit that shapes ends," and their leadership impelled by "conviction." These words conveyed something like a religious conversion and suggested that Barnard, himself converted to the proposition that only corporate management could realize the dream of a cooperative commonwealth, wanted to proselytize.

However, the cooperation that Barnard visualized was on the terms set by a corporate elite. Perrow correctly characterized Barnard's apologia for them as reflecting a "company town" mentality. It is not too farfetched to suggest that his leadership model for the managerial state was fashioned after ATT. In any event, Barnard wanted managerial leadership to be properly prepared for its obligations. By their good works in private institutions, the public would be convinced that they were indeed the better sorts for securing prosperity, progress, and peace in the land.

So in the end Barnard's paean to the higher virtue of private institutions turned upon inspiring a public act of faith in their leaders. But what was it about them that should win this confidence? What collective attributes ought they to have? What were the inspirational qualities of their professional practice? The stakes were high; the legitimacy of corporate leadership in the new managerial order was the prize.

LEADERSHIP ATTRIBUTES

Although historical forces in America may have been partly responsible for the rise of a professional management elite, their acceptance by the public was not predetermined. The elite managers had to merit it by the virtuousness of their lives and the expert practice of their profession. Barnard tried to show managers the way.

In a letter to Joseph H. Willits, Henry A. Moe, president of the Guggenheim Foundation, wrote: "And, have you ever thought what ought to be done about CB's [Chester Barnard's] ideas as to what studies might be made in respect to some of the suggestions in his publications on the study of leadership? I believe he suggested that I.Q. is not so important as vitality and endurance, persuasiveness, decisiveness and responsibility for executive leadership." Moe concluded his letter with the wistful observation that "perhaps all we can do today is to let the Barnards rise from the ranks, not train them in business schools, not even find how to train them or what they are actually like. I wish, however, that there were some ways to capitalize, as a research possibility, the kind of know-how that Mr. Barnard has."[7]

Barnard was too modest to make such a high claim for his own virtues. But he was concerned about the larger question of how good attributes of character could be identified, researched, and instilled in managers. Rather than merely listing such traits, he argued for an educational environment that would socialize future leaders in cooperative efforts, encourage them to live ascetic lives, improve their capacities for complex reasoning, and enhance their moral integrity.

The Education of Leaders

Barnard had well-formed views on education. His thoughts were expressed in correspondence with academic leaders, convocation addresses to graduates, and the case studies he presented to students at Harvard University. Some representative examples illustrate his views.

About the power of educational institutions to socialize students, Barnard said in an address at Pennsylvania State College, "The greatest opportunity for developing latent executive ability in students seems to lie in the various student-managed activities associated with college and university life."[8] Five years later, he repeated this theme in a letter to Amory R. Johnson, dean of the Wharton School. "Schools of business," he said, "should encourage student activities because they make much easier the translation of the student to the actor in the world of business affairs. The special importance of extra-curricular activities is that they socialize without the student knowing it."[9]

Barnard made his most important statement to academics at the University of Chicago in a colloquium that included the faculties of the business school and the social sciences.[10] All executive education, according to him, required five elements: broad liberal arts background, rigorous analysis of the complexities of formal organization, understanding of the nonlogical aspect of human behavior, the ability to persuade others in nonlogical terms, and the capacity to take a rational approach toward uncertainty in the decision process. Executive education should implant these attributes in students so that they would develop later into habits of character in the business world.

The commencement address that Barnard made to the graduating class at MIT in 1950, during the second year of his presidency at the Rockefeller Foundation, revealed his thoughts about managerial virtues.[11] He emphasized personal humility, warning the graduates that if they were excessively transported by their intellectual capacities and attainments, they might be led to an "overrating of one's self and an equally pernicious underrating of others."[12] He told the graduates that after they began their careers they needed to continue to develop their skills, knowledge, and judgment, concluding with the admonition, "Our society and everything in it that endures would never have been established except for the moral judgement that through the centuries gave meaning to man's striving for material progress. In such judgement lay the justification for the privilege of thought and action which we so highly prize."[13] Summing up, Barnard described professional management as a calling that demanded a certain guardianlike austerity from its practitioners. They had to be modest, physically sound, dedicated to their tasks, technically informed, socially skilled, decisive, and morally upright.

Barnard's ventures into academe included the presentation of case studies for instructing students in the skills of executive leadership. His most popular case was the "Riot of the Unemployed in Trenton, N.J.," and he used it six times at Harvard.[14] He stressed that nonlogical sentiments and emotions most often governed behavior, in this instance that of the delegates who represented the unemployed to the New Jersey Relief authorities.

He taught the Paretan lesson that managers needed to recognize the importance of the intuitive, nonlogical, and nonintellectual components of behavior. In practical management situations, people often disguised their feelings with logic, and they were only vaguely aware of doing so. Managers in action had to be able to distinguish between these motivations, not only for their own effectiveness but also because people usually were confused about real issues, and that created misunderstandings. People did not know what was in their own best interests, and management had to set them straight. Barnard felt that he achieved his greatest success in applying Pareto's concepts of residues and derivations by his handling of the Trenton riot.

Asceticism

During 1932, the worst year of the depression, Barnard spoke to the Newark Exchange Club upon being recognized by it for his work with the New Jersey Relief Commission. He said, "The protection of the economic rights of the individual requires the limitation of the economic privileges of the individual."[15] But such limitation had to be self-imposed, requiring individuals' short-term willingness to forego immediate consumption coupled with a long-term transcendence of material goods as a source of personal gratification.

> The individual must be willing to support his society first as a means to the utmost of his individual possibilities. And this I believe must be fundamentally voluntary support that comes from honest belief in the dignity of community service, of true appreciation of the utility and the satisfaction of cooperative effort arising out of, but above, individual interest that comes from a social esprit de corps, from an economic patriotism, from a conviction of mutual prosperity.[16]

Barnard hammered on the point of personal sacrifice throughout the 1930s and into the 1940s, in a commencement address to the graduates of the Polytechnic Institute of Brooklyn, in a letter to sociologist Talcott Parsons, and in his speech to telephone company employees on the eve of war.[17] But Barnard's strongest appeals for asceticism are found in his book, and we have noted already how negatively he regarded material incentives as the bases for motivation and persuasion. In a very real way, he shared Frederick W. Taylor's opinion that it was not good for people to have too much.

Although Barnard preached asceticism for the nation, he held that the managerial elite also must practice it. Pride of work, the cooperative spirit, and loyalty were higher incentives from which managers ought to receive satisfaction that was superior to the material wealth obtained from their jobs. Granting that the prestige of their positions enabled managers to make more money to impress others with a certain display of opulence, Barnard felt that it did not necessarily improve their performance. Rather, high living might have an opposite effect. Thus, Barnard's ideal practitioners were true ascetics as were the Guardians of Plato's polis. The greatest threats to this ideal were material blandishments, acquisitiveness, and unmodulated self-interest. Poor Barnard must have spun in his grave during the 1980s!

Complex Reasoning

Students also needed to be prepared to reason complexly as managers, because of their future responsibilities in organizations of profound intricacy and uncertainty.

But such ability was counterintuitive. People do not reason complexly when they conduct their daily affairs. Rather, they think about events in terms of simple cause-and-effect relationships. The need for food on the table at home prompts a trip to the market.

Such simplistic reasoning, however, was fatal to successful management. Managers had to engage in "pattern" reasoning, according to Barnard, because it was more appropriate to the systems of interdependence and interaction with which they had to contend. For example, a regional sales manager had to consider the interconnections of many factors in the pursuit of a profitable bottom line: motivation of sales force, division of territory, demography of consumers, product lines, the actions of competitors, and so on. Direct causation of performance was impossible to determine under these circumstances. So while simple cause-and-effect reasoning was adequate for everyday affairs, organizational systems demanded complex reasoning.

But contradictions between the logics and the conclusions reached by these types of reasoning posed two difficulties that Barnard addressed. One was the matter of awareness of the differences in these reasoning processes and the other was the difficulty communicating and justifying to others management's decisions reached by complex reasoning.

Relative to the first difficulty, managers engaged in both simple and complex reasoning. Danger arose when they applied cause-effect logic to a system that required complex reasoning. Management had to be aware of how and when to reason one way or another. But the problem was more complicated than this. Barnard believed that managers usually applied complex reasoning to systems with which they were familiar and were able in such cases to make an easy adjustment between simple and complex reasoning. "But the ease of doing so diminishes rapidly as familiarity with a particular complex system decreases, so that most people attempt to apply 'cause and effect' reasoning to complex systems with which they have little acquaintance."[18] This mistake led to errors in decisions and to disappointment with results. The solution seemed to lie with raising the awareness of managers about the types of reasoning they used in their decision-making through education, by experience of executive work, and by acknowledging the elusive factor of intuition.[19]

These two forms of reasoning could not be reconciled, but Barnard had a common-sense way to deal with them. If experience and intuition showed that it was expedient and effective to assume a simple correlation of a cause and an effect, then it would be appropriate to use this approach, otherwise a manager had to shift into a complex reasoning mode. "We use one method of reasoning under conditions in which our experience shows it to be effective, another for different conditions."[20] In other words, the manager should employ whatever method works best. Barnard felt that managers could never really know how complex systems produced results; they could only observe what went into them and what came out. Therefore, how managers chose to think about systems, simply or complexly, depended entirely on what seemed to help them the most to make decisions and to understand their consequences.

But this resolution raised the other, far more serious, difficulty. How do managers justify their complexly reasoned decisions to others? Management had to account for its "reasonableness" to employees, stockholders, customers, and government regulators. But because of human limitations to know, infer, perceive, and describe what happened in complex systems, such demonstrations were difficult for management to make.[21] Furthermore, the problematic nature of communicating compounded the accountability problem. Barnard observed that managers were often accused of duplicity because what they said did not correspond to their actions. However, managers really did not intend to deceive. Language thwarted their efforts to express those abstract reasons and intuitions underlying their decisions.

He expanded on this point in a long letter to his daughter, who was an economics major at Smith College. She had asked her father to explain monopolistic pricing. Barnard responded that single-variable economists did not have a glimmer of understanding about the way administered pricing worked. Complex organizations required managers to think systemically and intuitively, but he confessed that language prevented him from really explaining to her what went on in managers' minds when they made pricing decisions in monopolies. He wrote, "We must use language inadequate to our problem." This problem with language led businessmen into making statements that were false and misleading except to those inside the organization, "in on the know." This shortcoming of language produced misinterpretations and cries for regulation based on "negative" principles.[22]

In general, Barnard believed that managerial ability to reason complexly was distilled from experience, arcane knowledge, and intuitive understanding of organizations. But whatever it took to reason complexly was available only to management. Therefore, the reasonableness of managerial decisions could not be contested, vesting great discretionary power in management. Adolph A. Berle wrote that this power "though limited is in large measure absolute [authorized by] the legal 'presumption' that management action is taken for the best interests of the corporate institution."[23]

Barnard's analysis of complex reasoning was intricate,[24] although his aims were clear. How better can one justify management discretion in a democratic society than to argue that the way managers reason is inaccessible to an ordinary person's comprehension, and, indeed, beyond the language's ability to convey? Barnard, in effect, justified unaccountable management power this way, rendering his belief in management's moral virtues all the more important. Those virtues ensured that power was used responsibly in behalf of those who depended on managerial leadership.

ATTRIBUTES OF PROFESSIONAL PRACTICE

"Executive work," Barnard wrote, "is not that *of* organization but the specialized work of *maintaining* the organization in operation.[25] "Maintenance" meant to him something much different than it did to certain contemporary writers, such as James P. Thompson, who depicted it as the mundane bureaucratic chore of keeping the internal affairs of an organization tidy.[26] For Barnard, maintenance was nothing less than management's ultimate responsibility to assure organizational survival. This work entailed decisionmaking, accountability, governance, and the political use of organizational power. The first two are discussed next, the last two in chapter 10.

Decisionmaking

Since we have already mentioned Barnard's theory of individual decisionmaking, there is no need to retrace those steps here. It is worth repeating that Barnard made a clear distinction between subjective individual versus objective organizational decisions. The theory of exchange pertained to the former, while the theory of opportunism applied to the latter.[27]

Barnard borrowed John R. Commons's idea of strategic factors for his theory of organizational decisionmaking. The concept was perfectly straightforward because it recognized that in any organization literally dozens of variables influenced decisions. However, among all those variables were just a few of overwhelming importance, accounting for most of the variance in organizational action. These variables were the factual data of organizational life. The manager had to identify those strategic factors with the greatest leverage over the outcomes of a particular decision. The issue was not what the manager fancied but what the facts dictated.

Barnard based the separation of individual and organizational decisions upon a means and ends analysis. Individual decisions to participate in and produce for organizations entailed subjective goals and the perception of whether or not the available inducements led either to their attainment or to their frustration. However, "the acts of organizations are those of persons dominated by organizational, not personal, ends."[28] Thus, organizational decisions were driven by an enterprise's needs, not by the needs of the people in it.

Barnard did not anthropomorphize organizational decisionmaking. Organizations as such did not decide anything. Managers decided, but they did so in behalf of organizations. Thus Barnard concluded that the logics of individual and organizational decisionmaking had to be different, resulting in distinct kinds of behaviors.

Barnard stressed that these two types of decisions were interrelated. Subjective individual decisions influenced impersonal organizational decisions and vice versa, and while these decisions could be split apart for analytical purposes, the two in reality were closely connected. For example, the strategic factors that a manager might choose to select for a decision could be based upon personal preferences, not upon an objective assessment of what was good for the organization. However, Barnard hedged, noting that the higher a manager stood on the organizational ladder, the less likely it was that this would happen. His explanation was fascinating. The more exalted the position, the more the manager's personality took on the personality of the organization.[29] "The most important single contribution required of the executive . . . is loyalty, domination by the organization personality."[30]

He shed more light on such domination in his correspondence with Herbert Simon, relative to his review of the manuscript for *Administrative Behavior*. Especially important were Barnard's observations about the role of assumptions in decisionmaking. He told Simon that the use of "the word 'factual' obscures the element of estimate and assumption [in decisionmaking]. Your treatment suppresses from view the enormous extent to which assumptions are elements of decisions and the extent to which the selection of assumptions is itself the occasion for decision."[31] If decisionmaking was as much a valuation of premises as it was a calculation of facts,[32] then it followed that organizational domination of managers' personalities ensured their decisions were made in the interests of the organization and not according to personal whims. "The great mass of decisions are private, rarely expressed, frequently cannot be made articulate, and are decisions of choice between assumptions and between speculations as to the consequences of concrete action."[33]

Barnard concluded that organizational decisionmaking was at once a matter of rational calculation and of personal valuation. But he stressed the latter, perhaps to counterbalance the narrow conceptions of economic rationality that pervaded management thinking at the time. Simon, in fact, poked Barnard a bit about his insistence upon the nonlogical and intuitive aspects of decisionmaking. He said that Barnard's usual insight had failed him.[34] Not to be put off, Barnard responded that managers lacking information to make rational choices had to rely on intuitive judgments of the situation, and they had a certain aesthetic quality.[35] Organizational decisionmaking was an art as well as a science, and in aesthetics intuition prominently figured.

Accountability

Outside of its simplest form of upward reporting in a chain of command, management accountability is a worrisome issue. Impersonal market forces do not discipline management effectively in monopolistic or oligopolistic industries. Politically, managers are not held accountable because there are no mechanisms, such as voting procedures, to bring them to task for poor judgment or shaky performance. The legal system sometimes works in egregious cases of corruption, but for the most part the prudent business judgment rule absolves many management sins. Government regulation is often misdirected and dysfunctional since some regulators are hampered by former connections with the industry they are supposed to regulate or by inadequate preparation to monitor effectively formulation of industrial policy. Finally, there is the language barrier. It ensures that no one in business, government, education, or labor can articulate to anyone else how organizations work, how decisions are made, and why certain goals are selected and not others. These management "realities" have changed little from Barnard's time. Therefore, it is no wonder that Barnard decided that management was mainly accountable to itself, a conclusion that remains depressingly valid.

But such great discretionary executive power preordained a major confrontation with democratic values. And the two sets of principles are not reconcilable, although many have tried and some are still trying[36] to reconcile them. Barnard realized this and finessed the problem. "At every turn," he averred, "the executive is confronted, both as respects the environment of the organization and its internal constitution, with requirements, prohibitions, limitations, disabilities, inertia, obstruction, recalcitrance, disintegrating influences that restrict choices."[37] Therefore, no matter how autocratic management may seem, or how towering hierarchical authority may appear, executive power was far from absolute. That being the case, why worry about the incompatibility of executive discretion and democratic theory? Actually discretion often seemed to be a positive force for advancing freedom, because competent and moral management practice created for the people more choices of material goods and greater opportunities for self-expression and psychological satisfaction. Therefore the public would not care about abstract democratic principles as long as their institutions were expertly and virtuously managed.

But what was the nature of management virtue, and how should it be used to govern the organizations of the managerial state? Barnard's approach to this question is examined in the next two chapters.

9

The Moral Obligations
of the Elite

One might think that as executive discretion increased, so should management accountability, certainly not absolutely proportionately but commensurately. However, such are not the ways of managerialism. Discretion and accountability are inversely related in managerial societies, confirming the King of Id's dictum, "He who has the gold rules." No immutable logic or deterministic social force compelled this to be the case. Rather it resulted from the conscious application of executive power to concentrate organizational control in management, and keep it there.

However, democracy imposes some inconveniences, such as the justification of power in institutions that are critical to public welfare and that embody esteemed social values. Therefore, from Barnard to the present-day discretionists,[1] the argument has been that executive power is legitimate because it is not absolute. Their litany of limitations,[2] intoned before the altar of legitimacy, repeats:

- · legal mandates define management's fiduciary responsibilities toward property owners
- · the court system provides legal oversight and review
- · professional norms regulate practice, and management expertise is often self-justifying
- · competition in free markets disciplines management, as do the countervailing interests of pluralistic groups.

This list contains enough truth to be compelling, if not altogether convincing. Consequently, the issue of legitimacy has not disappeared, perhaps because of the curious nature of executive power. It is at once subordinate to higher authorities and largely unaccountable to them. Thus, all of management's moral obligations stem from an ambiguous relationship in which executives are free and not free from accountability to the authorities (God, nature, the people, government,

145

stockholders, creditors, etc.) that grant them the right to rule.[3] Therefore, when executives are freed from constraint to use their power, the public is compelled to trust in their skills, good character, and nobility of purposes for the assurance that right things will be done.

But this formula for noblesse oblige is not heartening in democratic societies. The critical legal scholar Gerald E. Frug, for instance, has argued at great length that the discretionists' litany of limitation was merely a fairy tale supporting the unsupportable. Without participatory democracy, Frug contends, organizations are unproductive of democracy's most important moral outcome: citizen virtue through self-government.[4] The shortcomings of the limitation argument were not lost on Barnard or the political scientist Harvey C. Mansfield, Jr. Both invoked another justification of executive power, the legitimizing potential of the moral virtues. Mansfield wrote, "The perceived need of executive power constitutes an admission of the need for virtue."[5]

Although Mansfield wrote about the executive power of the American presidency, the extension of his argument to management is fairly direct, with one extremely important exception. The presidency, constitutionally "situated and fortified" has often had a morally cleansing effect on the person holding that office. Its awesome majesty limited by constitutional checks and balances frequently has caused the person in it to rise ethically above himself. The office has made the man!

However, it is reasonable to wonder if the moral virtues will moderate the uses of executive power in organizational situations not so constitutionally fortified. One must have doubts. Consequently, the present management surge toward ethics implies the need to elevate the virtue of practitioners. If this does not happen, then public uproar, translated into legal restrictions, will reduce executive discretion by increasing accountability. Barnard foresaw these threats and that led him to argue emphatically for management morality as the last, and most important, defense against the erosion of autonomous executive power.

Thus, management as a moral discipline occupied a critically important space in Barnard's thought. He first presented his formal speculations on this subject in chapter 17 of his book, although he admitted that he had "little conception of the general problem"[6] before going to the RF. This experience had a major impact on the growth of his ideas in moral philosophy. However, Barnard's basic opinions about theology and morality were consistent for most of his life. Having established his bona fides as an authority on ethics in his book, he became a natural source to whom John D. Rockefeller, Jr., and the Foundation's board of trustees could turn when deliberating the place of ethics and morals in its funding policies.

Barnard's last published words about the moral issues in management came six years after he retired as president of the RF.[7] Thus, Barnard attended to the ethics and morals issue for two decades and searched for ways to bring the subject down to earth for practitioners. Nevertheless, during all this time he held firm to his beliefs in the essential morality of cooperation and management's obligation to achieve it.[8] Time and time again he returned to his testimony of faith found in the last paragraph of his book.

> I believe in the power of the cooperation of men of free will to make men free to cooperate; that only as they choose to work together can they achieve the fullness of personal development; that only as each accepts a responsibility for choice can they enter into that communion of men from which arise the higher purposes of individual and of cooperative behavior alike. I believe that the expansion of cooperation and the development of the individual are mutually dependent realities, and that a due proportion or balance between them is a necessary condition of human welfare.[9]

BARNARD'S EXISTENTIALISM AND
LEAP OF FAITH

When Barnard wrote about ethical issues, Western philosophy had already abandoned Christian absolutism as a basis for moral argument. Consistent with this mood, Barnard believed that Christian ideals and values failed to provide moral guidelines for people in formal organizations. Lacking ethical criteria for resolving organizational dilemmas, such as conflicts in loyalties and moral codes, Christian principles did not suit the ambiguous and uncertain environment of modern times. Barnard attributed this lack to the origins of Christianity. "Christian ethics had developed in agricultural, pastoral, and nomadic societies and were chiefly expressed in terms intelligible to the people of such societies."[10] Bucolic metaphors had little meaning to urban dwellers. What did New Yorkers know, Barnard asked, about the "care of the flock, lost sheep, black sheep"?[11]

As an alternative to Christian values, Barnard turned to a moral perspective that was compatible with existential philosophy and his own Yankee deism. Although he never mentioned the existentialists, his beliefs were similar to many of theirs, relative to the freedom of individual choice and commensurate individual moral responsibility for the choices made.

Some existentialists believed that moral responsibility was "the dark side of freedom," and Barnard held a similar idea. He thought that the subjective and contingent qualities of individual decisionmaking limited freedom and made it impossible for an executive to know where moral responsibility lay or what was the right thing to do. The higher an individual rose in an organization, the greater this uncertainty.

Traditional laws and ethical rules offered little comfort, guidance, or even relevance to those who were forced to resolve moral conflicts in the organizations. This situation was generalized to the human condition by such extreme existentialists as Sartre and Camus, who contended that universal anguish would arise among the people as they "lucidly" recognized the absurdity of their lives in the absence of cosmic guarantees.

Barnard rejected this extreme, but he did go to another. His was a Kierkegaardian vision in which the experience of human interdependency in cooperative systems created the need for people to make a leap of faith that affirmed the morality of the organizations to which they belonged and in which they found the source of their own moral development. The closing paragraph of his book, quoted above, was a marvelously existential statement of faith.

Nevertheless, the type of cooperation that Barnard visualized posed a serious dilemma. While cooperation was, a priori, a moral enterprise, individual executive moral rectitude was not predetermined to be characteristic of their practice. Instead executives' acts of moral responsibility came from their will to be controlled by a personal code consistent with the cooperative code of the organization. In other words, managers must first be committed to cooperative principles, and then they must convert others to the same principles. Good management, thus, was an act of virtue if it flowed from the free will of individual managers to regulate their conduct to conform with organizational codes. Those managers who based their practices on this commitment became the moral exemplars of the organization.

However, cooperation was not so morally inexorable that it drove managers into this path of righteousness in spite of themselves. Self-interest always contended with the cooperative good. So Barnard argued that management was a calling, something akin to a religious conversion, requiring a life of selfless commitment to a profession of transcendent social importance. Managers who accepted this calling and regulated their conduct accordingly were those with highly developed moral characters.

The idea that managers' personal moral characters could be enhanced was in some ways similar to the tenets of some existential philosophers. As David Norton pointed out, the highest stage of moral development, in Kierkegaard's philosophy, was faith in God.[12] But for Kierkegaard's god, Barnard substituted faith in cooperation. However, Barnard did not suppose for one moment that people would follow those who defaulted on their avowed principles. Managers had to practice the cooperative virtues in order to lend credence to their claims of legitimacy. Once these claims were established, people then would be inspired to subordinate their individual interests to the welfare of the cooperative whole. Within the boundary of these semi-existential notions Barnard framed his practical moral philosophy.

The central question in moral philosophy for more than 2,500 years was, what are the requisite conditions of a worthy life? Traditional discourse in ethics pertained to character, integrity, education, and moral enlightenment. However, beginning with Hobbes, this discourse changed. Hobbesian problematics, otherwise known in management as contingency theories, required that ethics be approached from an "administrative point of view." Hobbes retreated from the morally enhanced self and reduced "ethics to a code of minimal standards of behavior ... that cannot be ignored without social disaster."[13]

Philosophical discourse thence turned from the virtues of character toward moral minimalism. It became less concerned with what constituted a worthy life and more interested in the diagnosis of ethical dilemmas, perplexities, and quandaries whose solutions were found in rule systems. Barnard exemplified this reductivism, and if present trends in the management field of business ethics are of any significance, morality has become equated with rule responsibility.

For instance the Bennis and Nanus slogan about leaders doing right things raises the obvious moral question of what is right. In modern management, that tends to be rules that ensure the collective well-being of the organization rather than what enhances the moral character of organizational members. Thus, ethics all too often heed organizational technicalities, legalities, and public relations and ignore employee moral development. This state of affairs grew directly from Barnard's approach to moral responsibility as instrumental practices that protected management's discretion.

Whether or not managers did right things depended on their moral status. And although an individual's moral codes might be high, if his or her behavior was not controlled by these codes, a person might be judged irresponsible, another way of saying that the road to hell is paved with good intentions. Therefore, both personal control and high moral status were necessary for responsible executive practice. In Barnard's opinion, the confluence of these conditions in an executive's behavior produced a moral exemplar, or a "qualified moral agent" in Aristotle's words.

These exemplary people were permitted to inculcate morals in others, elevating the role of management guardianship to a position that had previously been reserved for teachers, ministers, rabbis, and priests. Managers would emphasize "fundamental attitudes, loyalties to the organization or cooperative system, and to the system of objective authority," encouraging employees to subordinate their "individual interests and minor dictates of personal codes to the good of the cooperative whole."[14]

Barnard told two peculiar stories to illustrate his points about responsibility. The first was a hypothetical case of a conscientious worker at a water plant, a person who was devoted to many organizations besides his company. Although these associations might present this worker with problems of conflicting loyalties, he, being a responsible individual, would do all that he could to reconcile these demands. However, if the "disturbing fact of alcohol" was introduced in this situation, the now boozing employee would become irresponsible to all of the codes that formerly controlled his behavior, even though his moral status remained high.

Barnard told a second story, presumably based on an actual incident, about a woman who worked as a telephone operator in a small exchange. Looking out of the window one day, she saw her nearby house, one she shared with her invalid mother, burning. Her mother was in it! Even so, she stuck to her switchboard, motivated, according to Barnard, by the "*moral* necessity of uninterrupted service."[15]

Behind these curiously naïve tales was an important point, and it pertained to the virtue of conscientiousness in the performance of duty. As Edmund L. Pincoffs argued, quandary ethics is addressed to the conscientious person because it stresses the solution of problems that arise from personal conflicts with organizational rule systems.[16] The moral lessons in Barnard's stories were: do not become paralyzed with the drink and unable to work effectively; do not leave your post, even though staying on might be considered pathological from other points of view.[17] From the standpoint of the subordinate employee, conscientiousness coupled with obedience were the prime organizational virtues.

The importance of all of this was patently clear. The complexity of modern organization required the elaboration of rules to prevent breakdown and disorder. This in turn necessitated employing the type of person who would be rule responsible, as well as one who would not panic when confronted with a crisis of conscience. Barnard's notion of moral creativity arises with respect to the latter employment criterion, and it conforms closely with Pincoffs's observation that where no rule exists to resolve conflicts with respect to ethical conduct, the conscientious person would create one that "is consistent with other rules that he accepts."[18] Since there is little in Barnard's writing that gives much weight to other virtues such as friendship, compassion, love, or sympathy, it must be concluded that conscientiousness was central to his moral philosophy.

Rule responsibility and rule creativeness were thus the quintessential tests of management morality. But because management was uniquely situated in organizations, it had to be the final and sole arbitrator of what was right and how to achieve it. Therefore, the amount of discretion needed to fulfill these moral obligations had to be considerable, and, as Barnard judged it, accountability to external sources for decisions about ethical quandaries only confused people and inhibited the successful performance of management functions.

Barnard joined the Rockefeller Foundation in 1940, midpoint in the evolution of these ideas. For the next dozen years until 1952, events at the Foundation were major influences on the development of his moral philosophy. The issues debated at RF during this period confirmed his views about organized religion and the necessity of finding an existential faith in management as a substitute for it. This was a stormy time for the trustees, a period during which Barnard contended with some remarkable people, as the following record of his tenure there attests.

"THE MORAL DEFICIT"

Europe and many countries in the Far East, in particular Japan and China,[19] were physically and morally shattered by World War II, a situation that was troubling to some trustees and officers. Urged by John D. Rockefeller, Jr., John Foster Dulles, and John D. Rockefeller III, the Foundation's board of trustees began an investigation of how the Foundation might help civilization overcome the "spiritual and moral deficit" created by this vast conflict. Barnard was at the center of the unfolding story of the Ethics and Morals Project and how RF might help humanity redeem its moral debt.

In 1942, when an Allied victory still was in doubt, the Federal Council of Churches established its Commission on a Just and Durable Peace with Dulles as chairman. The first conference sponsored by the commission was held in Cincinnati, Ohio, with Barnard attending as a representative of the YMCA. This conference, the published proceedings of which included remarks by Dulles, the Harvard philosopher William Earnest Hocking, and Henry P. Van Dusen, head of the Union Theological Seminary,[20] marked the indirect beginnings of the Foundation's interests in ethics and morals.[21] As it turned out, Dulles, Van Dusen, Hocking, and Barnard had considerable influence on the Foundation's venture into moral philosophy.

Immediately after the war, in December 1945, the board of trustees, at its regular annual meeting in Williamsburg, adopted a resolution to appoint a committee from its membership "to review the policies and programs of the Rockefeller Foundation in the light of changed conditions."[22] Barnard chaired this committee. During its investigations, both Dulles and John D. Rockefeller III called for the committee to consider the subject of ethics and morals. The committee did, and it turned to Hocking for advice around the middle of 1946. Hocking confirmed the board's feeling that there was, indeed, a "sag in American moral texture."

Since he was preaching to the choir, it was foreordained that Hocking's opinions would be influential. For example, he argued that the democratic virtues of freedom and equality did not commensurately emphasize obligation. For its part, Christianity tended to emphasize the "soft" virtues of sympathy and unselfishness. As Hocking put it, "The pacifist controversy is only a special case of a very general difficulty."[23] Beyond the soft virtues, Hocking declared that pugnacity and self-assertion were essential for building personal character and community. These views no doubt made a favorable impression on the board, which was composed of successful business and professional men.

But Hocking warned also of the prevailing distrust in America of absolute values, attended by the denigration of conscience and the transcending idea of "the will of God." These traditional guideposts of moral virtue had given way to relativism and positive science as the main sources of knowledge and truth. The culmination of these trends produced a disparagement of the soul and a trivialization of happiness as a goal of living. To Hocking, the final irony was that people who should know better, psychiatrists and college curriculum makers, in all of their ardent talk about integration, failed to recognize that the root of the word was found in "integrity." No wonder, he concluded, that Americans were morally adrift.

But what might the Foundation do about it? Hocking suggested several areas where its grants would help, such as studies of the ethics of inequality and the ethics of group life. However, he favored research on the "ethics of the impersonal relationship," such as those found in business and in the competitive market system. Here the aforementioned virtues of self-assertion and pugnacity were most salubriously represented and practiced. He said, "Submission to an impersonal judgement with all its hardness and calculation, is a mark of maturity." The genius of business made "pugnacity, competition, and defeat-and-victory . . . phases of the morality of the system."[24] Barnard thought highly of these views, taking time from his crowded business schedule to visit Hocking at his summer home in New Hampshire for a personal conversation concerning the RF's future contributions to the area of moral philosophy.

In its final report, Barnard's committee recommended to the board that ethics and morals must not be passed over and that the entire subject required further investigation before policies were made. While concurring with the general thrust of this report, Barnard was uncomfortable with certain details.

Raymond B. Fosdick did not favor an excursion into moral philosophy. But Dulles was of a different mind and actively lobbied for the establishment within the Foundation of a division of moral philosophy. He wrote to Barnard that the Foundation from its origins was based upon Christian principles and that these principles were subjected to two primary threats, from Germany and from the Soviet Union. These "essentially atheistic" confrontations, according to Dulles, "challenge our system of personal freedom because . . . it is not possible to have personal freedoms except in a religious and theistic society."[25]

John D. Rockefeller, Jr., shared Dulles's opinion that the RF was obligated to fund ethics and morals projects, and, as Barnard put it, "succeeded in getting me elected [in December 1946] as a committee of one to pursue the subject."[26] After a delay, caused by his business obligations, Barnard and Joseph H. Willits began to solicit opinions from many leaders in business, politics, economics, and philosophy. During this survey, Barnard moved more and more into Fosdick's camp, particularly on the matter of direct grants to religious institutions. He concluded that for the Foundation to enter moral philosophy was for it to "walk among eggs" as it maneuvered around sectarian differences.

By 1949, Barnard, then Foundation president, warned specifically of establishing relations with theological schools and faculties and cautioned against moving too quickly into the fields of ethics and morals. The board of trustees had reached no consensus on the subject, and Barnard stated that "in fairness to the Trustees who have a definite contrary view we are obliged to proceed with great caution."[27] One dissenter was Barnard's old friend, Walter Gifford, who Willits reported as saying "that the proper subject for RF attention was not morals and ethics, but the common cold."[28]

As a member of the Federal Council of Churches' Department of the Church and Economic Life, in addition to his wide acquaintanceship, Barnard knew many people who had given much thought to contemporary morals. As mentioned above Barnard and Willits polled these people for their opinions.[29] The correspondence that resulted lacked not only a focus on what the Foundation should or should not do but also an agreement on the nature of humanity's moral deficit.

Nevertheless, the ethics and morals question was very much in the fore of policy debate at the Foundation in 1949, as it had been from the end of the war. Van Dusen knew about these deliberations from the start, first through Dulles and Hocking and later as a member of the board when he was elected to it in April 1947. Van Dusen's interest was not altogether detached, since both the Federal Council of Churches and the Union Theological Seminary (UTS) stood to benefit financially from RF support if the board decided to move definitively into the sphere of moral philosophy.

Van Dusen, however, jumped the gun. In a speech before the New York Academy of Dentistry in 1947, he said, "One of the great foundations has recently voted a fundamental reorientation of program" toward moral philosophy.[30] This speech created a tempest at the Foundation when it was published, and Barnard tried to calm the waters.

Although Van Dusen had not mentioned the RF by name, it would have not required much investigation to know that he was referring to it. Never one to shirk onerous tasks, Barnard chided Van Dusen for his ill-considered comments and poorly timed article. Said Barnard, "I think it is usually regarded as wise for individual directors or trustees not to make public announcements as to the policy or programs of the institutions with which they are connected."[31] He pointed out to Van Dusen, in no uncertain terms, that the board had not voted a program reorientation nor had it decided whether or not it would direct its attention and financial resources to the issue of the spiritual and moral deficit. He made it clear that many of the trustees were "still of the opinion that Mr. Fosdick's judgement is correct,"[32] a view toward which he himself leaned as he explored the labyrinth of sectarian moral philosophy. And so the situation remained throughout Barnard's presidency: the board debated the issue, but no progress was made to establish a division of moral philosophy. Neither were grants approved to religious institutions for studies or conferences other than those provided by the Humanities and the Social Science divisions when moral philosophy overlapped their usual interests.[33]

Dulles was unhappy with this inaction and voiced his dismay to the trustees in April 1951. He said that while philanthropic support for science and the material aspects of civilization was growing, similar contributions for the development of the spiritual strength of the nation had languished. He was particularly upset because support for the education of people in the Christian ministry was not forthcoming to the degree he thought necessary to further the cause of the faith upon which Western civilization was based. The RF was as guilty of this neglect as were the other sources of private funding. Summing up, Dulles said, "The result is a growing distortion of the fabric of our society. We are expanding material power without expanding correspondingly, the capacity to subject that power to moral controls and to use it for moral purposes."[34]

Embedded in Dulles's blanket indictment of philanthropy were two specific concerns. The first was the threat of godless communism. By 1951, while at the United Nations, but soon to become secretary of state, he firmly believed that communism was rapidly emerging as the supreme test for the free world. It pitted Christianity against the atheistic forces in the East, already in place in the Soviet Union and growing in ascendancy in Mao's China.[35] Putting it starkly, Dulles argued that "those who have prospered out of our Western civilization should ponder their responsibility to preserve and pass on the spiritual values of their inheritance."[36] Dulles challenged the board of trustees; the RF had an obligation to secure and advance Christian goals and it was not doing so.

It also bothered Dulles that the Foundation's charter was not being followed. Pointing out that the RF's charter's "permissive clause" allowed it to carry on programs of grants for proposed and existing religious or missionary activities,[37] lawyer Dulles wondered why it had done so little to aid them. Such support, it seemed to him, had been mandated by the charter as part of the senior John D. Rockefeller's original intentions.

This blast caused a stir among the trustees and the officers.[38] After a six-month delay, during which time he was gathering information, Barnard responded to Dulles's remarks. He wrote in a letter addressed to all of the trustees that he was disturbed by Dulles's allegations because they seemed to impugn his integrity as well as that of the board members. According to Barnard, the ethics and morals question had received full and careful consideration over the years, and the Foundation under his administration had moved cautiously into the field. He expressed the hope that these deliberations would continue and that some decisive steps would be taken by his successor.

Soon after Dean Rusk became president, Van Dusen, on the behalf of UTS, submitted a grant proposal for funding an institute on interdenominational education. Rusk was friendly toward this application and in a long supporting letter to the board of trustees reviewed the history of the Foundation's involvement with religious organizations in general and with the ethics and morals question in particular. In preparation for their regular annual meeting in April 1953, Rusk asked the trustees to consider two specific matters. The first was the merits of the UTS proposal. The second was to reconsider the Foundation's policies toward funding organizations with a clear-cut sectarian orientation: in the case of UTS, liberal Protestant Christianity.[39]

The UTS proposal raised red flags at the Foundation, chiefly within the Social Science Division. Willits counseled Rusk to move cautiously, observing that under any circumstances the "general financing of religious institutions should be 'out' for RF."[40] However, this did not preclude funding research on values, nor did it eliminate the possibility of studying specific problems such as the educational standards of religious personnel.[41] Willits told Rusk that he thought the Foundation would be best advised to support objective historical and social science research on values and to avoid pumping "financial gas into this or that earnestly advocated specific venture,"[42] such as he believed the UTS proposal to be.

Herbert A. Deane, a social science consultant to the Foundation, was even more pointed in his objection to this proposal. Protestant Christianity, in his opinion, did not have a corner on the ethics and morals market. The moral principles of professing Christians were not necessarily better than those of non-Christians. Furthermore, and this seemed to be his telling point, "many Protestant groups in this country do not look with favor on UTS or its 'modernist' brand of Protestant theology." Unless the Foundation was prepared to support similar institutes in "fundamentalist Protestant seminaries . . . and at Jewish and Roman Catholic Seminaries," this request should be denied.[43]

But the dissenters did not prevail, and in 1954, the proposal of UTS was approved, with a grant of $525,000 to fund its institute. This grant, interestingly enough, came from a general Foundation appropriation, unrelated to a specific division.[44] Thus, the work of Dulles and Van Dusen was partially vindicated both by the substantial grant and by the reversal of RF policy,[45] against the judgment of Fosdick, Barnard, and Willits. Dulles's larger proposal to establish a division of moral philosophy within the RF was never implemented.

MORAL DEFICITS AND MANAGEMENT OBLIGATIONS

The moral deficit, while an infelicitous condition of civilization in general, was not an affliction of the leadership elite, or so it seemed in the rarified atmosphere of the RF boardroom. Barnard most assuredly believed that a morally superior management had the obligation to help humanity overcome this problem, and his twelve years with the Foundation sharpened this point of view.

But he was ambiguous toward the ethics and morals project. On the one hand, he was aligned in principle with the position of Fosdick, Willits, and Gifford, which opposed Foundation support of projects proposed by religious organizations. He agreed as well with John D. Rockefeller, Jr., that the Foundation's entry into ethics and morals should be on a practical level that promised tangible benefits for "all mankind." However, curing the world's moral sickness was of a different order than the prevention of malaria or the discovery of penicillin. Practicality in this area, as in the social sciences, was elusive but necessary to men of affairs. On the other hand, Barnard was sensitive to the moral deficit problem. He believed, as did the other people in his circle, that the war had created a sag in Americans' moral character and that the wealthy and powerful had an obligation to engage in its moral uplift; management after all was a moral discipline.

However, Foundation policy had to be circumspect, and in this regard he gave Rusk two pieces of advice: steer clear of entanglements with religious groups, and support noncontroversial empirical studies such as those in comparative values and conflicts in moral codes. Regarding the latter, Barnard referred Rusk to the memorandum he had written to the board of trustees in 1946,[46] concerning the moral problems of organizations and the individual's relationship to them. Since there were few recognized moral codes (other than certain legal precepts) that defined these relationships, the definition of moral obligations of corporate management to employees and the community was open and researchable. This topic was proper to fund, as were more important issues concerning conflicts in loyalty that often arose between individual employees and the organization.

Barnard's Rockefeller years exemplified his remarkable consistency on philosophical issues. In his alliance with Hocking, Fosdick, Willits, and Gifford, he found support for his opinion that traditional Christianity offered little to people in organizations. His stand against Foundation grants to religious groups was, therefore, compatible with his more general evaluation of the inadequacy of Christian values in the solution of moral quandaries. Their place had to be filled by the modern moral principle of cooperation.

So while Barnard disagreed with Dulles on how to spend Foundation money, and while he did not see eye to eye with John D. Rockefeller, Jr., on some Foundation policy goals, he was nevertheless in their camp with regard to the nature of the postwar world. It was an existential fact that society would be controlled by professional managers who represented the interests of the private sector elite. No leaders from other institutions could inspire the people's faith in cooperation as they were in the position to do.

Barnard's experience at the RF reinforced his belief that traditional religious institutions could not reconcile social harmony and material progress in modern managerial states. In this respect, he opposed John Foster Dulles. Instead, as president of the RF, Barnard found affirmation for his opinion of the essential morality of cooperation if it was pursued by a virtuous managerial elite. Given this perspective, it followed that management had to have maximum discretion. Anything less prevented the achievement of a cooperative commonwealth from which all would benefit. Therefore, the people had to have faith that executives did the right things with their vast discretionary power. To demonstrate that this faith was warranted became management's supreme moral obligation.

10

The New Order of National Power and Organizational Governance

Barnard opened his book with a passage from Aristotle's *Metaphysics* and closed it with a selection from Plato's *Laws*. Aristotle extolled the general for establishing order in an army, and Plato in turn praised the pilot because his art enabled him to guide ships safely through dangerous waters. These classical images summarized many of Barnard's most important themes: leadership, expertise, uncertainty, moral obligation, and discretion. No wonder he thought these selections were appropriate, representing as they did the application of the highest management virtues in organizations. What were armies or ships but metaphors for organizations?

Plato and Aristotle most certainly did not have management in mind when they wrote about generals and pilots. That was Barnard's interpretation to explain management's new place in the social hierarchy and its political responsibility to maintain the stability of the social order. Barnard's psychology, sociology, and moral philosophy of organization were preludes to this political insight, applauded by the distinguished French political philosopher Bertrand de Jouvenel.

He complemented Barnard, writing: "You make the point that your strikingly original thinking has made its impact upon sociologists, not upon political scientists. That precisely is what amazes and worries me. Your thinking is political philosophy of the highest order; the fact that it has not revolutionized political science seems to me a judgement upon the latter." And later in the same letter de Jouvenel observed that "perhaps organizational politics would describe the school of which I for one gladly acknowledge you as founder and master. As one speaks of a Keynesian revolution in economics, I feel one could speak of a Barnardian revolution in political science."[1]

This revolution had three aspects. First, it stimulated a debate about democracy and freedom between political theorists and management apologists.[2] Second, it delineated the "appropriate" distribution of national power between corporate management and the federal government. And third, it codified management doctrine with respect to the administration of justice systems within organizations. These dimensions of Barnard's political revolution are the subjects of this chapter's inquiry.

ORGANIZATIONS AND THE ECLIPSE OF FREEDOM

The values of individuality and community have dominated the American ethos. De Tocqueville, visiting America fifty years after the signing of the Declaration of Independence, wrote of how Americans seemed to oscillate with marvelous inconsistency between them.[3] These values, critical to the national identity, have fueled the essential dynamic of American life, the tension between principles of freedom and principles of order. Herbert McClosky and John Zaller, in their Twentieth Century Fund study, conducted in the early 1980s, reconfirmed de Tocqueville's observations and noted as well that the tension between these principles gave a dialectical aspect to the American experience.[4] Some sense of this tension is conveyed by comparing familiar words that are associated with these values and that suggest the rich variation in the American dialectic.

Individuality (Principles of Freedom)	Community (Principles of Order)
1. Liberty	Justice
2. Independence	Interdependence
3. Competition	Cooperation
4. Obligation	Entitlement
5. Inequality	Equality
6. Autonomy	Obedience

The importance of the dialectic cannot be overemphasized, since it has preserved freedom and order as independent principles in this country.[5] In the American regime values,[6] freedom was held to be the precondition of individual civil intelligence and moral development, whereas order was the basis for community, sustained by justice, that guaranteed equality of rights and citizen egalitarianism. The interplay and tension between these principles were debated by the Founders in the *Federalist* papers and institutionalized by them in the Declaration of Independence, the Constitution, and the Bill of Rights. The American dialectic acted as a defense against the tyranny either of the individual or of the community, and its safekeeping may have been the Founders' chief regime value.

Managerialism departed from this founding premise, and dialectical tensions did not figure into its ideal of how the individual ought to interact with the organizational community. Tension meant conflict, and that was an inadmissible idea in cooperative systems. Consequently, the dialectic had to be replaced by a new mind set, one that held that harmony, not conflict, was the "natural" state of human relationships. The doctrine of mutuality of interests encompassed this idea, and Barnard completely accepted it as the grounds for suppressing the tension between order and freedom.

Machiavelli taught that the people do not desire to rule, but desire only not to be ruled. This sentiment defined the political problem for Machiavelli that according to Mansfield was, "how to rule the people without their developing the intolerable sensation that they are being ruled."[7] This approach characterized Barnard's philosophy of management rulership, since he believed employees desired freedom at work but were reluctant to accept the responsibilities that went along with it.[8] Barnard explained this human foible simply: just as people's capacity limited their ability to make choices, so also it limited their ability to be free. Therefore, they required order, direction, and control by others who knew better what was good for them. Nevertheless because of the perversity of human nature they resisted management decisions and directions.

Freedom, according to Barnard, entailed a trade-off of one sort of freedom for another,[9] and he observed that freedom applied differentially to a variety of human experiences, such as religion, culture, economics, and politics. Therefore one might argue, for example, that political freedom may have to be sacrificed for economic freedom. He commented that some countries with highly centralized political authorities claimed to be free societies either because their economic systems permitted a wide range of consumer choice or because they tolerated all religious faiths or because they protected the cultures of ethnic minorities.

The parallels between this example and management were obvious. Management gave employees jobs, thereby providing them with the economic opportunity to exercise free choice as consumers. All it asked from employees in return was obedience to management authority. On the surface, this trade-off theory was not Machiavellian. The concentration of freedom in one area at the expense of it in another merely acknowledged that the loss of freedom was not necessarily a zero-sum game. The expanded opportunities for freedom elsewhere made palatable the sacrifice of individual autonomy in organizations. However, the theory takes on Machiavellian overtones with the knowledge of Barnard's advice to management about how to influence the way employees think about their personal motives in relation to the needs of management for order. He wrote, "The distinguishing mark of executive responsibility . . . is the process of inculcating points of view, fundamental attitudes, loyalties, to the organization or cooperative system, and to the system of objective authority, that will result in subordinating individual interest and the minor dictates of personal codes to the good of the cooperative whole."[10]

So in the modern managerial scheme of things, organizational imperatives eclipsed freedom; management needs overshadowed democracy. Naturally Barnard argued that this was the price paid for democratic freedoms in other areas, the trade-off theory. But he was not content to let it rest there, feeling it necessary to justify his position by elaborating on the difficulties that democracy made for management. Facing the issue squarely, Barnard wrote, "I can only repeat that the democratic process tends strongly to increase the . . . intensity of [conflict] . . . by its emphasis on the abstract justification of decisions," concluding that "where such conflicts are very numerous and intense, and especially where they lead to class conflicts, non-democratic authority supported by mystical conceptions (divine right, racial superiority, inspired leader) may be the only practicable alternative to the disintegration of the organization."[11]

To be fair, Barnard applied this prescription to just the most extreme circumstances or emergencies. In the usual course of events, democratic peoples had to believe that the professional managers in their nations' organizations did the right things. And insofar as the dialectical tension between order and freedom was concerned, all he offered had distinctly Orwellian overtones, "The most general condition of freedom is order."[12]

Therefore, political freedom always took second place to order in Barnard's theories. But this would not be such a bitter pill for people to swallow as long as their attitudes had been properly adjusted to the idea that their interests and management's were mutual.

THE DISTRIBUTION OF NATIONAL POWER

Private interests had dominated public interests in America for years. But FDR's election changed that, and Barnard did not like it one bit. Looking at the international situation in Russia, Germany, and Italy, in 1936, he stated, "In all these cases there is social integration on a vast scale, involving government domination of individual political, economic, racial and religious interest."[13] Although he admitted these trends in the United States were comparatively moderate, he detected danger in New Deal policies that seemed to be heading the nation in the direction of government tyranny.

Despite his rhetoric, Barnard did not have a simple antigovernment view. He recognized that government, as business, was a primary institution in the managerial state, and he held that government power was a contingency problem in industrial nations. The extent of power of any central government should be determined by the type of people it ruled and the amount of resources at its disposal. The United States did not require a strong national government because it had ample resources and literate, hard-working citizens. However, since the federal government had become a major force in American life, Barnard believed that its functions had to be delineated. This amounted to a functional division of labor between business and government.

Barnard's opinions about business-government relations did not deviate one millimeter from the line established by Theodore N. Vail and followed by Walter S. Gifford. Armed with his staff experience in dealing with state regulatory agencies and with Vail's and Gifford's philosophy, he could comment with authority on the respective functions of government and business from the point of view of corporate management. The depression, however, was a major test for these ideas. Business had to fight the stigma of being responsible for it while it tried to stem the intrusion of government into its affairs.

The economy looked bleak in 1930, when Barnard was asked by a business magazine to remark on the subject of how industry could help the nation get out of the economic slump.[14] His ideas were expressed in two words, stabilization and integration. Although they might have sounded hollow to people in line at soup kitchens, they contained the essential aspects of his beliefs about economic recovery. Stabilization required industry to bring its productive capacity into line with demand for commodities and to introduce capital improvements and efficiency measures whenever possible. But stabilization would not be effective if implemented on a piecemeal basis. Intra- and interindustry coordination was needed and that meant monopoly had to become a high priority in national industrial policy. Barnard said, "Monopoly, merger, integration, trade association or some form of intelligent regulation of supply to the level of sane and stable demand . . . is getting to be a necessity, a factor of tremendous importance in making our mechanical age do its job and serve the people."[15]

The program that Barnard endorsed presumed a drastic revision of national policy, away from the protection of competition toward a cooperative state of the type that Herbert Hoover envisioned. Barnard, in fact, referred to a speech in Cleveland, before the American Bankers Association, in which Hoover had said that combatting the evil tendencies of economic excesses and overproduction that led to the depression would "require courage, foresight, and a greater degree of cooperative effort than has yet been achieved."[16]

Thus, Barnard repeated a familiar refrain. The government should be a benign and facilitative partner with industry in helping it integrate. The practical side of integration required changing federal policies on the enforcement of antitrust laws. Barnard concluded his interview with a most ringing appeal. *"We need stability desperately.* WE SHALL NEVER GET IT UNTIL WE ACHIEVE INTEGRATION AND THAT MAY POSSIBLY MEAN A MUCH WIDER APPLICATION OF THE PRINCIPLE OF REGULATED MONOPOLY THAN WE HAVE NOW."[17]

Ironically, the New Deal offered to deliver exactly the kinds of policy changes Barnard wanted, only the initiative for implementation was placed in the hands of government instead of with private enterprise, and Barnard most certainly did not want that.

The prospect of government intervention put business on the defensive and caused its spokesmen to take their case into forums of public opinion, where they argued for keeping the balance of national power in the private sector. Barnard manned the barricades in the 1930s along with many other corporate executives. Although the appeals made by most of these executives were scarcely more significant than Chamber of Commerce pep talks, Barnard's were different. Unrelentingly analytical, intellectual, and cogent, the best example was his 1936 address to the CEOs of life insurance companies at their annual convention in New York city.[18] Barnard argued that the management of the United States' primary institutions performed two basic functions, planning and regulation. Rhetorically, he asked the executives in the audience, upon what principle should government govern?

He gave the answer in the form of two options: "The central [government] authority prescribes what must be done and so precludes freedom to do otherwise, [or] government specifies what may not be done, and so leaves an immense range of choice available."[19] Barnard, of course, favored the second option because it implied regulation. When a government mandated what *must* be done, it had to plan, and that was unacceptable to Barnard.

He gave a number of reasons for this opinion, and praised the foresight of private enterprise for making goods available, providing jobs, and increasing Americans' standard of living. These successes were accomplished without government planning, and, he noted, where there was centralized planning, generally results were worse and living standards were lower.

However, government was not any better prepared than private enterprise to anticipate the future of the national economy. The central government, therefore, should stay out of planning, leaving to private enterprise, disciplined by a free market, the function of exercising the foresight necessary to allocate resources. Ten years later he made a similar point in his review of Wootton's book. "The pink advocates of planning,"[20] as he called them, did not realize that when government attempted to exercise foresight, it laid the dead hand of bureaucracy on economic efficiency. So, Barnard held unwaveringly to the opinion that limited regulation was an appropriate function of government but that planning was best left to professional managers in corporations, responding to market forces.

The interesting aspect of this argument is that Barnard in the past had seldom mentioned the market as a factor in management decisions. The most obvious reason was that competition did not occupy his everyday concerns as president of New Jersey Bell Telephone. Pricing worked most effectively when it was administered, and his early work on telephone rates confirmed this view. But beyond this, Barnard preferred monopolies because he believed that they were the only rational answer to industrial coordination. The rough and tumble world of competition was less healthy for the nation's economy than the stable environment of regulated monopoly.

Barnard also felt that forecasting, essential to planning, was a poorly developed technique. Plans ultimately had to be hit or miss propositions. Although this criticism of planning applied to both public and private organizations, government had the power of the state to enforce wrong-headed plans. Consequently, vesting the authority for national planning in it was an extremely dangerous proposition. In response Barnard recommended to the insurance executives that national policy rely on competition. Let the free market allocate resources and guarantee that corporate executives retain the discretion to respond to market forces. Soothing words for the insurance executives, however, they marked a considerable change in his attitude in five years.

Barnard's flip-flop on competition, while curious, was not inexplicable. In 1931 Hoover's friendly administration favored corporate management discretion to achieve industrial "cooperation." However, by 1936 implementation of cooperative policies had shifted toward government. Then competition arose in Barnard's mind to become the favored alternative to national planning. Thus, Barnard's views on planning changed with the political winds. Because the last thing he wanted to see was the concentration of planning power in the federal government, he trotted out the free market argument to justify the status quo of corporate management discretion.

Within these same five years, Barnard's ideas about regulation changed somewhat, at least to the extent that he admitted to an expanded role for government in this arena. However, Barnard's notions of regulation were peculiar to the telephone industry where it fell within the jurisdiction of the states in which the Associated Companies operated.

The Associated Companies made a comparatively modest contribution to ATT's profit picture. Overall Barnard frequently mentioned that a 6 percent return was the expectation for a Bell system operating company. However, the major sources of corporate profits were long-distance operations (ATT corporate was the operating company for the "long-lines") and the utterly unfathomable system of transfer pricing between Western Electric (that made telephone equipment) and the Associated Companies. These two highly profitable enterprises, integrated within the Bell System, were not closely regulated by the ICC on the national level. One might speculate about Barnard's reaction if he had been questioned on this matter. Regrettably, he never was.

Barnard's position on the distribution of national power was about what might have been expected from a spokesman for private enterprise. However, he was too honest intellectually to settle for a simple business-booster approach to this intricate problem. Therefore, a certain ambivalence crept into his ideas on business-government relations. On the one hand he wanted corporate management to be the moral authority in the managerial state. On the other, he realized that business had to share this authority with government to a greater extent than ever before. Consequently, he wondered how professional management might realign itself to these changed conditions.

We mentioned Barnard's partial solution of this problem above. The primary institutions divided between themselves the functions that each was most qualified to perform. Business would create material wealth by efficiently responding to market forces, and government would regulate its distribution. Although Barnard granted that the expansion of government regulation limited corporate management's discretion to some extent, it was not as restrictive as government domination of the planning function.

In a certain sense, this formulation constituted Barnard's parting nod to the old Hooverian ideals. Barnard realized that business and government had become inextricably linked in a network of administrative relationships. Businessmen and government officials could no longer glare at each other across the boundaries of their institutions or maintain a cozy arrangement where government existed merely to further narrow business interests. Rather, the situation as Barnard came to see it could be better characterized as one where professional managers, on both sides of the fence, worked together to reach accommodations that best served their respective organizations.

In this new context, moral authority rather had to take care of itself, and Barnard appreciated the fact that it was built on the shifting sands of economic conditions and public opinion. So while government was ascending in American life in the 1930s, its dominance might eventually wane as the dynamics of a pluralist society turned against it. As long as people stayed free to determine for themselves the standards of effective organizational performance, the "better sorts" would ultimately emerge as national leaders. Barnard had faith that they, in the course of events, would come from the private sector, but corporate management could hasten this day by demonstrating its moral responsibility, its competence, and its success in creating material well-being for the nation. In short, management had to prove its right to rule. The free market made such proof possible, and the government was a factor that often impeded it. These opposing conditions defined the new arena of national power for management, wherein private enterprise symbolically stood for freedom while government stood for order.

However, who ruled the nation was one thing, but who ruled the nation's organizations was quite another. And this brings us to the third major subject addressed by Barnard's political theories.

MANAGEMENT GOVERNANCE
WITHIN ORGANIZATIONS

Although individual freedom does not flourish in organizations, justice does because community order depends on it. Justice means fairness, and it is central to employee satisfaction, motivation, and performance. A vast contemporary literature in social psychology addresses the importance of equity in employee relations.[21]

Barnard grasped this fundamental idea in both its psychological and governance aspects. He analyzed justice in the classic Aristotelian manner by dividing it into distributive justice, which concerned employee interests in the allocation of organizational resources, and corrective justice, which pertained to employee rights in the redress of grievances. He held that the implementation of both sides of justice had to be centralized in management because it had the responsibility to preserve organizational order. Any dilution of management's discretion to decide what was equitable compromised cooperation and organizational performance.

The Justice Ideal

Barnard distinguished between the administration of justice in the United States as a government entity versus its management within organizations. Relative to distributive justice he commented:

> From a structural point of view the organization of the United States of America is especially noteworthy, but from the viewpoint of executive functions it is intended to be defective; that is, the system of States Rights of dual sovereignty and the separation of legislative, judicial, and executive departments precluded a common center of authoritative communication in American government as a formal organization.[22]

Thus, the constitutional model that decentralizes power, while laudable in American government, was undesirable for American business organizations. The economical allocation of resources required a "common center" in order to be efficient. That center had to be management, because it had the skills and the overall perspective necessary for making satisfactory distributions. However, management would not be arbitrary or unfair in its distributive decisions, not only because the morale of all corporate stakeholders depended on fairness but also because management's heightened moral sensitivity instructed it in the right things to do.

As the constitutional model did not apply to distributive justice in organizations, neither did it to corrective justice. Barnard wrote:

> But there is another aspect of moral creativeness that is little understood, except in the field of jurisprudence. This is the inventing of a *moral* basis for the solution of moral conflicts. . . . This function is exercised in the cases that seem "right" from one point of view, "wrong" from another. The solution of such cases lies either in substituting a new action which avoids the conflict, or in providing a moral justification for the exception or compromise. We are accustomed to call the first solution 'executive,' the second 'judicial.' They are both executive functions in the broad sense . . . were it not for the separation of power in American government, we should better recognize that the judicial process is a highly specialized executive process.[23]

Were Barnard's readers not "confused," as he suggested, by the separation of powers in American government, they would understand that the judicial and executive functions in organizations were indistinguishable. Management wore two hats, as he saw it; one when it made organizational "law," the other when it resolved disputes that arose under the law. Therefore, regardless of the procedures for the resolution of disputes over rights, employees had to depend ultimately upon management's "moral creativeness" for just settlement of their grievances and complaints. Separation of powers in corrective justice, such as union griev-ance procedures or third-party arbitration, was proscribed.

Despite the excitement caused by the participatory management movement after World War II,[24] the power to make distributive justice decisions is still firmly in management's hands. Corrective justice in organizations now seems to be less centralized than Barnard might have preferred, since management discretion in this area has been moderated by management initiated grievance systems (MIGS). However, a close examination of these systems shows that basic due process is grossly curtailed by them. For example, speedy reviews of cases are not guaranteed, administrative hearings are not open, the equivalent of a public de-fender is not provided by companies for their employees. Furthermore, MIGS are captive programs of corporate personnel departments, and they systematically exclude from their hearing boards people in the nonmanagerial ranks and the community at large. The most serious objection to these systems is that the last stage of MIGS procedures is held before upper levels of management, whose decisions are final. The vast majority of MIGS do not provide for an independent arbitrator.[25]

Barnard's ideas about organizational governance, therefore, are alive and doing well in today's corporations, a testament to his success in forging solid links between the abstract concept of justice and its application to management prac-tice. However, justice is not the whole story of organizational governance, and Barnard did not overlook the fact that liberty figured into it as well. But co-operation depended more on justice than on liberty, and this led him to stress the former and to have considerable hesitation about the latter in organiza-tions.

The Liberty Ideal

One of the more important issues debated among the American intelligentsia in the 1930s pitted those who argued for social regimentation, that is, Marxist pro-letarian discipline, against those who spoke for unbridled individual freedom, that is, free market economy. Describing this debate, Barnard wrote, "Those who carry the banners of individualism are crying for the right of the individual to choose; and those who trumpet so loudly for the state and society proclaim the folly of individual choice and seek to prevent it."[26] Barnard saw merit on both sides of this argument but certainly not in the extreme positions that polarized the opinions of the proponents of one point of view against the other. He stood for an alternative to social regimentation and individualism that combined the goods of each into a "third way." He seemed to have discovered this alternative in Hoover's idea of ordered freedom, because it provided a contingency approach to the liberty–justice, freedom–order dilemma that management theory confronted.

Barnard contended that the weight given by management to freedom and order in organizations depended on such concrete circumstances as technology, quality of work force, the regulatory environment, the competitive situation, and so on. For example, limited individual freedom was desirable if it could spark technical and financial innovations that contributed to the prosperity of the company. No doubt this opinion was shaped by Barnard's experiences at ATT. Remember that ATT's scientists at Bell Labs had considerable independence to select and to pursue their research projects. And also recall the example of Gifford's success in designing ingenious financial schemes to raise money for funding ATT's modernization and expansion after World War I. None of this was lost on Barnard, and consequently he valued his company's policies that permitted such freedoms to exist. But all corporations were not so favorably situated as ATT, and therefore Barnard felt that freedom had to be restrained. Otherwise it might destroy the unity of an organization's purpose by overloading it with too many opinions that would distract it from the efficient and effective pursuit of goals. In short, freedom had to be managed properly in order for it to be beneficial to an organization.

Apart from the positive effects that freedom had on organizational performance, it did not stand as a desirable goal in its own right. Freedom, in Barnard's opinion, was always conditional, instrumental, and subordinate to organizational and managerial considerations. If employees benefited from it in a civil or moral sense, this was a happy, but secondary, outcome. The harshness of these contingent views of liberty was tempered by Barnard's assumption that cooperation, if achieved, would enhance employees' moral character, heighten their job satisfaction, and, in the bargain, improve organizational performance. Thus the normative gulf between social regimentation and individual freedom disappeared, replaced by the ordered freedom of the cooperative system.

Barnard believed that freedom in organizations, on balance, created mischief. But more than this, liberty and management discretion were inversely related; a free people was far more likely to demand accountability from its leaders than those people who had no choice but to follow orders. However, Barnard may have thought that he had adequately dealt with the issue of accountability. After all, if managers were competent and trustworthy, why would accountability be necessary?

Perhaps the most telling of all Barnard's attitudes about liberty was his ambivalent feeling about the value of political freedom in society at large. In correspondence with Herbert Simon, he wrote, "I probably give a somewhat higher value to political democracy than you, not only for the reason that you approve of it but because I think the exercise of political democracy adds something to the dignity of the individual . . . but I am unable to go this far with respect to all people . . . what I believe to be an abject fact [is] that all peoples do not want political democracy."[27]

The abject fact Barnard referred to was that most people do not have the capacity to be free. Therefore, democracy, while an abstract good, was not for everybody. This idea, common in Barnard's circle of acquaintances, led him to try to devise means for putting into practice Machiavelli's formula. Thus, it seemed to Barnard that the managerial elite had to impose order on the people for their own good, but in subtle ways that disguised the pivotal role this elite played in American life.

As Barnard's theories of national power and organizational governance valued justice over liberty, cooperation over conflict, order over freedom, and community over the individual, they bestowed on corporate management the greatest possible discretion, with the least possible accountability. The managerial elite had the freedom, and the rest had to settle for the cooperative system.

Barnard cast a very long shadow upon the evolution of modern management theory and practice, particularly with respect to his substitution of the cooperative system for a dialectical image of human relationships in organizations. And as McClosky and Zaller hinted, Americans seem to be embracing a new ethos that blends the conflicting ingredients of individualism and community into a new brew that is consistent with managerial ideology.[28] So Barnard may have had it right all along: the modern order of the managerial state has its own imperatives that require the suppression of individualism and the substitution of communitarian values in the American ethos.[29]

11

The Exhaustion of Managerialism

The century began with a tacit agreement between the guardian class of managers and the American public. If the guardians modernized the nation in line with Progressive standards, then the public would recognize their legitimacy to rule it in concert with the politicians. So in 1934 Walter Lippmann argued that the best arrangement was for America to be run by an informed and competent managerial class, controlled by federal and state legislative consent.[1] This new apportionment of the power of governance had already been set in motion by 1917, and by the 1930s the political aspect was understood. However, the managerial factor was not, and it was in this connection that Barnard redefined the Progressive ideals in management terms. Furthermore, he showed what skills the guardians needed and what virtues they should practice so that the promise of the Progressive managerial order could be kept. Barnard, thereby, legitimized the management revolution, institutionalized its values, and codified its thought.

But in time all revolutions dissipate, leaving behind self-interested caretakers whom Franz Kafka called the "slime of bureaucracy." And so the managerial paradigm that Barnard had assiduously cultivated and evangelized at midcentury turned sour at the century's end. Contemporary managerialism disappoints material aspirations for a better life, it despoils idealism, and it suffocates individuality. The compact has been sundered, and as a result, confidence in management has declined relentlessly since the early 1970s. The public's opinion seems to be that the guardians are not benefiting the nation and that their interests are not consistent with the interests of those whom they are supposed to serve. In short, public consciousness has sensed a failure in leadership. But in addition to this failure there may also be an exhaustion of the very ideas that inspired the managerial revolution. So we are left to speculate about the fate of managerialism and Barnard's contribution to it. We should wonder, as historian Lyford P. Edwards did in 1927, whether any "class . . . will permanently be allowed to exercise power over society without being responsible to society for the way power is exercised."[2]

THE DECLINE IN CONFIDENCE

Whether one reads the popular press or studies empirical surveys, a recurring theme has held center stage for twenty years: Americans no longer feel that it is their obligation or responsibility to believe what their leaders tell them or to do what their leaders ask of them. President Carter called this attitude a crisis of confidence, and President Reagan considered it to be public cynicism. Both were right, and similar comments have been made by pollsters, experts in public and private management, and social observers who all agree that the confidence gap is associated with American leadership, not with American institutions.[3] This is a crucial distinction.

Are public feelings about its leadership a reflection of a more generalized malaise about institutions in particular or life in general? Such does not seem to be the case. For example, polls have shown consistently that confidence in American institutions is 50 to 70 percent higher, since 1972, than it is in the leadership of those institutions.[4] Furthermore, people seem satisfied with their jobs. In one survey, 75 percent of those questioned "liked their jobs very much,"[5] and polls of self-described "happiness" disclosed that only one in seven were "unhappy" while the rest said they were either "very happy" or "pretty happy."[6]

Therefore, the public's loss of confidence is specific in its object. Its complaint is with the leadership elite, not with life in general, the job, or institutions. So we must next consider the nature of the leadership failure and the exhaustion of the ideas that drove it for more than seventy years.

Failure of Leadership

Management leadership is failing for two reasons. First, it promised a level of competency in practice that it cannot deliver. Second, it has defaulted on its moral obligations. The first condition was apparent in the 1970s, the second in the 1980s, and together they have seriously compromised management's claim of the privilege to rule. As a result, Americans are less likely to accept the proposition that their personal interests are in congruity with those of their leaders. This negative perception undermines the all-important management doctrine of mutuality of interests, and it lacerates the cooperative spirit that is needed to make managerialism work.

The ineptness of management began to be seen in sharp relief in the days following the OPEC oil embargo of 1973. This event focused attention on two crucial American industries where management incompetence set a chain reaction in motion that seriously affected the public welfare. The oil industry was mouse-trapped by the embargo. Although its management had ample warning of the impending oil crisis, its failure to respond adequately contributed directly to an inflationary spiral that reached double digits by the end of the Carter administration. Management in the automobile industry fared no better. Because of its systematic refusal to redesign cars to improve their quality and fuel efficiency, the consumer rebelled and bought German and Japanese cars in abundance. The auto industry now exemplifies American noncompetitiveness in the global market-place.

General Motor's restructuring cutbacks, announced just before Christmas 1991 with consumer confidence at its lowest level in years, will close twenty-one plants, lay off thousands of blue- and white-collar workers, and result in the disappearance of 70,000 jobs from the economy by 1993. All the while, Ralph C. Stempel, the company's CEO, is drawing a salary of over a million dollars a year.

The oil and automobile industries are easy targets for criticism, but no less important are the dramatic failures of financial institutions and junk bond em-pires. Whereas once the management of the financial industry held the highest public confidence, compared to all other sectors of American business, now the public disillusionment with it is great, especially as taxpayers are being dunned for billions to cover management blunders in real estate loans and investments in high-leverage bonds.

Management incompetence in manufacturing and research and development has led to inferior domestic goods and to the exploitation abroad of American innovations in management techniques and in new products. For example, Amer-icans invented quality circles and VCRs, but the Japanese have successfully applied one to make the other. The fault for the malfunctioning Hubble space telescope was attributed by a congressional investigating committee to a break-down of quality control in manufacturing. But the most humbling of all recent management failures is the inability to produce an effective new weather satellite. In order to avoid an interruption in national weather coverage, NASA is contem-plating the use of European or Japanese satellites to tide the weather service over the period between the demise of the ones in orbit and the launch of a new high-technology system.

Thus, virtually no segment of large business has been left untouched by the floundering of management's vaunted expertise, and while more may be expected of it than human practitioners can possibly achieve, the public has been led to anticipate excellence in management practice. All the greater then is its disap-pointment when management, with all of its MBA degrees, does not live up to its own billing. But most devastating to public confidence and to management legit-imacy is the realization that management's claim to monopolize organizational expertise is one of the larger fictions of this century. Barnard's enthusiastic pro-mulgation of it reduces our faith in his vision.

A moral dimension has to be added to the competence failure. As high-paying blue-collar jobs and capital assets have emigrated abroad, the CEOs of many major American corporations have paid themselves eye-watering salaries and generous financial perks. Golden parachutes have guaranteed that senior execu-tives will not suffer the consequences of their ineptness. Robert N. Bellah and his coauthors of *Habits of the Heart* summarized the general moral decline during the

1980s.[7] The get-it-now attitudes that emphasized short-term success, instrumentality, manipulation in human relations, and selfishness have characterized management's moral decline in that decade.

It helps to remind oneself of some of the scams and rip-offs of the recent past. For example, Harold S. Geneen, CEO of ITT for seventeen years, stated, "Among the boards of directors of Fortune 500 companies I estimate that 95% are not fully doing what they are legally, morally and ethically supposed to do."[8] Or as one controller responded to a survey conducted by the Controller Council, an affiliate of the National Association of Accountants, "We as business managers seem to be following the accepted norm today, which is, 'Let's see how much we can get away with.'"[9]

Press coverage of business scandals during the 1980s supported these opinions. The May 26, 1986, cover of *Newsweek* declaimed, "A $12 billion stock scandal stuns the financial world and raises questions about the values of a new generation of America's best and brightest who are making millions doing deals." The February 15, 1985, *Wall Street Journal* reported a possible connection between a Boston bank and organized crime. A story in the August 15, 1984, *Journal* told of the pervasive use of golden parachutes, where managers protected themselves from takeovers or adverse company conditions. Reports of mismanagement in the banking industry, padded expense accounts, fictitious bills, excessive bonuses for top executives, utility and airline bankruptcies, leveraged buyouts, and the downside rigidity of executive salaries were commonplace. The E. F. Hutton check overdrafting practices, General Electric's contract frauds, and the use of insider information for private gain by investment bankers were all grist for the 1980s scandal mill. *Time*'s issue on ethics of May 25, 1987, reported, "White collar scams abound: insider trading, money laundering, greenmail, greed combined with technology has made stealing more tempting than ever. Result: What began as the decade of the entrepreneur is becoming the age of the pinstriped outlaw."

Government executives were no purer than their corporate counterparts. Throughout the 1980s, influence buying by trade associations and political action committees was widespread. Incumbents received five times as much support money as their challengers. Former government officials turned up as lobbyists, consultants, or holders of government contracts such as reported in the Michael Deaver affair. More than a dozen employees in the Reagan White House took up lobbying and received up to $250,000 a year as retainers for their services.

To cover up blatant cases of fraud, waste, and abuse, the Reagan administration engaged in a disinformation campaign that attempted to reduce the flow of information in the name of national security. Former CIA director, William Casey, threatened to prosecute news organizations for violating security regulations. Observers of this process documented more than seventy-five actions of the Reagan administration that threatened the freedom of the press. Allan Alder of the ACLU contended, "This administration has far surpassed any previous administration in demonstrating its disdain for the public right to know what it is doing."[10]

In summarizing these events in the public sector, *Time* in its ethics issue observed, "A relentless procession of forlorn faces assaults the nation's moral equanimity, characters linked in the public mind not by any connection between their diverse dubious deeds but by the fact that each in his or her own way has somehow seemed to betray the public trust."

Clashing with Lippmann's vision of a democratic legislature overseeing professional managers, Morris Fiorina wrote, "Wasteful, deceptive, disingenuous, paternalistic, and captive bureaucrats work in harmony with wasteful, deceptive, disingenuous, paternalistic, and captive Congressmen."[11] Richard G. Darman, deputy secretary of the Treasury, commented in a 1986 speech that the government bureaucracy and business management had become a "corpocracy" that was "bloated, risk-averse, inefficient, and unimaginative."[12]

Much of this mean-spirited, self-serving management behavior in the 1980s became daily fare served up to the public by the media. As the powerfuls' miscreant conduct was exposed, Americans became more and more alienated from their leadership and cynical about its intentions. Thus Barnard's presagement was fulfilled, but in a negative way. Too many defalcations by managers of their moral responsibilities jeopardized their moral authority and, thereby, the legitimacy of their claim to leadership. Cleaning management's moral mess of the 1980s seems to be one of the main projects of the 1990s.

The Deflation of Progressive Ideals

More than a hundred years ago, the public, tired of corruption in government, embarked on Progressive reform. And although this reform was vague and generalized, it quickly became defined by the means that were used to implement it. By 1900 Progressive leaders were identified by their commitment to efficiency and science as the instruments for improving management expertise and heightening rational practice in all organizations, regardless of whether they were business corporations or government agencies. Soon science and efficiency became central to management thought, and as early as 1886, Henry Towne equated engineering, economics, and management because they drew from the same source, technical rationality.

The concept of technical rationality amalgamated efficiency and science in management theory and practice. Peter Drucker defined management in a way that would have satisfied the most ardent Progressive fifty years earlier. In 1954 Drucker wrote, "Management, which is the organ of society specifically charged with making resources productive, that is, with the responsibility for organized economic advance, therefore reflects the basic spirit of the modern age."[13]

Thus, expertise meant, in its most elementary sense, the successful management of the equation of efficiency relative to organizational inputs, $E = O/I$. This economic function of allocating resources was so important in management ideology that the philosopher Alasdair MacIntyre held that managers believed that they, to the exclusion of anyone else, had a systematic expertise in "controlling a certain [economic] aspect of social reality."[14]

The practical skills connected with this expertise relied heavily on the supposedly value-neutral generalizations discovered by the social sciences. It was the assumption that with the benefit of formal education, practical experience, and organizational socialization, managers would gain specialized knowledge and skill that would enable them to be efficient in their tasks.

This ideal was deflated because the very social sciences upon which management depended have not produced objective, quantifiable generalizations that are predictable with any degree of consistency. The best that a social science can do is to explain about one-third of any economic or social behavior. Furthermore, meta-analyses conducted in the 1980s of such well-traveled research areas as leadership behavior, job previews, and job design as predictors of job performance, absenteeism, turnover, and job satisfaction suggested that 75 to 90 percent of the variance in the criteria is unexplained.[15] So even those areas in which scientific researchers perceive their work to be effective do not provide management with powerful foundations on which to base its claims for expert authority.

But the main reason for the deflation of the scientific ideal is management's reliance on social scientists who are in the thrall of positive science. Their present orthodoxy can be traced to Herbert Simon, who argued in 1947 for the need to measure administrative concepts "with sufficient experimental control to make possible the isolation of the particular effect under study." The propositions that resulted from the application of such scientific rigor "must correspond to empirically observable facts or situations." Simon emphatically believed that a science of administration must separate fact from value, for "there is no place for ethical assertions in the body of science."[16] Simon touched all the proper bases of logical positivism, which, he felt, must serve as the model for management's scientific research. This argument was widely accepted and applied because of the belief that a scientific agenda would make management practice more efficient.

For this to be the case, there had to be a direct link between the research findings of positive science and the practice of management. But no convincing link existed. Waiting for social science to deliver valid and useful concepts to management was rather like waiting for Godot. As Barnard had warned when he was at the Rockefeller Foundation, the strict application of the methodology of positive science to management was likely to have unproductive, disappointing results.

Beyond the technical limitations of the social sciences is the relationship between scientists and practitioners. As Barnard observed, they did not communicate with each other because scientists tended to emphasize the methodologically elegant instead of the managerially relevant. Since Barnard's time the barriers separating science from practice have grown vastly higher. Overspecialization has fragmented the social sciences, and the dedication of scientists to methodological orthodoxy has created a stultifying strictness in research. Practitioners too are not without blame. In areas such as personnel management and industrial-organizational psychology, management has co-opted scientists, making them, in historian Loren Baritz's words, "servants of power."[17] As matters now stand, scientists have lost credibility because of their failure to produce valid conceptual generalizations, and management has lost honor by its haste to "buy" researchers to conjure up behavioral techniques that confuse manipulation with the efficient use of human resources.

Expertise and science not withstanding, the greatest deflation of Progressive ideals occurred in management's moral integrity. Although Barnard knew that managers made critical decisions about the allocation of resources, he also realized that the true tests of those decisions lay beyond science, rationality, and the law and within the realm of personal morality. Barnard sounded a tocsin about moral heedlessness that management ignored. Public trust was betrayed by many managers in the 1980s, putting the ideal of moral responsibility to shame. And a stream of moral lapses continues to jangle the nation's sensibilities in the present decade, as the Treasuries market scandal at Salomon Brothers demonstrated.

The dark side of Barnard's Progressive vision is showing as the millennium draws near. The management elite is not expert at running organizations, nor is it rational and visionary in its decisions. Worst of all the elite is not trustworthy. Therefore, as Barnard feared, public confidence in its management leadership has waned, resulting in a decline in its legitimacy to rule. This condition forewarns of fundamental reforms in the American managerial state, similar to those epic reforms that took place early in this century. However, the new aim will not be at the modernization of the nation but may be at honor, justice, and democracy in the administration of the republic's institutions. But one cannot be sanguine about this prospect because Barnard had similar expectations for cooperation. We have been there before and it did not work out.

The Bankruptcy of Cooperation

Democracy was an essential part of Progressive idealism. Its hopes for social mobility, public education, merit-based advancement, and wide distribution of power were formed by notions that individuals were free to choose among alternatives, had roughly equal access to opportunities, were the agents of their own destinies, and knew better than anyone else what was good for them. However, as we saw in the last chapter, these ideas contradicted managerial values and the collectivistic imperatives of organizations.

Barnard resolved those difficulties, theoretically at least, by substituting management omniscience about "the good" for individual self-determination, management virtue for accountability, and most importantly, cooperation for democracy. However, he did not entirely dispense with democracy. Rather he wanted it controlled by management, for he realized that it was a powerful means for ratifying management decisions by nonmanagers.[18] But this "proper use" of democracy depended on fabricating new human material by psychological manipulation. Once done, people then would join willingly with management, on management's terms, in the creation of a cooperative (collectivistic) system. Barnard thought that building cooperation this way was a benign, even-handed, nonexploitive use of executive power. Such social engineering was more than an adequate substitute for democracy. Reluctant to abandon management's discretion and independence of action to the uncertainties of democratic procedures, Barnard sought the "perfection" of individual employees and the effectiveness of organization in the manipulative flimflams required by his cooperative ideal.

Thanks to Barnard, and other opinion leaders of his times, American management has dreamed the dream of cooperation. Since the end of World War II the number of atrocities committed in its name are legion. Human relations, democratic leadership, the managerial grid, sensitivity training, organizational development, cultural enactment, and imaginization are a few of the expensive follies that claim to create a rich collective life for employees while increasing their cooperative predispositions toward management. However, it is doubtful that these techniques have profited anyone other than management consultants. Nevertheless, they are interesting artifacts since they attest to the persistence of cooperation in managerialism's ideology.

Few, besides management practitioners, consultants, and orthodox scholars, were particularly smitten by this indulgence, unless one counts the Japanese, for whom Barnard already is a legend. Most Americans approach cooperation pragmatically, as a contingency problem. Sometimes one should cooperate with one's boss as a matter of self-interest, but other times a confrontational stance is necessary. However, most of the time a certain neutrality toward or distance from management and the organization is the best prescription for personal sanity and survival. But the idea of being absorbed by the collective apparatus of the formal organization, as Barnard thought necessary for full cooperation, was a stupefying proposition for the average American employee. The managerial ideal of cooperation appeals to few except managers. Thus Barnard's faith in cooperation was not confirmed. American workers were not as pliable as he wished them to be, and they could easily detect when management tried to use its power surreptitiously to influence their attitudes and behavior.

And so for these and many other reasons, the ideas and the ideals, the theories and the practices, the hopes and the promises of our managerial state are in disarray. If we attempt to answer Bertrand de Jouvenel's three questions, we might gain some deeper understanding of our present situation. He wrote: "Perhaps societies are governed in their onward march by laws of which we are ignorant. Do we know whether it is their destiny to avoid the mortal errors which beset them? Or whether they are not led into them by the same dynamics which carried them to their prime? Whether their seasons of blossom and fruitfulness are not achieved at the cost of a destruction of the forms in which their strength was stored?"[19]

THE RESTORATION OF CONFIDENCE

The title of this section implies that there are steps that could be taken to save the managerial paradigm of values and practices, but it begs the question of whether or not managerialism ought to be saved. However, let us suppose for the moment that it should and ask what minimal reforms are needed to patch up management's reputation and legitimacy in the public eye.

The answer to this question is evident: reverse the aforementioned conditions that led to the decline of confidence. The practical task of doing so, however, is monumental, and there may not be the necessary strength of mind, body, character, and will left in the managerial elite to execute it. Nevertheless, it might be helpful to touch on some areas where repairs are most needed.

Discretion and Accountability

Since managers have the privilege of power, they must be accountable for its use. Yet accountability in any form should not be so stifling that it smothers executives' incentive to take independent action or to make critical decisions.

This principle has been recognized for a long time in public regulatory policy and in the legal interpretations of it. Nevertheless, the fine balance between over and under regulation constantly needs adjustments at the margin. The difficulty with regulatory remedies of indecent amounts of management discretion is that they create rules that in turn breed more rules as management finds ways to circumvent the original ones. A society that relies on statutes or agency regulations to enforce accountability inevitably becomes rule laden. And while laws may achieve some desirable and beneficial limits of discretionary power, they do not fundamentally change management values or behavior. That is why Barnard thought that government regulation was the least noxious form of government activism.

It did not occur to Barnard that there was another potential avenue of public accountability within the legal system. Managers, theoretically, can be held personally liable for their actions in criminal or civil court proceedings. However, establishing culpability is virtually impossible, since managers are protected by the prudent business judgment rule in the private sector.[20] The relaxation of these rules would increase individual accountability, but the courts have not shown much inclination to enforce it. It is very difficult to prove management malpractice, malfeasance, or nonfeasance. All and all, in an already pathologically litigious nation, one might rightly question a reform that takes it further in this direction. Nevertheless, executives' intentions are always at the heart of their use of discretionary power, and the court system is the only place where such intentions can be determined. If the abuse of power becomes too flagrant, increased litigation may be the price management will have to pay.

More regulation and more litigation are answers that are too obvious and too

Draconian. Reforms of justice systems within organizations, while not substitutes for legal oversight, may be a more beneficial approach to the moderation of executive power. However, management travels on this route mostly by its own volition and peril, because the farther management goes along it, the more it violates one of Barnard's cherished principles, the concentration of all organizational governance functions in management.

Reform of organizational governance places more control of justice systems in the hands of those who have a stake in the success of the organization, particularly the employees. In practical terms, employees, and others perhaps, would participate fully in resource allocation decisions, and they would have access to judicial procedures, independent of management control, for redressing grievances.

Already management has introduced the latter in many large organizations. However, systems of procedural due process, installed by management initiative, are subject to overwhelming management influence. These devices for protecting the rights of stakeholders against management depredations are in their formative stages. But they are further along than those justice systems concerned with interests. As legislative processes, these systems depend for just outcomes on power equalization between management and nonmanagers in and out of an organization. Thus any of the steps that might be taken toward meaningful governance reform such as employee ownership, steps that limit management's discretion and increase its accountability, entail dispersing of power to those who are most affected by it.

Competency and Rationality

Barnard took it for granted that managers knew the operation of the enterprises they were managing. Such technical knowledge and competency in its application was for him a necessary, but not sufficient condition, for getting and keeping an executive position. The first part of the Bennis and Nanus slogan presumes the same thing. "Managers are people who do things right. . . ." Alasdair MacIntyre might argue that the infinitive form, to manage, implies a functional morality:[21] to manage means to manage well.

Therefore, management is supposed to be composed of people who use their skills, based on practical knowledge, to make things work as they should. Managers who run factories, deans who run business schools, administrators who run hospitals, financiers who run banks, and publishers who produce and sell books are expected to know how mechanics, scholarship, patient and care-giver relationships, economics, and aesthetics apply to their jobs. An oversimplification, perhaps, but the point is that such elementary knowledge and practical competencies cannot be taken for granted as Barnard supposed.

The depressing fact is that many executives are responsible for activities about which they have little working knowledge. Should less technical knowledge be expected from an executive than from a newly commissioned West Point second lieutenant? While the latter may know a lot about military strategy and history, he or she does know how each weapon in an infantry platoon functions, how it is maintained, and how it is used to maximize the capabilities of the unit as a fighting force. The restoration of confidence in management depends a great deal on its relearning what it once knew how to do: to achieve quality and efficiency in product design and service delivery as well as in the operations used to create both.

How technical skill is obtained is not as important as whether a manager has it. Nevertheless, there are only three sources of competency—self-education, experience, and formal education—and of these just formal education is appropriate to comment on here, because it is the only aspect of competence that can be measured and reformed in any standardized way.

Modern reformers of management education could do much worse than to follow Barnard's ideas. The purpose of college, he believed, was to prepare broadly educated people and to socialize them through extracurricular activities because they produced lasting networks of associations useful in post-university life. This Harvard College model worked well for Barnard, but does it apply to the age of the MBA?

Harvard's first MBA class coincided with Barnard's class of 1910, and he died years before the national explosion of MBA programs and degrees. Of course, Barnard approved of Donham's successful efforts to establish an elite MBA program at Harvard, but had he lived he most likely would have been appalled by the proliferation of MBA programs at third- and fourth-rate universities.

Since the majority of MBA programs exist because the career credentials they provide are demanded, they are the worst of the educational world, as Barnard saw it. They do little to impart useful skills, they do not socialize students (many programs are offered at car-hop universities at night), and they make feeble efforts to provide a comprehensive general management education. Undergraduate business programs might have been an even greater abomination to Barnard because their vocational orientation deprives students of the opportunity to experiment with ideas and to experience a type of learning that is critical for their character development.

Universities will not abandon management education. However, their commitment to it may diminish since corporate clients are becoming disenchanted with its "products." Already the bloom is fading on the MBA rose, and we may expect fewer programs and students in these courses in the next ten years. This is a good thing since universities are not corporation farm clubs and do not function well in that role. Companies are now realizing this, and more MBAs are having trouble finding jobs. Alternatively, companies are spending billions on their own "shadow" universities. They find that they can better train good undergraduate students in the skills they need in their work. As this trend continues, accompanied by declining MBA enrollments, one might hope that universities will rededicate themselves to the Barnardian vision of education.

Barnard was also concerned about the connection between science and management practice. The problem with this connection seemed to lie in what was meant by rationality. Rationality to scientists meant something different than it did to management. However, Barnard believed that the house of rationality had many rooms, and it bothered him that academic social scientists lived in just one of them, the one having the name "positive science" attached to the door. This created in the academy what he called a "false idea" of science. Since rationality could take many forms, he felt that the trick was to find the form that best led to the truth about a phenomenon under study. This required the development of a social science epistemology that went beyond the positive science model.

Little progress has been made in this enterprise, and it is truly amazing now to see how much the academy has been engulfed by a stifling commitment to a single orthodox social science methodology that excludes more knowledge than it creates. Students are required to learn what their professors know "scientifically" to be true; Ph.D. candidates are forced to hone their empirical techniques so they can do regression equations in their sleep; assistant professors must publish empirical research in approved journals in order to become tenured; and those with tenure must continue with this activity if they want to be promoted and receive salary increases.

This frenetic activity within the academy has very little to do with anything that happens in the management world outside of it. But restoring confidence in scientific rationality certainly does not mean that research should be more useful to practitioners. The servants-of-power syndrome must be avoided. It does mean, however, that the criteria for selecting research topics should change. Too often subjects are chosen because they are trivial enough to be studied with elaborate empirical techniques. However, important policy questions defy examination by such narrow methods, and they are perhaps more susceptible to investigations using the criteria of art and aesthetics. As Peter Drucker has frequently pointed out, management is a moral discipline. The sooner researchers realize this and alter their methods accordingly, the richer and more relevant will their studies be.

Integrity and Moral Character

The restoration of confidence in the integrity of the leadership elite is the chief project of the management field for this decade. Management has a moral deficit to overcome, and its problem is to find ways to reduce the proclivity of practicing executives to commit ethical transgressions. This project, therefore, pertains to the other half of the Bennis and Nanus slogan: how are people encouraged "to do right things?"

Implicit in this part of their slogan is a modifying phrase, "in the face of pressures to do otherwise." Those who successfully resist such pressures are people of virtue, people of high moral character. Ultimately, then, the management ethics project is an attempt to heighten employees' moral character through training, education, and morally upgraded organizational atmospheres. As they have done so often in the past, the guardians have again turned mistakenly to sympathetic and willing academics in business schools who will give them counsel, for a price, about how to accomplish the most elusive goal of helping people become better sorts.

Business schools jumped on the ethics bandwagon around the mid-1980s for several reasons. First, there was a vague uneasiness in management education that it was not doing enough to raise students' ethical awareness. Second, the consulting opportunities for self-appointed management "ethicists" abounded. And third, business schools, as their corporate clients, foresaw that considerable public relations capital could be gained from demonstrating that they were doing something to advance people's moral development. The difficulty with these reasons, aside from the fact that they are often drawn from crass and cynical motives, is that business schools have no tradition, experience, or special expertise in moral philosophy, the discipline underlying ethics.

As a result faculties are reluctant to address issues of virtue and moral character as legitimate and practical goals of ethics programs in their schools. Most frequently heard in faculty discourse about program objectives is that "we want to sensitize students to ethical issues." Because this purpose is mundane, so are the pedagogical means used to achieve it. Schools of business rely on familiar techniques for transmitting ethical ideas and attitudes, such as case studies or television tapes of incidents depicting ethical dilemmas. Foundering students led by floundering faculty muddle about in these contrived quandaries and never actually address the most important question in moral philosophy, what are the requisite conditions for a worthy life?

Realizing that business schools are ill suited to provide moral education, many faculty members oppose making ethics an integral part of the curriculum. Students, for their part, are not especially inclined to learn more, in required courses, about what they think they know already, particularly when the time might be spent better, in their opinion, on such subjects as marketing, operations management, accounting, and finance. Therefore, it takes a very special teacher to fire student enthusiasm for the subject, and there are few such ethics professors in business schools. As Socrates observed in *The Meno*:

But if we have ordered all our enquiry well and argued well, virtue is seen as coming neither by nature nor by teaching; but by divine allotment incomprehensibly to those to whom it comes—unless there were some politician so outstanding as to be able to make another man a politician. And if there were one, he might almost be said to be among the living such as Homer says of Teiresias among the dead, for Homer says of him that he alone of those in Hades has his mind, the others are flittering shades. In the same way also here on earth such a man would be, in respect of virtue, as something real amongst shadows.

Simply said, business schools cannot be expected to be fountains of moral guidance for practicing managers, and management should save their companies' money. Endowing their ethics programs or hiring their ethicists will not redeem moral debts.

Barnard had a keen sense of a similar institutional problem and that accounted for his hesitation about the Rockefeller Foundation becoming involved in moral philosophy. Not that he was opposed to ethics, he attested to his concern in the chapter of his book that dealt with executive responsibility. But he was leery of specialized organizations getting embroiled in affairs that were best left to philosophers and theologians. However, he did not despair over the ethics question because he thought that the best way for management to demonstrate its virtue was by its practice. He believed in a functional morality, which puts a different spin on the Bennis and Nanus slogan, since it suggests that people who do things right also do right things within the limits of their organizational responsibility.[22] In other words, competent practice defines the nature of executive virtue, much as it defines virtue in medicine and law.

Leaving integrity and moral character here returns us, full circle, to the last section on competence and rationality. Although this is not a bad place to end, it creates a kind of existential hunger, one that afflicted Barnard throughout his life. He knew that the functional morality of the technica could not fully compensate for the moral failure of individual managers. However, it was a problem with which the institutions of corporate management, education, and philanthropy could not adequately cope. Moral character was a private and individualized affair, whose development was assisted by the venerable confederation of family, community, religion, and the state. Society and government, he commented, "must always remain the outposts against the unknown."[23] They mirrored the social values of the common will, and if that will was informed by the virtue of cooperation, the moral development of the individual would take care of itself.

Cooperation within Organizational Enclaves

Individuals cooperate with each other because they believe they have common interests and compatible goals. As a small-group phenomenon, the primal act of cooperation is democratic and nonhierarchical. Barnard was perfectly aware of these primitive origins of cooperation. He went wrong in his attempt to adapt them to a collective ideology as substitutes for democracy. Furthermore, Barnard's "theology" of cooperation was flawed. That cooperation is an inherently moral act is an unsupportable premise. If this premise fails, as it often does in practice, then the entire chain of reasoning that led Barnard and Donham to conclude that the managers of large organizations must be moral cannot be convincing.

Barnard's ideology of cooperation ought to be abandoned, but some of his ideas about the origins of cooperation might be usefully reconstructed as principles of individualism, voluntarism, and subsidiarity. These principles are consistent with the central elements of the American ethos because:

- individualism counters tendencies toward pernicious collectives that are managed for the benefit of a favored elite class
- voluntarism emphasizes the values of local self-determination of autonomous community group
- subsidiarity stresses the importance of intermediate institutions that buffer individuals and small groups from the overwhelming power of large government and private corporations.

Social enclaves are the means by which these principles of social action are implemented within formal organizations. As semiautonomous groups, which are based upon expert knowledge and technical skill and which are a part of larger structures, social enclaves are a nonhierarchical antidote for unmoderated management power and discretion. The social theorist A. G. Ramos argued that organizations delimited by enclaves reduced management power, decentralized authority, increased organizational diversity, placed decisions in the hands of the people who were responsible for action, and generally improved overall organizational performance and employee satisfaction. His "new science of organizations" celebrated pluralistic interests, social and individual differences, balanced power between the leaders and the led, and organizational decentralization.[24]

There is some evidence that delimited organizations are appearing, and Henry Mintzberg's description of professional bureaucracies is a case in point.[25] Organized around expertise, not hierarchical positions, these organizations create semiautonomous islands of skills within larger structures. They are exemplified by contract research groups, law offices, health maintenance organizations (HMOs), and universities. But the imperative that drives organizations to become professional bureaucracies is not altruism but the market. Such organizations seem better adapted to certain environments, and therefore more efficient than conventional hierarchies.

Ramos worried about this problem because of modern organization theory's affinity with market-determined solutions of organizational puzzles. He thought that in addition to a market-driven organization theory, there were at least three other organization theories: one driven by ideas (ideational), another by the affective nature of groups and communities, and a third by the desocialized propensities in human nature. Only when managerial ideology acknowledges that people are incomplete and unfulfilled without the opportunities for both instrumental and substantive organizational experiences will it be able to create a natural, unmanipulated, cooperative spirit among individuals.

It is ironic that Ramos, a Brazilian, captured in his treatment of organizations the dialectical essence of the American ethos. Ramos's views raise conflict to the same ideological plane as cooperation. Not only is this position more realistic, it is likely to be more fruitful in the reconstruction of the managerial paradigm.

The managerial paradigm might be saved if management discretion were moderated by increasing management accountability and by dispersing management organizational governance power; if management improved its technical competency; if the integrity and moral character of management practitioners were revived; and if its ideology of cooperation drew for inspiration upon the concept of social enclaves. Attaining these four goals presents a Herculean project of reform. But if the management paradigm is not saved, then what must follow it portends a Jupiterian shift in management's wind and weather.

Epilogue: The Management of Crisis and Tribulation

Warren Bennis was reported to have said that the centralized command management systems of large business organizations sprang from the military experiences of many of their top managers in World War II. "They believed in three words: control, order and predictability. It was the Army pyramid. The hierarchy, line of command and division of labor."[1] This description is an inadequate explanation of current management practices in America's mature companies. Bennis might have been more illuminating had he said that many past national crises and public tribulations prompted solutions based upon hierarchical structures and autocratic management styles of leadership and that these solutions tended to persist even after a particular emergency had ended. At least this observation would have been more consistent with the historical record because present management woes are, to a significant degree, the fallouts from the menacing events management has confronted over the last one hundred years.

For example, professional management originated in Progressivism's attempt to restore integrity in government and confidence in the economic system that had been imperiled by the inefficiencies and the corruption of the old order. The crisis of World War I underscored the virtues of national industrial coordination during emergencies and hastened the country's modernization by professional technocratic managers in the 1920s. The fear of foreign ideologies added impetus to this movement. The decade of the 1920s ended with the stock market crash, and the depression that followed it dashed Hoover's vision of a managerial state founded on voluntarism and privatism. However, the managerial state itself survived because it adapted to new principles based on government intervention and activism. These principles were managerial in nature and they were stimulated by the fear of economic privation brought on by the Great Depression. World War II and the Cold War reconfirmed what by then had already been established in managerial values and in public opinion: modern organizations, and indeed modern societies, required, as Barnard said, "an authoritative source of communication" to issue commands, to secure coordination, to inspire faith in cooperation, and to create a belief in a common cause.

That authoritative source, in Barnard's thinking, was the managerial elite, but the values of its members leaned toward repressive bureaucratic systems. This fact was recognized by the management field, and it attempted to ameliorate it with organizational humanism and limited versions of industrial democracy. However, none of those innovations, beginning with the Hawthorne studies, can stand up to close inspection. In one way or another they have succumbed to the domination of managerial values. As Robert Michels concluded, "That which is oppresses that which ought to be."[2] Thus, all approaches designed to achieve an atmosphere that was thought to be liberating and ennobling—starting with the early attempts to use the behavioral sciences for social engineering to the present fancy of applying moral philosophy to management practices—have instead been co-opting and manipulating.

On the other hand, present management values and practices are not understandable exclusively in terms of past crises and fears. This interpretation puts far too fine an edge on the complex and multivariate process of executive decision-making. Management actions also result from strategic decisions taken in anticipation of economic conditions, consumer demand, new technologies, international markets, and so on. So it is correct to say that besides the past the future is also valid for explaining management behavior. Nevertheless, troubling events encourage management, and governments, to concentrate organizational authority, to centralize executive power, and to impose tight formal controls on operations. Boiled down, the "lean and mean" American management response in the early 1990s to a weakened domestic economy and to foreign competition is to centralize reactions to crisis situations. The answer to present difficulties seems to be the same as it has been for decades: strengthen the hands of the guardians of the managerial state.

In 1955, speculating about America's next twenty years, Peter Drucker wrote, "This question of the legitimacy of management may well be the toughest yet to be answered by the modern industrial society."[3] Now that question is being answered. Managerialism is bankrupt and the country is in a period of moral, psychological, and economical disjunction. This sounds the warning of a crisis of faith in the ruling class, and its reverberations may signal a passage whereby managerialism will be replaced by a new ideology of organizational control, and that augurs a transformation in the nation's institutional order.

To date since the end of World War II, every major totalitarian managerial state and its supporting bureaucracy (except China's) has broken down by war or by revolution. Some say that this breakdown was caused by the waning of centralized power; others suggest that it demonstrates people's ever-present longing for freedom; and still others argue that after lying dormant during much of this century, age-old ethnic and racial animosities are resurfacing. But whatever the reasons, it is clear that millions of people are rejecting their former authoritative sources of administrative communication decisively and by revolution.

Although the United States did not drift into the "absolute collectivism" of some totalitarian European countries, the disheartening fact is that its once bright alternative of "free collectivism" is growing dim. Could Walter Lippmann comment on our present adversities, he would undoubtedly address the fate of the nation's managerial state and the destiny of its guardian class of managers upon whom rests the responsibility for so much that has gone wrong. The current climate in the United States favors a revolution in the structure and values of its institutions and leadership in the same manner as it did 100 years ago.

However, this conclusion seems too narrow. Is it really a matter of management elevating its standards of moral conduct and competency or are we facing revolution? Neither of these alternatives appears likely before the century's end. Instead, the public may lower its expectations of management virtue and performance. Heightened national cynicism in the 1990s may bring the public's estimation of its leadership to the level of refinement that it took the French several centuries to cultivate. And surely, it is accurate for people to conclude that their well-being is just tangentially related to managerial trustworthiness, competence, and vision. Barnard's solution to leadership legitimacy is not especially pertinent in a post-industrial world. What matters most now is power, and that power flows to those in administrative positions.

So what we might reasonably anticipate in this decade is more of the same, for as long as management is able to provide people with an acceptable standard of living, they will support the status quo. Management's power to control the production and distribution of material incentives, not management virtue and not psychological manipulation, is what determines quality of life for Americans. Thus, an intermediate agreement may be forged to replace the old one. The people will accept corruption and incompetence from the guardians in exchange for goods and services, and the political and legal system will guarantee that this new compact has official sanction.

This prospect for the millennium is far from what Barnard and the other visionaries of the 1920s and 1930s had dreamed for the nation. Theirs was a new ideological order animated by rationality, cooperation, and functional morality. But, as de Jouvenel suggested and as we have now come to realize, the forms that caused managerialism to blossom and bear fruit are precisely the forms that have led to its decline. And if society is indeed moved by laws we do not understand, then it may be best not to try to save managerialism but to let it go into that part of limbo reserved for failed experiments in social engineering. But the shedding of one elitist ideology does not guarantee that it will be replaced by another that is more efficient, just, or democratic. Nevertheless, we can hope the essence of an ideology to come will recognize that people, despite their shortcomings, function best when left alone.

Notes

INTRODUCTION: THE VOICE OF THE NEW MANAGERIAL STATE

1. Dwight Waldo, *The Enterprise of Public Administration* (Navato, CA: Chandler and Sharp, 1980), p. 10. Waldo called *administrative* states cultural mutations. I prefer the term *managerial* state and use it throughout this book to describe the pluralistic network of elite professional managers who run the significant institutions and organizations in this country.

2. Richard P. Adelstein, "'The Nation as an Economic Unit': Keynes, Roosevelt, and the Managerial Ideal," *Journal of American History* (June 1991): 161.

3. Similar interpretations of the American governance system have been given by John Kenneth Galbraith, in *The New Industrial State*, 3d ed. (Boston: Houghton Mifflin, 1978), chapters 26 and 27, where Galbraith subsumes the concept of the administrative state under the rubric "planning system." See also Edward O. Laumann and David Knoke, *The Organizational State: Social Change in National Policy Domains* (Madison: University of Wisconsin Press, 1987).

4. Kevin Phillips, *Politics of Rich and Poor* (New York: Random House, 1990).

5. Guy Alchon, *The Invisible Hand of Planning* (Princeton: Princeton University Press, 1985), pp. 33–50.

6. Dwight Waldo, *The Administrative State*, 2d ed. (New York: Holmes and Meier, 1984), p. 97.

7. David L. Norton, *Democracy and Moral Development* (Berkeley: University of California Press, 1991), p. 164.

8. See Charles J. Fox and Clarke C. Cochran, "Discretion Advocacy in Public Administration Theory: Toward a Platonic Guardian Class?" *Administration and Society* 22 (August 1990): 249–71.

9. Herbert Hoover, *The Challenge to Liberty* (New York: Charles Scribner's Sons, 1934), pp. 28–29.

10. Quoted in Adelstein, "The Nation as an Economic Unit," p. 178.

11. Walter Lippmann, *The Method of Freedom* (New York: Macmillan Company, 1935), p. 32.

12. Ibid., pp. 37–38.

13. Quoted in James K. Feibleman, *An Introduction to the Philosophy of Charles S. Peirce* (Cambridge: MIT Press, 1970), pp. 280–82.

14. Chester I. Barnard, *The Functions of the Executive* (Cambridge, MA: Harvard University Press, 1938), p. 284.

15. See George Orwell, *1984* (New York: New American Library, 1961), Appendix "The Principles of Newspeak," pp. 246–56, and "Politics and the English Language," in *The Collected Essays, Journalism, and Letters of George Orwell* (New York: Harcourt Brace Jovanovich, 1968), 4:127–39.

16. Brant Short, "The Rhetoric of the Post-Presidency: Herbert Hoover's Campaign Against the New Deal, 1934–1936," *Presidential Studies Quarterly* 21 (Spring 1991):347.

CHAPTER 1. THE MANAGERIAL AGE

1. Stephen Skowronek, *Building a New American State* (Cambridge: Cambridge University Press, 1982).

2. Guy Alchon, *The Invisible Hand of Planning* (Princeton: Princeton University Press, 1985).

3. Ellis W. Hawley, *The Great War and the Search for a Modern Order* (New York: St. Martin's Press, 1979).

4. Alchon. *Invisible Hand*, pp. 6, 67–68.

5. Now classics in public administration and business management, their books are: Dwight Waldo, *The Administrative State*, 2d ed. (New York: Ronald Press, 1948); Herbert Simon, *Administrative Behavior*, 2d ed. (New York: Holmes and Meier, 1984); and Peter F. Drucker, *The New Society: The Anatomy of the Industrial Order* (New York: Harper and Brothers, 1950).

6. Alfred D. Chandler, Jr., *The Visible Hand* (Cambridge, MA: Belknap Press of Harvard University, 1977), p. 4. Twenty-three years earlier, Drucker made a similar statement: "Rarely, if ever, has a new basic institution, a new leading group, emerged as fast as management since the turn of this century. Rarely in human history has a new institution proven indispensable so quickly." Peter F. Drucker, *The Practice of Management* (New York: Harper and Brothers, 1954), p. 3.

7. Sigmund Diamond, *The Reputation of the American Businessman* (Cambridge, MA: Harvard University Press, 1955), esp. the conclusion, pp. 176–82.

8. Henry Adams, *The Education of Henry Adams: An Autobiography* (Boston: Houghton Mifflin, 1918, 1961), p. 499.

9. Woodrow Wilson, "The Study of Administration," *The Political Science Quarterly* 2 (June 1887): 197–222.

10. Herbert Hoover, *The Ordeal of Woodrow Wilson* (New York: McGraw-Hill, 1958), p. vii.

11. Wilson, "The Study of Administration," p. 210.

12. This change in organizational leadership has been extensively documented. See for example, Mabel Newcomer, "The Big Business Executive," *Scientific American Special Report*, 1965. Newcomer's study found that around 45 percent of top managers in big business came from the wealthy class in 1900; by 1964 this economic class accounted for less than 10 percent of top managers. Post-1964 studies confirm Newcomer's finding and document a continuation of this trend.

13. Mentioned by Professor Alberts in a conversation with me after a colloquium on Chester I. Barnard at the University of Washington.

14. Gaetano Mosca, *The Ruling Class* (New York: McGraw-Hill, 1939), p. 71.

15. John H. Schaar, "Legitimacy in the Modern State," in Philip Green and Sanford Levinson, eds., *Power and Community*, p. 289 (New York: Pantheon Books, 1970).

16. Wallace B. Donham, "The Social Significance of Business," *Harvard Business Review* 5 (1927):419.

17. Quoted in Paul Johnson, *Modern Times* (New York: Harper and Row, 1983), p. 88.

18. Reported in Barnard's privately published pamphlet, "Observations and Reflections on a Brief Call at Leningrad and Moscow," July 1939, BL, Barnard Collection, carton 1.

19. Ibid., pp. 8–9.

20. Ibid., p. 30.

21. Peter Fearon, *War, Prosperity, and Depression* (Oxford: Philip Allan Publishers, 1987), p. 13.

22. For an excellent account of Baruch's role in the WIB see James Grant's biography, *Bernard M. Baruch: The Adventures of a Wall Street Legend.* (New York: Simon and Schuster, 1983), esp. pp. 164–80.

23. Hawley, *The Great War.*

24. Robert D. Cuff, *The War Industries Board* (Baltimore: Johns Hopkins University Press, 1973), p. 265.

25. Alchon, *Invisible Hand*, p. 22.

26. The Bolshevists had a similar view of how this new order would further socialism in Russia. However, their efforts to put it in action were hampered in the early years of the revolution by civil war and factional strife among the socialists. Mussolini, who originally was a socialist, tired of its endless internecine squabbles and turned toward fascism as an alternative. For the first couple of years, Mussolini's government of Italy was fairly liberal, and aspects of it would have appealed to the free-trade economist Vilfredo Pareto, who Mussolini claimed as the source of his ideals.

27. Johnson, *Modern Times*, p. 242.

28. Joseph Brandes, "Product Diplomacy: Herbert Hoover's Antimonopoly Campaign at Home and Abroad," in Ellis W. Hawley, ed., *Herbert Hoover as Secretary of Commerce* (Iowa City: University of Iowa Press, 1981), pp. 185–210.

29. Melvyn P. Leffler, "Herbert Hoover, the 'New Era' and American Foreign Policy," in ibid., p. 150.

30. Herbert Hoover, *American Individualism* (New York: Doubleday, Page and Company, 1922).

31. Ibid., p. 44. These opinions are echoed today. W. Edwards Deming, the management consultant who advised the Japanese on how to restore their industries after World War II, stated that there should be more cooperation and less competition in American industry. He said, "it is absurd that the Government, under the guise of antitrust law, discourage cooperation to improve products and reduce prices." Few contemporary management experts have captured so succinctly the heart of Hoover's image of his associative state. Elizabeth M. Fowler, "University Heeds Advice on Management," *New York Times*, March 7, 1989, sec. D).

32. Chester I. Barnard, *The Functions of the Executive* (Cambridge, MA: Harvard University Press, 1938), pp. 294–95.

33. Given at a conference, October 24, 1940, Cooperative Study of Teacher Education, "Requirements of Leadership in a Democratic Society," p. 11, BL, Barnard Collection, carton 1. Barnard noted in this speech that freedom could be eliminated by democratic process. Although he did not mention Hitler and the Nazi rise to power in Germany, it must have been in the back of his mind.

34. See Barnard, "Review of Barbara Wootton's *Freedom Under Planning*," *Southern Economic Journal* 12 (January 12, 1946):299–300.

35. Those policies developed while he served as secretary of commerce in the Harding and Coolidge administrations and one term as president.

36. Quoted in Dwight Edwards Robinson, *Collective Bargaining and Market Control in the New York Coat and Suit Industry* (New York: Columbia University Press, 1949), p. 103.

37. See ibid., chapters 4 and 5.

38. Rexford Tugwell, *Industrial Discipline* (New York: Columbia University Press, 1933), pp. 218–19.

39. See Barry Dean Karl, *Executive Reorganization and Reform in the New Deal* (Cambridge, MA: Harvard University Press, 1963) for an excellent discussion of the Committee for Administrative Management, the motivation behind its founding, and the character and thought of Brownlow, Merrian, and Gulick.

40. Stanley M. Milkis, "The New Deal, Administrative Reform, and the Transcendence of Partisan Politics," *Administration and Society* 18 (February 1987):433–72.

41. Luther Gulick, "Politics, Administration, and the New Deal," *The Annals* (1933):55–56.

42. George C. Homans and Charles P. Curtis, Jr., *An Introduction to Pareto* (New York: Alfred A. Knopf, 1934), p. 249.

43. Donham, "Social Significance of Business," p. 416.

44. John A. Rohr, *To Run a Constitution* (Lawrence: University Press of Kansas, 1986), p. xi.

45. Hoover, *American Individualism*, p. 67.

46. James Burnham, *The Managerial Revolution: What Is Happening in the World* (New York: John Day Company, 1941).

47. See Wilson's address, before the American Bar Association in 1910, reprinted in William Z. Ripley, *Main Street and Wall Street* (Boston: Little, Brown and Company, 1927), pp. 3–15.

48. See Ripley, ibid.

49. Adolf A. Berle, Jr., and Gardiner C. Means, *The Modern Corporation and Private Property* (New York: Macmillan Company, 1933), esp. book 4, pp. 333–58.

50. George Orwell, *James Burnham and the Managerial Revolution* (London: Socialist Book Center, 1946), published earlier under the title *Second Thoughts on James Burnham*. But as Crick pointed out, Orwell may have been coming around to grudging acceptance of Burnham's proposition about the division of the world into three major national power centers, with each center ruled by a "self-centered oligarchy" (see Bernard Crick, *George Orwell* [Boston: Little, Brown and Company, 1980], p. 342).

51. See ibid.

CHAPTER 2. THE MANAGEMENT REVOLUTION

1. See Frederick W. Taylor, *The Principles of Scientific Management* (New York: Harper and Brothers, 1911, 1919). Taylor stressed the universality of his scientific management principles and felt that they could be applied with equal advantage to government, church, home and family, philanthropic institutions, and to the farm (p. 8).

2. Dwight Waldo, *The Enterprise of Public Administration* (Navato, CA: Chandler and Sharp, 1980), pp. 10–11.

3. Henry Towne, "The Engineer as an Economist," *Transactions,* 7, pp. 428–32, ASME, 1886.

4. Woodrow Wilson, "The Study of Administration," *Political Science Quarterly* 2 (June 1887): 197–222.

5. Frederick W. Taylor, "A Piece-Rate System," *Transactions*, 16, pp. 856–903, ASME, 1895.

6. Frank B. Gilbreth, *Primer of Scientific Management* (London: Constable and Company, 1912).

7. Lillian Gilbreth, *The Psychology of Management* (New York: Sturgis and Walton, 1914).

8. The idea that there was no essential conflict between the legitimate aims of employees for wages and of employers for profit had been around for a long time. See Charles Babbage, *On the Economy of Machinery and Manufacturers* (London: Charles Knight, 1835). This idea became known as mutuality of interests, whose common denominator was productivity. The scientific management pioneers claimed that their techniques would increase productivity and thereby contribute to social harmony through the satisfaction of the materialistic aspirations of workers and owners. It was management's task to "create" a mutuality of interests by scientifically raising efficiency so that higher productivity could work for the benefit of all.

9. See Otto Friedrich, *Before the Deluge* (New York: Harper and Row, 1972), pp. 99–104; Antonio Gramsci, *Prison Notebooks* (New York: International Publishers, 1971); and Nikolai Lenin, "Scientific Management and the Dictatorship of the Proletariat," in John R. Commons,

ed., *Trade Unionism and Labor Problems*, pp. 179-98 (Boston: Ginn and Company, 1905).

10. Stephen Skowronek, *Building a New American State* (Cambridge, MA: Cambridge University Press, 1982), pp. 269-70.

11. See William J. Cunningham, "Scientific Management in the Operation of the Railroads," in Clarence B. Thompson, ed., *Scientific Management*, pp. 580-99 (Cambridge, MA: Harvard University Press, 1914). Actually, the term *scientific management* was coined by Brandeis and Harrington Emerson in a hotel room in New York City where they met to prepare for the ICC hearings.

12. Raymond E. Callahan, *Education and the Cult of Efficiency* (Chicago: University of Chicago Press, 1962), p. 73.

13. Jesse R. Sprague, "Religion in Business," *Harpers* 155 (September 1927):436.

14. John F. Goucher, "How to Apply Efficiency Tests to the Church," a speech to the General Conference of the Methodist Episcopal Church, 1912.

15. Bruce Barton, *The Man Nobody Knows* (New York: Bobbs-Merrill Company, 1924; Triangle Books, 1940). Judas was the exception in this exemplary management team. Barton grudgingly conceded that he was probably not such a bad fellow, being the treasurer for a crowd of idealists. His problem was that he had the weakness of "a small-bore businessman" (p. 178).

16. Frederick W. Taylor, "The Principles of Scientific Management," in *Scientific Management* (New York: Harper and Brothers, 1947), p. 59. The "Principles" was originally published in 1911.

17. Quoted by Frank B. Copley in his biography, *Frederick W. Taylor: Father of Scientific Management* (New York: Harper and Brothers, 1923), p. 53.

18. See Loren Baritz, *The Servants of Power* (Middletown: Wesleyan University Press, 1960), pp. 45-46.

19. Raymond B. Fosdick, *The Story of the Rockefeller Foundation* (New York: Harper and Brothers, 1952), pp. 194-98.

20. Quoted in ibid, p. 200.

21. An expanded account of Mayo's early connections in America may be found in the sympathetic biography by Richard S. C. Trahair, *The Humanist Temper* (New Brunswick, NJ: Transaction Books, 1984).

22. Fritz J. Roethlisberger and William J. Dickson, *Management and the Worker* (Cambridge, MA: Harvard University Press, 1939).

23. Henri Fayol, *General and Industrial Management* (London: Pitman, 1949). Urwick took the publishers of this edition to task for changing the last word in the title of Fayol's book from "Administration" to "Management." He thought administration was a general term more consistent with Fayol's point of view, whereas management was used mostly in connection with business organizations.

24. Ibid., p. ix.

25. Ralph C. Davis, *Industrial Organization and Management* (New York: Harper and Brothers, 1928, 1940).

26. Mary Parker Follett, *Dynamic Administration* (London: Pitman, 1926, 1941), pp. 146-48.

27. James D. Mooney and Alan C. Reiley, *Onward Industry* (New York: Harper and Brothers, 1931). Later revised by Mooney and republished under the title *The Principles of Organization* (New York: Harper and Brothers, 1947).

28. Unity of command is the principle that subordinates must have one and only one superior to whom they are responsible; determinate hierarchy asserts that wherever the authority of one function leaves off, the authority of the next function should pick up so that there will be no gaps or overlaps in the command structure of the organization.

29. Luther Gulick and Lyndall Urwick, eds., *Papers on the Science of Administration* (New York: Columbia University Press, 1937).

30. Lyndall Urwick, "Organization as a Technical Problem," in ibid., p. 49.

31. Ellis W. Hawley. *The Great War and the Search for a Modern Order* (New York: St. Martin's Press, 1979), p. 83.

32. The concept "elite class" is very difficult to validate from an objective perspective. One is seldom confident whether the research on this subject actually concerns an objective, identifiable class or whether the reported elite is simply an artifact of the research design and method. I use the term broadly without pretense of scientific precision, and in the same spirit as C. Wright Mills, *The Power Elite* (New York: Oxford University Press, 1957).

33. Michael Useem, "The Social Organization of the American Business Elite and Participation of Corporate Directors in the Governance of American Institutions," *American Sociological Review* 44 (August 1979): 553-72. See also Gwen Moore, "The Structure of a National Elite Network," *American Sociological Review* 44 (October 1979): 673-92.

34. Thomas J. Peters and Richard H. Waterman, Jr., *In Search of Excellence* (New York: Harper and Row, 1982). The title of this book is suggestive. While many people may seek excellence in a variety of occupations, the most important and truly worthy are those who achieve it in large American corporations, or so Peters and Waterman imply.

35. Chester I. Barnard, *The Functions of the Executive* (Cambridge, MA: Harvard University Press), p. 224.

36. Horace Coon, *American Tel and Tel* (New York: Longmans, Green and Co., 1939), p. 192.

37. James Burnham, *The Managerial Revolution: What Is Happening in the World* (New York: John Day Company, 1941), p. 123.

38. Adolf A. Berle, Jr., and Gardiner C. Means, *The Modern Corporation and Private Property* (New York: Macmillan Company, 1933), p. 247. These words ought to sound alarms in contemporary ears. In the 1980s, leveraged buyouts, corporate mergers, golden parachutes, and greenmail seem to confirm Berle's and Mean's prediction.

39. Burnham, *The Managerial Revolution*, pp. 88-95.

40. Berle and Means, *The Modern Corporation and Private Property*, p. 356.

CHAPTER 3. BARNARD'S HARVARD CIRCLE

1. George C. Homans, *Coming to My Senses* (New Brunswick, NJ: Transaction Books, 1984), p. 132.

2. Chester I. Barnard, *The Functions of the Executive* (Cambridge, MA: Harvard University Press, 1938).

3. Reaching beyond Harvard, Henderson had considerable indirect influence on the development of American sociology through his students. Bernard Barber, a sociologist and one of Henderson's students in the late 1930s, documents that Henderson's ideas about social systems and social equilibrium are an integral part of contemporary sociological theory. See the introduction of Bernard Barber, ed., *L. J. Henderson on the Social System* (Chicago: University of Chicago Press, 1970). Similar points are made by Cynthia Eagle Russett, *The Concept of Equilibrium in American Social Thought* (New Haven: Yale University Press, 1966).

4. George C. Homans and Orville T. Bailey, "The Society of Fellows, Harvard University, 1933-1947," in Crane Brinton, ed., *The Society of Fellows* (Cambridge, MA: Harvard University Press, 1949). Quoted in Barber, *L. J. Henderson*, p. 7.

5. Henderson to Barnard, July 6, 1940, BL, Barnard Collection, carton 1.

6. Homans and Bailey, "Society of Fellows," p. 8.

7. For a full account of the founding and activities of the Society of Fellows see Brinton, ed., *The Society of Fellows,* and Homans, *Coming to My Senses,* chapter 8.

8. George C. Homans, *English Villagers of the Thirteenth Century* (Cambridge, MA: Harvard University Press, 1941). Barnard commented, "It seems to me your treatment leaves out of

account the function of the feudal system as an organizing principle revealed both in rationalizations and the institutions involved in it. . . . Payments made to lords seem to me . . . to be properly understood as a price involved in the maintenance of the system" (Barnard to George C. Homans, July 22, 1941, BL, Barnard collection, carton 1, pp. 2, 3). This quotation clearly reflects Barnard's commitment to the idea of "an organizing principle" that we noted in chapter 1. Also it seems that what Barnard had in mind about the feudal lord's maintenance function (and his reward for performing it) clearly parallels his views about the system maintenance role of modern managers and the economic "rent" they were paid to do this job. See Barnard, *Functions*, p. 215.

9. See "The Anatomy of Society," in Homans, *English Villagers*, chapter 25.

10. Specifically, the concepts of communication, willingness to serve, common purpose and effectiveness—efficiency. See Barnard, *Functions*, pp. 182–83. Barnard's theory of formal organization is discussed at length in chapter 7 of this book.

11. Both of these concepts are used extensively by Barnard in his book, see *Functions*, esp. chapter 9 and pp. 223–27.

12. W. Lloyd Warner et al., *Yankee City Series*, 6 vols. (New Haven: Yale University Press, 1941–1963).

13. Homans, *Coming to My Senses*, pp. 131–32.

14. Although Homans did not participate directly in the Hawthorne studies, he wrote a lot about those efforts. See George C. Homans, *Fatigue of Workers*, Report of the Committee on Work in Industry, National Research Council (New York: Reinhold Publishing, 1941).

15. Franz Borkenau, *Pareto* (New York: John Wiley and Sons, 1936), p. 10.

16. Ibid., p. 10.

17. Ibid., pp. 10–11.

18. Ibid., p. 126.

19. Lawrence J. Henderson, *Pareto's General Sociology* (Cambridge, MA: Harvard University Press, 1935), p. 45.

20. Published in English under the title *The Mind and Society*, trans. Andrew Bongiorno and Arthur Livingston, 4 vols. (New York: Harcourt, Brace, 1935).

21. Parsons to Barnard, December 5, 1950, BL, Barnard Collection, carton 1.

22. Henderson, *Pareto's General Sociology*.

23. Barber, *L. J. Henderson*, p. 34.

24. Homans, *Coming to My Senses*, p. 104.

25. George C. Homans to Barnard, February 5, 1946, p. 3, BL, Barnard Collection, carton 1.

26. This point is made by Barber, *L. J. Henderson*, pp. 23–26.

27. Henderson and Pareto figure importantly in Parsons's own monumental work, *The Social System*. He noted in particular his use of Pareto's concept of system and its extension to his own structural-functional analysis. In his preface and throughout his book, Parsons acknowledges his debt to Henderson and Pareto for the notions of systems and equilibrium (see Talcott Parsons, *The Social System* [London: Free Press of Glencoe, 1951].

28. George C. Homans and Charles P. Curtis, Jr., *An Introduction to Pareto* (New York: Alfred K. Knopf, 1934). A considerable portion of this book explores Pareto's concepts of residues and derivations, dwelling at length on two categories of residues—"persistent aggregates" and "instinct for combinations." The authors believed that these categories were particularly useful in explaining behavior. Much was also made of them by the scholars engaged in the Hawthorne studies.

29. Wallace Stegner, *The Uneasychair: A Biography of Bernard De Voto* (New York: Doubleday and Company, 1974).

30. Bernard De Voto, "A Primer for Intellectuals," *Saturday Review of Literature* 9 (April 22, 1933): 545–46.

31. Kingsley Davis, "Letter to the Editor," *Saturday Review of Literature* 9 (May 20, 1933):607.

32. Bernard De Voto. "Sentiment and the Social Order," *Harper's Monthly Magazine* 167 (October 1933): 569-81.

33. The scheduled lecturers in Sociology 23 in the spring semester of 1938 were Henderson, Brinton, Homans, Mayo, Roethlisberger, T. N. Whitehead, Nock, Parsons, President Lowell, Hanford, Herring, Copeland, Dean Donham, Chapple, Arensberg, Monsell, Dill, McFarland, Lee, Bock, Bullock, Kluckhohn, Isaacs, Williams, Barnard, Fergusun, Wilson, and Henderson (BL, Barnard Collection, carton 1). Barnard embarked on a project in 1945 to edit and publish Henderson's lectures. This undertaking generated a considerable amount of correspondence between Barnard and many of the principals mentioned above about their recollections of Henderson's views on Pareto. It is clear that they were not as transported by Pareto as Henderson but were willing to indulge his passion. Barnard did not finish his editorial project on Henderson. As late as 1957, Barnard had not completed editing the lectures for publication but claimed in a letter to Curtis that the manuscript was almost finished except for minor revisions. Barnard complained to Curtis about a certain inertia when it came to scholarly matters. Barnard felt that Henderson himself would not have published the lectures without great revision and that he was "diffident" about altering Henderson's work (Barnard to C. P. Curtis, June 24, 1957, BL, Barnard Collection, carton 1, file marked "Correspondence"). Henderson's lectures eventually were edited by Bernard Barber and published in 1970. Particularly valuable in Barber's introduction are the titles of lectures given by the speakers in Sociology 23. The range of the subject matter covered in this course is staggering and makes one pine for the days when breadth of education was treasured. See Barber, *L. J. Henderson*, p. 41.

34. Reprinted in Chester I. Barnard, *Organization and Management* (Cambridge, MA: Harvard University Press, 1949), pp. 51-79.

35. Barber, *L. J. Henderson*, p. 86.

36. Fritz J. Roethlisberger, *Management and Morale* (Cambridge, MA: Harvard University Press, 1941), p. 91.

37. Elton Mayo, *Social Problems of an Industrial Civilization* (Boston: Division of Research, Graduate School of Business Administration, Harvard University, 1945), p. 82.

38. Elton Mayo, *The Human Problems of an Industrial Civilization* (Cambridge, MA: Harvard University Press, 1933).

39. See Wallace B. Donham, "Essential Groundwork for a Broad Executive Theory," *Harvard Business Review* 1 (October 1922): 1-10; "The Social Significance of Business," *Harvard Business Review* 5 (July 1927): 406-19; "The Failure of Business Leadership and the Responsibility of Universities," *Harvard Business Review* 11 (July 1933): 418-35; and "Training for Leadership in a Democracy," *Harvard Business Review* 14 (Spring 1936): 261-71. Between 1922 and 1937, eleven of Donham's articles were published in the *Harvard Business Review*. The above four articles best represent his managerial ideals and strategies for the Graduate School of Business.

40. Donham, "Failure," p. 420 (emphasis added).

41. Ibid., p. 420.

42. This concern is yet another example of Donham's intellectual link with Henderson, Mayo, and Pareto.

43. Donham, "Essential Groundwork," pp. 1-10.

44. Wallace B. Donham, "Business Teaching by the Case Method," *American Economic Review* 12 (March 1922): 53-65.

45. Donham, "Essential Groundwork," p. 1.

46. Ibid., p. 8.

47. Melvin T. Copeland, *And Mark an Era* (Boston: Little, Brown and Company, 1958), pp. 75-76.

48. Wallace B. Donham, "Social Significance," pp. 406-19.

49. Ibid., p. 419.

50. Lawrence J. Henderson, "Business Education as Envisaged by the Scientist," *Harvard Business Review* 5 (July 1927): 420-23.

51. Donham, "Social Significance," p. 409.

52. Donham to Barnard, December 31, 1945, p. 2, BL, Barnard Collection, carton 1.

53. Ibid., p. 2.

54. Ibid., pp. 2-3.

55. Donham, "Failure," p. 423.

56. Copeland, *And Mark an Era*, p. 148.

57. Donham, "Failure," p. 429.

58. Ibid., p. 429.

59. Ibid., p. 425.

60. Peter Miller and Ted O'Leary, "Hierarchies and American Ideals, 1900-1940," *Academy of Management Review* 14 (April 1989): 258-59.

61. Donham, "Training for Leadership," p. 266.

62. Ibid., p. 266.

63. Ibid., p. 262.

64. Ibid., p. 263.

65. Ibid., p. 263.

66. Barnard to C. P. Curtis, December 14, 1954, BL, Barnard Collection, carton 1, file marked "Correspondence." *The Boston Sunday Globe* for September 16, 1956, carried a feature story on the history of the Beacon Hill Reading Club organized by Rose Standish Nichols, a stately Boston Brahmin, world traveler, gardening enthusiast, and a champion of global thinking. Pitirim Sorokin was among the visitors to her salon and on one occasion gave a talk on "The Institute of Creative Altruism" at Harvard. Sorokin was, no doubt "going public" with his dislike of the Fatigue Lab's work.

67. Barnard to Curtis, December 14, 1954, BL, Barnard Collection, carton 1, file marked "Correspondence."

68. Some authors have stressed the labor control aspects of the Hawthorne studies. For example see James Mulherin, "Sociology of Work in Organizations: Historical Context and Pattern of Development," Ph.D. diss., Berkeley: University of California, 1980, and Loren Baritz, *The Servants of Power* (Middletown, CT: Wesleyan University Press, 1960). Although there can be little doubt about this element of the Hawthorne studies, it should not distort the image of their wider importance in development of management as a professional discipline.

69. Mayo, *The Human Problems,* p. 54.

70. Mulherin, "Sociology of Work in Organizations," p. 141.

71. The mistakes in and shortcomings of the empirical findings of the Hawthorne studies have been discussed by R. H. Franke, "The Hawthorne Studies Revisited," *American Sociological Review* 44 (1979): 861-67; R. H. Franke, "The Hawthorne Experiments: First Statistical Interpretation," *American Sociological Review* 43 (1978): 623-43; and D. Bramel and R. Friend, "Hawthorne, the Myth of the Docile Worker, and Class Bias in Psychology," *American Psychologist* 36 (August 1951): 867-78.

72. The Hawthorne effect refers to the unanticipated experimental outcomes that arise from researcher "interference" in an experiment.

73. Fritz J. Roethlisberger and William J. Dickson, *Management and the Worker* (Cambridge, MA: Harvard University Press, 1939).

74. Donham, "Failure," p. 434.

75. Wallace B. Donham, "The Theory and Practice of Administration," *Harvard Business Review* 14, (Summer 1936): 409.

76. Chester I. Barnard, "A Memorandum on the Nature of the Social Sciences," submitted to the Board of Trustees of the Rockefeller Foundation, 1942, RAC, Program and Policy Report, 1942-1943, p. 11 (mimeographed).

77. Donham, "Theory and Practice," pp. 405-13.

78. See Martin L. Fausold, *The Presidency of Hoover* (Lawrence: University Press of Kansas, 1985), pp. 4-5, 245.

79. See William B. Wolf, *Conversations with Chester I. Barnard*, ILR Paperback No. 12 (Ithaca, NY: Cornell University, School of Industrial and Labor Relations, 1972), pp. 2-3, 14-18.

CHAPTER 4. THE "EMPIRICAL" BARNARD

1. Henry Towne, "The Engineer as an Economist," *Transactions*, 7, pp. 428-32, ASME, 1886; and Woodrow Wilson, "The Study of Administration," *Political Science Quarterly* 2 (June 1887): 197-222.

2. Chester I. Barnard, *The Functions of the Executive* (Cambridge, MA: Harvard University Press, 1938), p. 131.

3. Mentioned in William B. Wolf, *The Basic Barnard*, ILR Paperback No. 14 (Ithaca, NY: Cornell University, 1974), p. 9.

4. Barnard to Henry F. Cutler, March 30, 1904, p. 1, Barnard file, NMHA.

5. Catalogue of Mount Hermon School, 1903, p. 19, NMHA.

6. Application for Admission, standard form, Mount Hermon School, 1904, p. 1, NMHA.

7. Ibid., p. 3.

8. Barnard to Cutler, March 30, 1904, p. 1, Barnard file, NMHA.

9. William B. Wolf, *Conversations with Chester I. Barnard*, ILR Paperback No. 12 (Ithaca, NY: Cornell University, School of Industrial and Labor Relations, 1973), p. 55.

10. Ibid., pp. 54-55.

11. Transcript of Barnard's record at Mount Hermon School, 1904-1906, NMHA.

12. A. B. Stearns to Frank E. Dunn, February 28, 1939, p. 2, NMHA. Stearns was publicity manager at NJBT, and Dunn was Mount Hermon's alumni secretary. Dunn asked Stearns for some Barnard anecdotes to use in a newsletter.

13. Barnard to Cutler, March 24, 1909, p. 2, NMHA.

14. Mentioned to the author in conversation with Julia Welch, Barnard's granddaughter.

15. Application for Employment, Western Electric Company, file marked "Gifford, Walter S.," 1904, B-1125, ATTA.

16. Charles W. Eliot, Harvard's president from 1869 to 1909, pioneered a three-year A.B. degree program that Walter Gifford pursued. Barnard also chose that program, entering Harvard in 1906 and leaving it in 1909. However, he is carried on the Harvard rolls for the "class of 1910," and he always considered himself as a member of that class. It was a large one for the time, with 617 entering freshmen, 80 percent of whom received degrees. This class may have been Harvard's most illustrious, at least in the world of ideas. Besides T. S. Eliot and Walter Lippmann, it included Alan Seegar (the poet), Robert Edmund Jones (who revolutionized American stage design), John Reed (author of *Ten Days that Shook the World*), Heywood Broun (essayist and newspaperman noted for his columns in the *World* on the Sacco-Vanzetti case), Norman Foerster (philosopher and essayist), Clarence Cook Little (biologist and president of the University of Michigan, 1925-1929), and Charles Harold Livingston (the philologist).

17. Barnard to Cutler, 1906, p. 2, NMHA.

18. Ibid., p. 2.

19. Quoted in Horace Coon, *American Tel and Tel* (New York: Longmans, Green and Co., 1939), p. 103.

20. For example see letter from Gifford to Vail transmitting a long report prepared by Barnard. This was a longitudinal study of Bell and Independent telephone companies comparing exchange rates, growth in number of stations (customer telephones in service), and maximum and minimum rates. This extensive report demonstrated the thoroughness of Barnard's work

almost immediately after he was hired by ATT, since it was written on August 20, 1909. It also demonstrates Gifford's willingness to give Barnard credit for the work and to bring his name to the attention of Vail (B-1375, 1909, folder marked "Effects of Competition on Development and Rates," ATTA).

21. Thayer was a corporate vice president. He succeeded Vail as president of ATT in 1919 and served as CEO until 1925, when Gifford replaced him.

22. See Barnard memorandum to H. B. Thayer, "Status of the Government Ownership Movement," May 15, 1914, Box 47, folder marked "Government Ownership," ATTA.

23. N. C. Kingsbury was another ATT vice president and the author of the Kingsbury Commitment, an agreement made during the "trust busting" days guaranteeing that the company would not try to acquire or control directly competing telephone firms. Nothing in this agreement prevented the company from taking over noncompeting firms. See Coon, *American Tel and Tel*, pp. 113-14.

24. Record of General Commercial Conference, Shawnee-on-Delaware, Pennsylvania, June 4-11, 1924, section 24, pp. 8-11, ATTA 185-04-01-02.

25. New Jersey Bell Telephone Company *Annual Report*, 1927, p. 3, NJBTR. Most of the documentation in this section is drawn from files at the headquarters of NJBT in Newark, New Jersey.

26. Chester I. Barnard, "Our Task and Opportunity," *The New Jersey Bell*, October 1927, pp. 1-3, NJBTR.

27. See *Annual Reports* for 1928 and 1929.

28. NJBT *Annual Report*, 1929, pp. 10-11, NJBTR.

29. Chester I. Barnard, "Moving Forward to Higher Standards," *The New Jersey Bell*, October 1932, p. 2, NJBTR.

30. "Summary of President Barnard's Talk to Employee and Management Representatives," August 18, 1933, NJBTR.

31. Ibid., p. 6.

32. Ibid., pp. 9-14.

33. Ibid., p. 10.

34. Ibid., p. 11.

35. Ibid., p. 12.

36. Ibid., p. 12.

37. Ibid., p. 14.

38. Ibid., p. 14.

39. *Annual Report*, 1933 to 1947, NJBTR.

40. Chester I. Barnard, "The Future Will Test the Fibre and Loyalty of all of us . . . ," *The New Jersey Bell*, October 1940, pp. 10-13 and 16, NJBTR.

41. Ibid., p. 13.

42. *Annual Report*, 1944, p. 3, NJBTR.

43. *Annual Report*, 1947, pp. 5-8 and 19-21, NJBTR.

44. Ibid., p. 19.

45. Chester I. Barnard, "The History and Economics of the Dial Program of the New Jersey Bell Telephone Company," memorandum for the Supervisory Organization of the Company, September 2, 1947, ATTA, folder marked "C. I. Barnard"-110-11-01-02.

46. Ibid., p. 22.

47. Ibid., p. 22.

48. Ibid., p. 18.

49. A detailed account is given in a 1942 issue of ATT's in-house magazine. See "Organizing 'Fighting Industry' in 1917," folder marked "Gifford, W. S., Biography," ATTA, B-1125.

50. Reported in "Mr. Gifford Accepts President Hoover's Appointment to Unemployment Relief Work," *Southwestern Telephone News*, August 1931, p. 2, ATTA, folder marked "Gifford, W. S. Biography," B-1125.

51. For example see Chester I. Barnard, "Provision of Circuits for Connection to Radio Broadcasting Apparatus," *Commercial Letter #218*, April 11, 1922, ATTA, folder marked "Radio Bulletin #4, Radio Telephony," box 62. Barnard's report on radiotelephony was one of his last projects as a staff commercial engineer. He was promoted soon after it was written to a line management job at Pennsylvania Bell. Relative to Hoover's involvement in radiotelephony see letter to him from H. B. Thayer, president of ATT, requesting assigned frequencies between the 300 to 600 meter bands. H. B. Thayer to Herbert Hoover, January 23, 1922, ATTA, folder marked Radio Broadcasting Plans of ATT & RCA, 1921-22-24, Box 50.

52. This remarkable technological achievement, pictures transmitted over intercity telephone wires, is fully documented in the ATT archives. Most interesting for our purposes is the public relations material publicizing this event. Included are Gifford's and Hoover's remarks and the guest lists of people invited to the two demonstrations (a virtual who's who of American industry, science, and the press) (see ATTA, folder marked "Television 1927-1947," B-1062). No less interesting are the documents that record ATT's strategic decisions that led to its entry and then to its abandonment of the television business. Regarding the former decision, Gifford said, "We endeavor to develop all forms of communication that might be supplemental to the telephone" (ibid.). These records also portray the struggle for dominance between two major companies that had developed rival technologies. The Bell Labs designed an impractical electrical-mechanical system that was awkward in use and transmitted a low-quality image. RCA experimented with a fully electronic system that was far superior but not exploited commercially until after World War II. ATT withdrew from this new medium of communication, as it also gave up its excursion into the entertainment business. Again, in competition with RCA, ATT produced and marketed a sound system for the motion picture industry. For a discussion of the "talkie" saga see Sheldon Hochheiser, "ATT and the Development of Sound Motion Picture Technology," in *The Dawn of Sound*, ed. Mary Lea Bandy (New York: The Museum of Modern Art, 1989), pp. 23-33.

53. Barnard, "The Future Will Test," p. 16.

54. Chester I. Barnard. "Nine Weeks in the United States Treasury: October 6 to December 11, 1941," unpublished manuscript. I am grateful to Julia Welch, Barnard's granddaughter, for making this important and previously undocumented manuscript available to me. Unfortunately, I cannot do justice to its contents here and it merits close study because it records the early deliberations in government about how to finance America's war efforts.

55. Ibid., pp. 6-7. Barnard intended this record to aid his own recollections. Had he circulated it more widely, he probably would have not been quite so blatant in his ethnic and gender stereotyping. Furthermore, he would not have been as candid about his beliefs that the Communists were dominating the federal government and labor unions.

56. Ibid., p. 7.

57. Ibid., p. 7.

58. Ibid., p. 68.

59. William B. Hughes from Indiana Bell Telephone replaced Barnard as president of NJBT after Barnard retired. McRae had served as Barnard's second in command from NJBT's founding. He retired around the same time as Barnard.

60. Rockefeller Family Archives, RAC, Rockefeller Boards, folder 375.30.31, III, 2, 0.

61. Ibid.

62. Raymond B. Fosdick to John D. Rockefeller, Jr., March 10, 1948, ibid.

63. John E. Harr and Peter J. Johnson, *The Rockefeller Century* (New York: Charles Scribner's Sons, 1988), p. 450.

64. Others being considered for the presidency were John S. Dicky, president of Dartmouth and Lester B. Pearson, under secretary for External Affairs in the Canadian government. Both of these men had Rockefeller's strong support.

65. Harr and Johnson, *The Rockefeller Century*, p. 450.

66. Walter W. Stewart to John D. Rockefeller, Jr., March 5, 1948, Family Archives, RAC, Rockefeller Boards, folder 375.30.31, III, 2,0.

67. Fosdick had opposed funding Shartle's research grant proposal from the start. See Fosdick's diaries for 1946 and 1947, RAC, unit 1, shelf 4, box 19. These studies in leadership, now considered to be classic, established the autocratic versus democratic dimensions of leader behavior that are still used in leadership research. The RF grant, made by the Social Science Division in 1950, continued for some five years and was replaced by a much larger grant from the Kellogg Foundation in 1955.

68. Barnard stressed three themes in his report: population, communication, and cooperation. He said little new about the latter two, but dwelt at length on population and sexuality. He said that the sex drive in American males was far greater than necessary to sustain population and that led to moral problems, venereal disease, frustration, and crime. He concluded that "the sexual drives thus became one of the major maladjustments of society" and that celibacy may be the only answer. But that had its downside, too, since "continence may lead to emotional strain [that can] only with difficulty be distinguished from insanity" (President's Review, The Rockefeller Foundation *Annual Report 1948*, RAC, p. 16).

69. John D. Rockefeller, Jr., to Barnard, July 22, 1952, RAC Family Archives, RG2 (OMR), folder 375.

70. This information provided by Jared and Julia Welch, Barnard's grandchildren, in conversation with the author.

71. The authoritative source through 1957, the years relevant to our study, is J. Merton England, *A Patron for Pure Science* (Washington, D.C.: National Science Foundation, 1982). For a short and useful overview see George T. Mazuzan, "The National Science Foundation: A Brief History," (mimeograph, Washington, D.C.: National Science Foundation, n.d.). Both volumes are available at the headquarters of the National Science Board, Washington, D.C.

72. Minutes of Second Meeting of NSB, January 3, 1951, NSBA. Barnard's list mentioned: qualified as a scientist or experience administering scientific personnel; good understanding of national government; good understanding of the organization and practices of higher education; competent manager of moderate-sized organization with "high class personnel"; and adept at public relations.

73. England, *Patron for Pure Science*, pp. 124–27.

74. Chester I. Barnard, "Memorandum to Members of the National Science Board," September 22, 1955, NSBA, file marked "Reflections on the 35th Meeting of the NSB," p. 2, record number 165.

75. Ibid., p. 3. Record number 166.

76. England, *Patron for Pure Science*, p. 314.

77. Ibid., p. 313.

78. Harry Alpert to Alan T. Waterman, memorandum, May 22, 1953, NA, RG 307, box 20, folder marked "Social Science Research," p. 1.

79. Ibid., p. 2.

80. Harry Alpert, "The Role of the Foundation with Respect to Social Science Research," NSF Staff Paper, presented to the twenty-seventh meeting of the NSB, May 12, 1954, NSBR.

81. Based on a conversation with Hershey.

82. Based on conversations with Mitchell and Wolf.

83. See Rockefeller Family Archives, RAC Family Archives, RG2 (OMR), folder 375.

84. Ibid.

85. Mentioned by H. Roy Hershey in conversation with the author.

86. Barnard, *Functions,* p. 224.

87. The author is indebted to William Alberts for his analysis of NJBT's financial condition.

CHAPTER 5. BARNARD'S INTELLECTUAL DEBTS AND
HIS EPISTEMOLOGY OF THE SOCIAL SCIENCES

1. Paul Johnson, *Modern Times* (New York: Harper and Row, 1983), chapter 1.

2. Quoted in ibid., p. 123.

3. They were right in some instances. "Communist sympathizers largely succeeded in winning control of the Electrical, Radio and Machine Workers; the Transport Workers; the Maritime Union; the State, County and Municipal Workers; the Fur and Leather Workers; and the Woodworkers of America" (Foster Rhea Dulles, *Labor in America* [New York: Thomas Y. Crowell, 1949], p. 317). These industrial unions were affiliated with the CIO, and left-wing elements gained control of them largely by the parliamentary tactic of "boring from within." In spite of this, most rank-and-file members of these unions did not follow the party line and they ultimately purged themselves of communist leadership.

4. Chester I. Barnard, *The Functions of the Executive* (Cambridge, MA: Harvard University Press, 1938), p. 282.

5. Ibid., p. 283.

6. This interpretation was suggested in William B. Wolf. *The Basic Barnard,* ILR Paperback No. 14 (Ithaca, NY: Cornell University, 1974), preface and chapter 1. He reaffirmed it in recent conversations with me. But in fairness to Wolf, he also emphasizes Barnard's conceptual and integrative contributions to management thought and fully acknowledges the paradigmatic nature of his work.

7. Vilfredo Pareto, *The Mind and Society,* trans. Andrew Bongiorno and Arthur Livingstone (New York: Harcourt, Brace and Company, 1935), paragraphs 2060–66, 2079–2104.

8. Lawrence J. Henderson, *Pareto's General Sociology* (Cambridge, MA: Harvard University Press, 1935), p. 86.

9. Barnard, *Functions,* p. 79. Although Barnard stated in his draft copy for chapter 1 of the *Functions of the Executive,* 1936, BL, Barnard Collection, carton 1, p. 8, that he did *not* consider an organization either as a "mechanism" or as an "organism" in the sense of a living species.

10. Alfred North Whitehead, *Process and Reality* (New York: Macmillan Company, 1929).

11. Barnard, draft copy, chapter 1 of *Functions,* p. 17.

12. Elton Mayo, *The Human Problems of an Industrial Civilization* (New York: Macmillan Company, 1946), p. 170.

13. Kurt Koffka, *Principles of Gestalt Psychology* (New York: Harcourt, Brace Company, 1935), esp. pp. 682–84.

14. Barnard, *Functions,* p. 263.

15. Ibid. p. 283.

16. John R. Commons, *Institutional Economics* (New York: Macmillan Company, 1934).

17. Barnard, draft copy, chapter 1 of *Functions,* p. 15.

18. Commons, *Institutional Economics,* p. 67.

19. Ibid., pp. 89–90, 627–48.

20. Barnard, *Functions,* pp. 202–5.

21. Ibid., p. 205.

22. Talcott Parsons, *The Structure of Social Action,* 2d ed. (Glencoe: Free Press, 1949).

23. Barnard, *Functions,* p. 57.

24. See Barnard, draft copy of chapter 1, *Functions,* p. 15.

25. Pareto, *Mind and Society,* paragraphs 2066, 2067–68, 2203–36.

26. Fritz J. Roethlisberger and William J. Dickson, *Management and the Worker* (Cambridge, MA: Harvard University Press, 1939), p. 365.

27. Ibid., pp. 551–52, 567–68, 578–79.

28. Barnard, *Functions,* p. ix.

29. Ibid., p. ix.

30. Eugene Ehrlich, *Fundamental Principles in the Sociology of Law*, trans. Walter L. Moll, (Cambridge, MA: Harvard University Press, 1936).

31. Ibid., p. 488.

32. Barnard, draft copy, chapter 1 of *Functions*, p. 14.

33. Roberto Michels, "Authority," in E. R. A. Seligman, ed., *Encyclopaedia of the Social Sciences* (New York: Macmillan, Vol. 2, 1930).

34. This quotation is found in ibid., p. 319. Barnard quoted it in his book and noted that the italics were his doing. See Barnard, *Functions*, p. 164.

35. Michels, "Authority," p. 319.

36. Simon wrote mostly about limitations and restrictions to choice, as did Barnard. The precise term "bounded rationality" did not appear in Simon's influential book, *Administrative Behavior*. He wrote about the need for the "triangle of limits" to have more sides that "bound the area of rationality." See Herbert Simon, *Administrative Behavior* (New York: Macmillan Company, 1947), pp. 39-41, 243-44.

37. See Max Weber, *Theory of Social and Economic Organization*, trans. Talcott Parsons and A. K. Henderson (New York: Oxford University Press, 1947). Parsons, *Structure*; Emil Durkheim, *Le Suicide* (Paris: F. Alcan, 1930); Vilfredo Pareto, *Mind and Society*.

38. James D. Mooney and Alan C. Reiley, *Onward Industry* (New York: Harper and Brothers, 1931).

39. V. A. Graicunas, "Relationships in Organization," in L. Gulick and L. Urwick, eds., *Papers on the Science of Administration* (New York: Columbia University Press, 1937), pp. 181-87.

40. Barnard, *Functions*, pp. 108-10. The only table in Barnard's book, found on p. 108, presents Graicunas's ratios that show "relationships" increasing exponentially with simple arithmetic increases in numbers of people in administrative units. Barnard used the table to demonstrate "complexity."

41. Ibid., pp. 89-91, 106-9, 175-81, 217-26.

42. Pareto, *Mind and Society*, and Roethlisberger and Dickson, *Management and the Worker*, pp. 581-85.

43. One direct result of the Hawthorne studies was the interviewing program installed at the Western Electric plant of ATT. This program was used to tap into the nonlogical attitudes of employees that tended to be expressed within the informal networks of the organization's communication system. Management could use the information it gathered by interviews to modify its practices and to "correct" employee misconceptions. So critical was this program that Elton Mayo estimated that if faulty employee attitudes and misunderstandings could be dispelled by management, production would increase by 30 or 40 percent. He stated that the interview program was the first large-scale attempt by industry to get in touch with workers' feelings and to discover their relationships to morale and productivity. Mayo was, no doubt, cheerleading for the part that the Harvard researchers were playing in the interview program because these comments were addressed in a letter to G. A. Pennock, who headed the ATT end of the research at Western Electric. See Elton Mayo to G. A. Pennock, February 9, 1931, pp. 7-8, ATTA 159, folder marked "Correspondence and Comments concerning Hawthorne studies."

44. Barnard, *Functions*, p. 115.

45. See Mary Parker Follett, "The Process of Control," in L. Gulick and L. Urwick, eds., *Papers on the Science of Administration* (New York: Columbia University Press, 1937), pp. 159-70, in which she stresses that informal coordination by lateral relations among people is the most usual and effective means by which an organization is controlled when confronted by changes in the environment.

46. Roethlisberger and Dickson, *Management and the Worker*, pp. 387-91, 395-96, 405-6.

47. Barnard, *Functions*, p. 134.

48. Pareto, *Mind and Society*, paragraph 150.

49. Ibid., paragraphs 145–248, 249–366.

50. Noted by Barnard, draft copy, chapter 1 of *Functions*, pp. 16–17.

51. Junius F. Brown, *Psychology and the Social Order* (New York: McGraw-Hill, 1936).

52. Barnard, draft copy, chapter 1 of *Functions*, p. 17.

53. Barnard, *Functions*, pp. 75–76.

54. Chester I. Barnard, "A Memorandum on the Nature of the Social Sciences," submitted to the Board of Trustees of the Rockefeller Foundation, 1942, RAC Policy and Progress Reports, 1942–1943, mimeographed.

55. Raymond B. Fosdick, "Fosdick Confidential Diaries, 1938–1948," entry, November 16, 1945, "Memo to JHW," RAC, unit 37, shelf 4, box 19.

56. Barnard, "Memorandum," p. 7.

57. Ibid., p. 5.

58. Barnard, *Functions*, p. 291.

59. Barnard, "Memorandum," p. 4.

60. Barnard received several written responses from people within the Foundation to his memorandum. Willits's reply was the most extensive and detailed. He agreed that the social sciences needed integration but noted that before interdisciplinary connections could be drawn among them, much more had to be known about each in particular. This view was consistent with Willits's policy of support for theory-driven, rather than issue-driven, research. Indeed, this was the type of social science research usually funded by Rockefeller, even during Barnard's term as president. See Joseph H. Willits to Barnard, memorandum, April 2, 1942, RAC Policy and Progress Reports, 1942–1943.

CHAPTER 6. THE SEARCH FOR BEHAVIORAL CONTROL

1. Chester I. Barnard, "Report of the Special Committee on Policy and Programs," December 3 and 4, 1946, box 28–series 900–folder 155, RAC, p. 4.

2. Chester I. Barnard, *The Functions of the Executive* (Cambridge, MA: Harvard University Press, 1938), p. 40 (emphasis in original).

3. Ibid., p. 37.

4. From an early draft manuscript of Chester I. Barnard's book, *The Functions of the Executive*, "Introduction," BL, Barnard Collection, carton 1, p. 9.

5. Ibid., p. 10.

6. Barnard, *Functions*, p. 13.

7. Ibid., p. 14.

8. Not Barnard's word, but Herbert Simon's, who made much of the concept of bounded rationality in his theory of "satisficing" in decisionmaking. Nevertheless, the idea is the same, and it is one of the many debts that Simon owed Barnard. For example, in 1945 Barnard wrote Simon a long letter criticizing the manuscript for a book that was to become Simon's *Administrative Behavior*. This letter focused on the issue of decisionmaking, and relative to bounded rationality and satisficing Barnard said: "The great mass of decisions are private, rarely expressed, frequently cannot be made articulate, and are decisions of choice between assumptions and between speculations as to the consequences of concrete action." He goes on to point out that most major executive decisions are "composite" ones, that is, decisions jointly made by a group of executives such that in the end it is impossible to determine who was responsible for what in the final action. See correspondence between Chester I. Barnard and Herbert Simon, May 11, 1945, pp. 6–7, BL, Barnard Collection, carton 1, file marked "Correspondence."

9. Barnard, draft, chapter 1 of *Functions*, p. 7. As we discuss in chapter 9, these limitations to executive power are very important to the "discretionists," who see little danger of managerial absolutism because of them.

10. Ibid., p. 15.

11. See R. F. Nisbett and T. D. Wilson, "Telling More than We Can Know: Verbal Reports on Mental Processes," *Psychological Review* 84 (1977): 231–359; and E. J. Langer, "The Illusion of Control," *Journal of Personality and Social Psychology* 32 (1977): 311–28.

12. Barnard, *Functions,* p. 18.

13. Ibid., pp. 21–22.

14. Ibid., p. 21.

15. Ibid., p. 18.

16. Ibid., p. 17.

17. Ibid., p. 18.

18. See L. Festinger, *A Theory of Cognitive Dissonance* (Evanston: Row, Peterson, 1951); D. J. Bem, "Self-Perception Theory," in L. Berkowitz, ed., *Advances in Experimental and Social Psychology,* p. 6 (Santa Clara, CA: Academy Press, 1972); and K. E. Weick, "Cognitive Processes in Organizations," in B. M. Staw, ed., *Research in Organizational Behavior,* pp. 41–74 (Greenwich, CT: JAI Press, 1979).

19. Barnard, *Functions,* p. 19.

20. See A. G. Grumwald, "The Totalitarian Ego," *American Psychologist* 35 (1980): 603–18.

21. Barnard, *Functions,* p. 42.

22. Ibid., p. 86.

23. Ibid., p. 89.

24. Ibid., p. 83.

25. Ibid., p. 85.

26. Ibid., pp. 146–47.

27. Ibid., p. 247.

28. Ibid., p. 141.

29. Ibid., pp. 148–49.

30. Bendix elaborates on this point. His classic book, *Work and Authority in Industry,* puts the ideology of the human relations movement into a historical perspective. See Reinhard Bendix, *Work and Authority in Industry: Ideologies of Management in the Course of Industrialization* (New York: Wiley, 1956), pp. 308–19.

31. Elton Mayo, *The Human Problems of an Industrial Civilization* (Boston: Graduate School of Business, Harvard University, 1933; New York: Macmillan Company, 1946).

32. Barnard, *Functions,* p. 15.

33. Ibid., p. 15.

34. Ibid., p. 17.

35. The time frame was circa 1938. The results of the Hawthorne study had just appeared, and Barnard cited its early published version in his book. See Fritz J. Roethlisberger and William J. Dickson, *Management and the Worker,* Business Research Studies No. 9 (Harvard Graduate School of Business Administration, 1938). This research report was subsequently published by the Harvard University Press. Mainly through the proselytizing efforts of Mayo and Roethlisberger, the message of the Hawthorne studies got out. However, World War II intervened and it was not until after it that the full impact of these studies on management thought and practice was felt, some time in the late 1940s or early 1950s. Social psychology, via the Hawthorne studies, came into its own in management around then in the guise of the human relations movement.

36. Fritz J. Roethlisberger and William J. Dickson, *Management and the Worker* (Cambridge, MA: Harvard University Press, 1939), part 4, pp. 379 ff.

37. Barnard, *Functions,* pp. 223–24, 225–27.

38. Ibid., p. 115.

39. In practical terms, Barnard recognized that informal organizations were potential incubators of union organizing activities. Implicit was the notion that if the informal organization was

controlled, that is, infused with appropriate management values, the zeal for labor unions might be suppressed.

40. Thomas J. Peters and Richard H. Waterman, Jr., *In Search of Excellence* (New York: Harper and Row, 1982).

41. Barnard, *Functions,* p. 116.

42. Ibid., p. 111.

43. Ibid., p. 180.

44. Ibid., p. 271.

45. Ibid., p. 275.

46. Ibid., p. 167.

47. Ibid., p. 169.

48. Ibid., p. 55.

49. Mary Parker Follett flirted with this idea. She was interested in the "alignment" of group interests in larger systems, such as business firms and political parties, to achieve an integration among them that reduced conflict. See Mary Parker Follett, "Constructive Conflict," in *Some Classical Contributions to Professional Management,* General Electric, vol. 1, 1956, pp. 97–110. This article was based on a speech that Follett gave at a conference held by the Bureau of Personnel Administration in 1925. Barnard drew his ideas about "moral creativity" from Follett and highly regarded her work.

50. Barnard, *Functions,* p. 41.

51. Ibid., p. 107.

52. L. Miller and R. Hamblin, "Interdependence, Differential Rewarding and Productivity," *American Sociological Review* 28 (1963): 768–78.

53. Barnard, *Functions,* p. 134.

54. C. I. Hoveland to J. W. Willits, review of *The Functions of the Executive,* February 21, 1947, RAC 910 Policy and Programs, Psychology, 1947, p. 2. Hoveland's comments about Barnard on communication were based on Barnard's book, pp. 175 ff. He called Barnard's views "promising" and stated that little research had been conducted on these subjects. It is interesting that Hoveland singled out for comment the formal aspects of communication. Barnard, of course, was interested in the informal aspects as well.

55. Barnard, *Functions,* p. 175.

56. Ibid., p. 90.

57. Chester I. Barnard, "President's Review," The Rockefeller Foundation *Annual Report 1948,* RAC, pp. 16–19.

CHAPTER 7. ENGINEERING CONSENT IN FORMAL ORGANIZATIONS

1. The canon of classical theory was contained in the works of Mooney and Reiley, Gulick and Urwick, Weber, and Parsons upon whom Barnard drew for his theoretical constructs. He also used examples from his ATT experiences and from the military to illustrate some of his organizational views.

2. "Address by Chester I. Barnard after having been presented by the National Exchange Club with a medallion in recognition of distinguished service to the city of Newark during 1931–1932," BL, Barnard Collection, carton 1, p. 3. The service referred to in the title of this document was Barnard's work on the New Jersey Relief Commission during the early years of the depression. Barnard was extremely proud of his accomplishments with this commission in those dark days, using his handling of the "riot" of the Trenton unemployed as the basis of the "case study" he presented in Henderson's course, Sociology 23, Concrete Sociology, at Harvard.

3. Chester I. Barnard, *The Functions of the Executive* (Cambridge, MA: Harvard University Press, 1938), p. 19.

4. Ibid., p. 60.

5. Ibid., pp. 55–58.

6. Ibid., p. 57.

7. Ibid., p. 5.

8. Chester I. Barnard, "Persistent Dilemmas of Social Progress," address at the Newark College of Engineering, June 12, 1936, BL, Barnard Collection, carton 1.

9. Barnard, *Functions,* pp. 83–84.

10. Barnard to Henderson, August 7, 1940, BL, Barnard Collection, carton 1, file marked "Correspondence," p. 3.

11. The other two postwar problems were population and communication. See Chester I. Barnard, *First Annual Report to the Rockefeller Foundation,* RAC, 1949, p. 21.

12. See Chester I. Barnard, draft, chapter 1 of *Functions,* BL, Barnard Collection, p. 8. This manuscript, probably drafted in 1937, shortly after Barnard's Lowell Lectures, placed greater emphasis on organizations as "social networks of interaction" than the published version of his book. The idea of organizations as sets of systemic relationships that responded to internal and external social, individual, economic, technological, and political forces was central to this manuscript.

13. Ibid., p. 68.

14. Ibid., p. 75.

15. Ibid., p. 76.

16. Ibid., p. 79.

17. James D. Mooney and Allen C. Reiley, *Onward Industry* (New York: Harper and Brothers, 1931).

18. Barnard, *Functions,* p. 90.

19. Ibid., pp. 106–9.

20. Ibid., pp. 110–11.

21. Ibid., p. 112.

22. See V. A. Graicunas, "Relationship in Organization," in L. Gulick and L. Urwick, eds., *Papers on the Science of Administration* (New York: Columbia University Press, 1937), pp. 181–87.

23. Barnard, *Functions,* pp. 108–9.

24. Ibid., pp. 96–99.

25. Ibid., pp. 128–32.

26. Barnard made few references to specific technologies. But his observation on the telephone and its impact on specialization was on the point. He wrote that even for something as useful as the telephone, "society . . . requires . . . the labor of hundreds of executives, hundreds of lawyers, thousands of engineers, thousands of experts in the mechanics and organization arts . . . to attain a usefulness still regarded as incomplete" (Barnard, draft, chapter 1 of *Functions,* p. 5).

27. See Joan Woodward, *Industrial Organization: Theory and Practice* (London: Oxford University Press, 1965); H. E. Aldrich, "Technology and Organizational Structure: A Reexamination of the Findings of the Aston Group," *Administrative Science Quarterly* 17 (1972): 26–43; and D. J. Hickson, et al., "Operations Technology and Organization Structure: An Empirical Reappraisal," *Administrative Science Quarterly* 14 (September 1969): 378–97.

28. P. R. Lawrence and J. W. Lorsch, *Organization and Environment: Managing Differentiation and Integration* (Boston: Division of Research, Harvard Graduate School of Business Administration, 1967).

29. Barnard, *Functions,* pp. 136–37.

30. See Alfred D. Chandler, Jr., *Strategy and Structure: Chapters in the History of American*

Industrial Enterprise (Cambridge, MA: MIT Press, 1962); *The Visible Hand: The Managerial Revolution in American Business* (Cambridge, MA: The Belknap Press of Harvard University Press, 1977); and *Scale and Scope* (Cambridge, MA: The Belknap Press of Harvard University Press, 1990).

31. Barnard, *Functions*, p. 138.

32. Barnard was fond of telling homey anecdotes to illustrate his points. In an extraordinary letter to a disgruntled customer, unhappy about the costs of the "Bell Telephone Hour" (a radio show sponsored by ATT in the 1930s and 1940s) he described how telephone operators gave service in times of emergency when they were under no obligation to do so. He wrote, "Last week there occurred a disastrous explosion at Woolridge, NJ. Within *ten minutes* of that explosion *every single off-duty operator* of our Woolridge exchange had called the Chief Operator to see if she was needed to help out in the inevitable overload of our service." Barnard thought that the employees' faith in ATT's "cause" of telephone service prompted them to volunteer to work more than what was ordinarily expected of them. The "Telephone Hour" seemed to increase employee pride in their company and to compensate them for their dedication. Barnard ended his letter with the observation that the radio show added only about six or seven cents annually to this customer's bill. He actually took the trouble to figure it out. It is barely conceivable that a high-ranking officer in a giant corporation today would write a customer (or stockholder for that matter) such a comprehensive, thoughtful, and personal letter explaining company policy. This letter is evidence that Barnard himself had faith in the generalized purpose of service at ATT. See BL, Barnard Collection, carton 1, p. 4, folder marked "Company Correspondence," which contains selected examples of letters written by Barnard when he was president of New Jersey Bell Telephone.

33. Ibid., pp. 139, 141.

34. Ibid., p. 140.

35. Barnard's interest in nonmaterial inducements not only related to the cost of tangible rewards but also to his knowledge of social science research findings and Pareto's idea of residues as it pertained to nonlogical behavior.

36. Barnard, *Functions*, p. 144.

37. Herbert Simon, *Administrative Behavior* (New York: Macmillan Company, 1947).

38. Barnard, *Functions*, p. 144.

39. People make the best decisions they can under the conditions of "bounded rationality." Because of these limitations of choice, decisions are always less than optimum.

40. F. Herzberg, *Work and the Nature of Man* (Cleveland: World Publishing, 1966).

41. Barnard, *Functions*, p. 144.

42. Ibid., p. 144.

43. Ibid., p. 146.

44. Ibid., p. 149.

45. Ibid., p. 151.

46. Ibid., p. 152.

47. See Elton Mayo, *The Human Problems of an Industrial Civilization* (Boston: Graduate School of Business Administration, Harvard University, 1933), esp. Chapter 4.

48. Ibid., p. 152.

49. Ibid., p. 184.

50. Ibid., p. 164. Harbord was John ("Blackjack") Pershing's chief of staff in the AEF during World War I. He became RCA's first president after the war when the company was formed.

51. Ibid., p. 167.

52. Ibid., p. 170.

53. Ibid., pp. 170–71.

54. Rabin and Miller point out that Barnard's hypotheses about employee compliance rested on two conditions: the exchange relationship (discussed above) and the individual's sense of

responsibility (discussed in chapter 9). See Jack Rabin and Gerald J. Miller, "Moral Code, Compliance with Authority, and Productivity," *Public Productivity Review* 12 (Summer 1989): 423.

55. Ibid., p. 165.

56. Ibid., p. 169.

57. In view of his interest in the psychological engineering of consent, Barnard did not deny the importance of management's objective authority. Rather he believed that objective authority, based upon position in an organizational hierarchy, was sanctified by private property and by the rights of agency that flowed therefrom. The whole idea behind his exchange theory was to secure compliance with objective authority.

58. Harvey C. Mansfield, Jr., *Taming the Prince: The Ambivalence of Modern Executive Power* (New York: Free Press, 1989), esp. chapter 6.

CHAPTER 8. THE LEADERSHIP ATTRIBUTES OF THE MANAGEMENT ELITE

1. Warren Bennis and Burt Nanus, *Leaders: The Strategies for Taking Charge* (New York: Harper and Row, 1985), p. 21.

2. Chester I. Barnard, "Persistent Dilemmas of Social Progress," address at Newark College of Engineering, June 12, 1936, BL, Barnard Collection, carton 1, p. 5.

3. Perrow clarified this premise. He wrote that in Barnard's opinion, "People cooperate in organizations. They join organizations voluntarily. They cooperate toward a goal, the goal of the organizations. Therefore, the goal could not fail to be moral, because morality emerges from cooperative endeavors." See Charles Perrow, *Complex Organizations*, 3d ed. (New York: Random House, 1986), pp. 65–66. Perrow's is an accurate first approximation of Barnard's views about the relationship between morality and cooperation. However, as we will see in the next chapter, his ideas were more complicated than this.

4. Miriam Beard, *A History of the Business Man* (New York: Macmillan Company, 1938), chapters 24 and 26. They needed all the help they could get to justify "aristocratization" in democratic America. For example, possessing every trapping of aristocracy except titles of nobility, the men of great wealth vied with each other in arranging marriages for their daughters with European noblemen. Beard noted that in 1898 alone $196,155,000 was transferred to titled Europeans as dowries. Illustrative of this point, Beard mentioned an incident that grew out of the Gould-Vanderbilt railroad rivalry. When Gould slashed his freight rates, "Vanderbilt bought up Western cattle and shipped them cheaply over his rival's lines. Gould retaliated by shipping his daughter abroad, marrying Anna to a French count. But Vanderbilt almost immediately scored again by uniting his Consuelo to an English Duke," p. 705.

5. See David K. Hart and William G. Scott, "The Philosophy of American Management," *Southern Review of Public Administration* 6 (1982): 240–52.

6. Barnard to Herbert Simon, September 5, 1947, BL, Barnard Collection, carton 1, p. 2. Henry Morgenthau's legendary devotion to FDR was rewarded with a cabinet appointment to secretary of the treasury. Barnard's low regard for Morgenthau's administrative ability may have been in the back of his mind when he commented to Simon about political influence in the selection of government executives.

7. Henry Moe to Joseph H. Willits, February 1, 1947, RAC, RG 3-910-box 10-folder 90. Willits transmitted this letter to Fosdick, who was nearing the end of his tenure as president of the Rockefeller Foundation. Fosdick returned the letter to Willits, two days later, with the appended note, "With support from better men than I, I've long wished some way might be found to set CIB [Chester I. Barnard] to the questions he posed—as well as the science of administration." Fosdick may have been alluding here to his interest in Barnard as a possible successor.

8. Chester I. Barnard, "The Development of Executive Ability," Sackett's Industrial Conference, 1925, Pennsylvania State College, BL, Barnard Collection, carton 1.

9. Chester I. Barnard to Amory K. Johnson, September 9, 1930. BL, Barnard Collection, carton 1, file marked "Correspondence."

10. Chester I. Barnard, "Education for Executives," *Journal of Business* 18 (October 1945): 175–82.

11. Chester I. Barnard, "Skill, Knowledge, and Judgement," an address to MIT graduating class, 1950, RAC, RG3-910, box 10, p. 4.

12. Ibid., p. 4.

13. Ibid., p. 21.

14. Chester I. Barnard, "Riot of the Unemployed at Trenton, NJ, 1935," in *Organization and Management*, pp. 51–79 (Cambridge, MA: Harvard University Press, 1948).

15. Chester I. Barnard, "Address after having been presented by the Newark Exchange Club with a medallion in recognition of distinguished service to the City of Newark during 1931-1932," BL, Barnard Collection, carton 1, p. 4, mimeographed.

16. Ibid., p. 5.

17. See Chester I. Barnard, "What Other Purpose?" commencement address, The Polytechnic Institute of Brooklyn, June 19, 1936, BL, Barnard Collection, carton 1; and Barnard to Talcott Parsons, October 27, 1939, BL, carton 1. This letter to Parsons is important on several counts. In it Barnard explained the meaning of "organizational maintenance" as management conservation of organizational assets, and that this applied to all types of organizations regardless of whether they were business, civic, educational, or philanthropic. Executive self-discipline was critical to organizational maintenance, and that "quite generally fear of loss, conservation of assets, protection of position are far more powerful forces in most of the world's commercial work than is acquisitiveness." This opinion reflects one of Barnard's own "derivations," a product of his long exposure to conservative ATT policies.

18. Chester I. Barnard, "Requirements of Leadership in a Democratic Society," address at a conference on the Cooperative Study of Teacher Education, October 24, 1940, BL, Barnard Collection, carton 1, p. 3.

19. On the function of intuition in decisionmaking in complex systems, see Barnard to Herbert Simon, September 5, 1947, BL, Barnard Collection, carton 1, p. 1. More will be said about this letter and another one to Simon in the next section on decisionmaking.

20. Barnard, "Requirements of Leadership," p. 3.

21. Chester I. Barnard, "Notes on Some Obscure Aspects of Human Relations," speech given to Professor Philip Cabot's business executive group at the Harvard Graduate School of Business Administration, March 6, 1939, BL, Barnard Collection, carton 1, pp. 7–8.

22. Barnard privately published this letter as a pamphlet. See Chester I. Barnard, "Concerning the Theory of Modern Price Systems," March 10, 1941, BL, Barnard Collection, carton 1.

23. Adolf A. Berle, Jr., *The 20th Century Capitalist Revolution* (New York: Harcourt, Brace and Company, 1954), p. 63.

24. Barnard's clearest and most direct statement on this subject was in a long footnote in his book. He pointed out that understanding complex management situations can only be acquired by "intimate and habitual association" with them, and even then managers' understanding of complexity is not "practically susceptible, quickly to verbal expression." Barnard noted that when one attempted to analyze complexity in terms of a single variable, such as economic forces, one ran the risk of falling into Whitehead's fallacy of "misplaced concreteness." Such analysis, he said, was merely the beginning of purposive management action, not the end of it. See Chester I. Barnard, *The Functions of the Executive* (Cambridge, MA: Harvard University Press, 1938), p. 239.

25. Ibid., p. 215.

26. James P. Thompson, *Organizations in Action* (New York: McGraw-Hill Book Company, 1967).

27. See Barnard, *Functions*. Chapters 11 and 12 pertain to individual decisionmaking; chapters 13 and 14 are mostly about organizational decisionmaking. In chapter 13, "The Environment of Decision," he draws the distinction between individual and organizational decisions. Barnard's neglected appendix, "The Mind in Everyday Affairs," also concerns decisionmaking, wherein he expands upon the Paretan categories of residues and derivations and the role that they play in nonlogical behavior. He told the engineering faculty and students at Princeton, where this material was first presented as an address in 1936, that they should not expect most people to be as logical as they were trained to be in their approach to solving problems. See ibid., pp. 301-22.

28. Ibid., p. 185.

29. Ibid., pp. 281-82.

30. Ibid., p. 220.

31. Barnard to Herbert Simon, May 11, 1945, BL, Barnard Collection, carton 1, file marked "Correspondence." This is the letter to which Simon referred when acknowledging Barnard's review of a preliminary draft of his book. See Herbert Simon, *Administrative Behavior* (New York: Macmillan Company, 1947), pp. xv-xvi.

32. Simon mentioned later in an interview with Golembiewski that the decision premise was a pivotal concept upon which he based his entire theory of decisionmaking. See Robert T. Golembiewski, "Nobel Laureate Simon 'Looks Back': A Low Frequency Mode," *Public Administration Quarterly* 12 (Fall 1988): 284-85.

33. Barnard to Simon, May 11, 1945, BL, Barnard Collection, carton 1, file marked "Correspondence," p. 1.

34. Simon, *Administrative Behavior*, p. 190. Simon was particularly unhappy about Barnard's "Mind in Everyday Affairs," the appendix to his book. He blamed Barnard, along with others in the human relations movement, of trying to "make administrative ignorance a virtue."

35. Barnard to Herbert Simon, September 5, 1947, BL, Barnard Collection, carton 1, p. 1.

36. Such as Charles J. Fox and Clarke C. Cochran, "Discretion Advocacy in Public Administration Theory: Toward a Platonic Guardian Class?" *Administration and Society* 22 (August 1990): 249-71.

37. Chester I. Barnard, draft, chapter 1 of *Functions*. An early draft of the first chapter of *The Functions of the Executive*, BL, Barnard Collection, carton 1, p. 7. This passage summarizes Barnard's argument that management discretion is limited, and therefore managers are not as free as some think to dominate either the internal or external conditions of organization. It is regrettable that this justification of management discretion is not stated directly in the published version of Barnard's book, although the message is implicit in the text. Barnard recognized that management competence was itself limited and therefore he relied on moral virtue to justify management's unique position of power.

CHAPTER 9. THE MORAL OBLIGATIONS OF THE ELITE

1. See for example, Charles J. Fox and Clarke C. Cochran, "Discretion Advocacy in Public Administration Theory: Toward a Platonic Guardian Class?" *Administration and Society* 22 (August 1990): 249-71.

2. Gerald E. Frug identified five of these conditions as typical of the arguments for legitimizing management discretion. However, he did not notice the virtue argument that Barnard heavily relied upon. See Frug, "The Ideology of Bureaucracy in American Law," *Harvard Law Review* 97 (Spring 1984): 1277-1388.

3. A theme eloquently argued by Harvey C. Mansfield, Jr., *Taming the Prince: The Ambivalence of Modern Executive Power* (New York: Free Press, 1989).

4. See Frug, "Ideology of Bureaucracy," pp. 1278, 1386-88. Also see Carole Pateman, *Participation and Democratic Theory* (Cambridge: Cambridge University Press, 1990), and

Frederick C. Thayer, *An End to Hierarchy and Competition* (New York: New Viewpoints, 1981).

5. Mansfield, *Taming the Prince*, p. 297.

6. Chester I. Barnard, "Memorandum on Modern Problems of Morals and Ethics," manuscript, 1946, RAC Series 900, box 56, folder 303, p. 1.

7. Chester I. Barnard, "Elementary Conditions of Business Morals," *California Management Review* 1 (Fall 1958): 1–13.

8. The fundamental ideas in Barnard's moral philosophy were intact from 1938, when his book was published, until 1961 when he was interviewed by William B. Wolf. Barnard died two months after this interview. See William B. Wolf, *Conversations with Chester I. Barnard*, ILR Paperback No. 12 (Ithaca, N.Y.: Cornell University, School of Industrial and Labor Relations, 1972).

9. Chester I. Barnard, *The Functions of the Executive* (Cambridge, MA: Harvard University Press, 1938), p. 296.

10. Barnard to F. Ernest Johnson, March 28, 1946, RAC Series 900, box 56, folder 303, p. 2.

11. Barnard, *Functions*, p. 296.

12. David L. Norton, *Personal Destinies* (Princeton: Princeton University Press, 1976), pp. 64–79.

13. Edmund L. Pincoffs, *Quandaries and Virtues: Against Reductivism in Ethics* (Lawrence: University Press of Kansas, 1986), p. 31.

14. Barnard, *Functions,* p. 279.

15. Ibid. (emphasis in the original), p. 269. This incident had a happy ending. "The mother was rescued," Barnard said in a laconic footnote.

16. Pincoffs, *Quandaries and Virtues*, pp. 28–29.

17. Alberto Guerreiro Ramos took particular exception to Barnard's telephone operator example, calling her conscientious, rule-driven behavior "a striking illustration of the rejection of direct experience of reality." See Ramos, *The New Science of Organizations* (Toronto: University of Toronto Press, 1981), p. 99.

18. Pincoffs, *Quandaries and Virtues*, p. 29.

19. The Rockefeller Foundation supported medical and public health projects in many countries. However, China was a favored recipient of generous grants and endowments in these areas through the China Medical Board and the Peking Union Medical College. Fosdick reported that between 1921 and 1949 the Foundation contributed nearly $47 million to advance Chinese medicine. Therefore, it is little wonder that China figured heavily in the Foundation's postwar plans. See Raymond B. Fosdick, *The Story of the Rockefeller Foundation* (1952; reprint, New Brunswick, NJ: Transaction Publishers, 1989), pp. 88ff.

20. See *A Righteous Faith for a Just and Durable Peace* (New York: Commission to Study the Bases of a Just and Durable Peace, 1942).

21. Van Dusen remarked that Dulles underwent "something of a conversion" in 1937, doing an about face on the Christian churches' ability to affect the direction of world order. He moved from skepticism and cynicism to a complete commitment to the notion that Christianity could exert a positive influence in world affairs. Due largely to Dulles's leadership, the commission became a powerful voice in national policy toward Germany and Japan—a policy that rested on rebuilding and reeducating these former enemies and a 180-degree shift from the Treaty of Versailles! This policy had been central to the commission's program from the time of its inception. See Henry P. Van Dusen, ed., *The Spiritual Legacy of John Foster Dulles* (Philadelphia: Westminister Press, 1960), pp. 3–4.

22. Barnard to Henry P. Van Dusen, August 31, 1948, RAC, series 900, box 56, folder 303. Barnard's letter to Van Dusen has a helpful summary of events in the Foundation that led to its consideration of the possibilities of establishing a "Division of Moral Philosophy."

23. William E. Hocking to Barnard, September 6, 1946, RAC, series 900, box 56, folder 303.

24. Ibid., p. 7.

25. John Foster Dulles to Barnard, May 20, 1946, RAC, series 900, box 56, folder 304.

26. Memorandum from Barnard to Dean Rusk, June 11, 1952, RAC, series 900, box 54, folder 304, p. 1. Written just before his retirement from the Foundation, Barnard intended to orient Rusk to important policy issues still pending and to warn him of the pitfalls of sectarian support in ethics and morals projects.

27. Barnard to Branscomb, June 3, 1949, RAC, series 900, box 56, folder 304.

28. Joseph Willits to Dean Rusk, RF memorandum, August 4, 1953, RAC, series 900, box 59, folder 304. Gifford's remark was not entirely flippant. RF policy was to give grants to proposals that promised to be of "benefit to all mankind." Therefore, RF allotted a large portion of its resources to fund projects in medical science and public health. Given that the common cold was a plague of all mankind and one of the chief reasons for absenteeism at work, Gifford's comment made good sense.

29. Included among the many who responded were Walter Gifford, president of ATT; John S. Keir, president of Denison Manufacturing Company; Sen. Ralph Flanders of Massachusetts, and academics such as William Hocking, Fritz Roethlisberger, George Stigler, Frank Knight, and Jacob Viner.

30. Barnard to Henry P. Van Dusen, August 31, 1948, RAC, series 900, box 56, folder 303, p. 1.

31. Ibid., p. 1.

32. Ibid., p. 4.

33. These grants added up to a substantial sum. Between 1948 and 1951, roughly the years of Barnard's presidency, the Humanities and Social Science divisions provided $325,000 to fund research and lectures on the subjects of values and ethics. Although most of the individual grants were modest, some were notable, such as the social science division's grants of $100,000 to the Federal Council of Churches' Department of Church and Economic Life and $69,000 to the University of Notre Dame. See memorandum, November 28, 1951, RAC, series 900, box 56, folder 304. These grants were made under Barnard's presidential aegis, and the Federal Council grant was referred to by Barnard and others as the major achievement of his presidency in the ethics and morals field.

34. Statement by John Foster Dulles, minutes of meeting of board of trustees, April 2, 1951, RAC, series 900, box 56, folder 304, p. 2.

35. See John Foster Dulles, *War or Peace* (New York: Macmillan, 1950).

36. Ibid., p. 3.

37. This reference to the charter is mentioned in an excerpt from a letter from Barnard to the board of trustees, October 22, 1951, RAC, series 900, Policy and Programs.

38. Among other things, it created a flurry of memoranda pertaining to the support of philosophy and religion by private philanthropy. One interesting memo was written by Lelund C. DeVinney, Willits's second in command in the Social Science Division. As a counterpoint to Dulles's argument, DeVinney showed that one-half of all private giving went to support religious institutions. In 1950, this amounted to nearly $1.9 billion. See interoffice correspondence from DeVinney to Joseph Willits, October 18, 1951, RAC, series 900, box 56, folder 304, p. 4.

39. Joseph Willits to Dean Rusk, memorandum, March 24, 1953, RAC, series 900, box 56, folder 304, p. 4.

40. Ibid., p. 4.

41. Joseph Willits to Dean Rusk, memorandum, August 4, 1953, RAC, series 900, box 56, folder 304, p. 6.

42. Herbert A. Deane to Joseph Willits, memorandum, April 17, 1953, RAC, series 900, box 56, folder 304, p. 2.

43. RAC, Union Theological Seminary, 1952, series 200, Religious Studies, archives 2, p. 64.

44. Of course, Van Dusen had been arguing all along that this was not a policy reversal. Speaking of the "permissive" clause, which Dulles was fond of citing, he pointed out that the intentions of the incorporators of the Foundation were clearly not to eliminate sectarian causes from support. He dismissed the possibility of controversy that such a grant would raise with other religious groups by suggesting that any grant, regardless of the area, automatically excludes competitors who think they have just claims for support. See Henry P. Van Dusen to Dean Rusk, March 30, 1953, RAC, series 900, box 56, folder 304.

45. Chester I. Barnard to Dean Rusk, memorandum, June 11, 1952, RAC, series 900, box 56, folder 304, p. 2.

46. Barnard, "Memorandum on Modern Problems of Morals and Ethics."

CHAPTER 10. THE NEW ORDER OF NATIONAL POWER AND ORGANIZATIONAL GOVERNANCE

1. Bertrand de Jouvenel to Barnard, June 25, 1956, BL, Barnard Collection, carton 1, folder marked "Correspondence."

2. See for example, Sheldon S. Wolin, "Politics as a Vocation," *American Political Science Review* 63 (December 1969); and *Politics and Vision* (Boston: Little, Brown and Company, 1960), especially chapter 10. Wolin was particularly disturbed by displacement of political theory by organization theory by such scholars as Philip Selznick.

3. Alexis de Tocqueville, *Democracy in America*, trans. J. P. Meyer 1835; reprint, (Garden City, NY: Doubleday, 1967).

4. Herbert McClosky and John Zaller, *The American Ethos* (Cambridge, MA: Harvard University Press, 1984).

5. See William G. Scott and David K. Hart, *Organizational Values in America* (New Brunswick, NJ: Transaction Books, 1989); and William G. Scott, "The Management Governance Theories of Liberty and Justice," *Journal of Management* 14 (1988): 277-98.

6. The term *regime values* was coined by John A. Rohr, *To Run a Constitution* (Lawrence: University Press of Kansas, 1986), in which he argues for the constitutional legitimacy of the administrative state that he takes to mean an activist federal government.

7. Harvey C. Mansfield, Jr., *Taming the Prince: The Ambivalence of Modern Executive Power* (New York: Free Press, 1989), p. 140.

8. See Chester I. Barnard, "Review of Barbara Wootton's *Freedom under Planning*," *Southern Economic Journal* 12 (January 12, 1946): 290-300.

9. Barnard had a second theory of freedom, the "parceling out" theory based on the bizarre assumption that there was a fixed amount of freedom at any given time. This "lump of freedom" had to be rationed, with the managerial elite distributing it among various institutions. Barnard was less successful arguing for this point of view for the obvious reason that it was ridiculous. In any event it led him to the same conclusion as his trade-off theory. All of this is found in ibid., pp. 298-300.

10. Chester I. Barnard, *The Functions of the Executive* (Cambridge, MA: Harvard University Press, 1938), p. 279.

11. Chester I. Barnard, excerpt from draft of notes on "The Requirements of Leadership in Democratic Societies," October 1940, BL, Barnard Collection, carton 1, pp. 7-8.

12. Barnard, review of Wootton, p. 299.

13. Chester I. Barnard, "Persistent Dilemmas of Social Progress," address at the Newark College of Engineering, June 12, 1936, BL, Barnard Collection, carton 1, p. 22.

14. See an interview with Barnard, "Business Integration Essential to Stabilized Progress," *Journal of Industry and Finance*, 1930, in ATTA, 5S-05-01-09.

15. Ibid., p. 3.

16. Ibid., p. 4.

17. Ibid., p. 8 (emphasis in the original).

18. Chester I. Barnard, "Methods and Limitations of Foresight in Modern Affairs," address to Thirtieth Annual Convention of the Association of Life Insurance Presidents, December 4, 1936, BL, Barnard Collection, carton 1.

19. Ibid., p. 16.

20. Barnard, review of Wootton, p. 299.

21. For representative examples see J. S. Adams, "Inequity in Social Exchange," in L. Berkowitz, ed., *Advances in Experimental Social Psychology*, vol. 2 (New York: Academic Press, 1965), pp. 267-99; P. S. Goodman and A. Friedman, "An Examination of Adam's Theory of Inequity," *Administrative Science Quarterly* 16 (1971): 271-88; and Jerald Greenberg, "Looking Fair vs. Being Fair," in B. M. Staw and L. L. Cummings, eds., *Research in Organizational Behavior* (Greenwich, CT: JAI Press, 1990), 12:111-58.

22. Barnard, *Functions*, pp. 222-23.

23. Ibid., pp. 279-80.

24. See for example, Carole Pateman, *Participation and Democratic Theory* (Cambridge: Cambridge University Press, 1970); and Frederick C. Thayer, *An End to Hierarchy and Competition* (New York: New Viewpoints, 1981).

25. Terence R. Mitchell and William G. Scott, "America's Problems and Needed Reforms: Confronting the Ethics of Personal Advantage," *Academy of Management Executive* (August 1990): 23-35.

26. Barnard, *Functions*, p. 295.

27. Barnard to Herbert Simon, December 13, 1946, BL, Barnard Collection, carton 1, folder marked "Correspondence."

28. McClosky and Zaller, *American Ethos*, chapter 9.

29. Although individualism tends to come in and out of favor cyclically, the long-term effect has been a ratcheting up of communitarian values in the American ethos. This phenomenon has been commented on by numerous writers. See for example William H. Whyte, Jr., *The Organization Man* (New York: Simon and Schuster, 1956); and William G. Scott and David K. Hart, *Organizational Values in America* (New Brunswick, NJ: Transaction Books, 1989).

CHAPTER 11. THE EXHAUSTION OF MANAGERIALISM

1. Walter Lippmann, *The Method of Freedom* (New York: Macmillan Company, 1934).

2. Lyford P. Edwards, *The Natural History of Revolution* (Chicago: University of Chicago Press, 1927, 1970), p. 221.

3. See Seymour M. Lipset and William Schneider, *The Confidence Gap: Business, Labor, and Government in the Public Mind* (New York: Free Press, 1983).

4. *Gallup Report*, February 7, 1985, Princeton, NJ.

5. *Gallup Poll*, July 1985, Report #238, Princeton, NJ.

6. Lipset and Schneider, *Confidence Gap*, pp. 111-13.

7. Robert N. Bellah et al., *Habits of the Heart* (Berkeley: University of California Press, 1985).

8. H. S. Geneen, "Why Directors Can't Protect the Shareholders," *Fortune* 1101 (September 19, 1984): 28-32.

9. M. P. Fiorina, "Flagellating the Federal Bureaucracy," *Society* 20 (March-April 1983): 67.

10. Quoted in D. Bonafede, "Muzzling the Media," *National Journal*, July 12, 1986, pp. 1716-20.

11. Fiorina, "Flagellating the Federal Bureaucracy," p. 72.

12. Quoted in W. J. Moore, "Corporate Cover," *National Journal*, December 6, 1986,p. 2964.

13. Peter Drucker, *The Practice of Management* (New York: Harper and Brothers, 1954), p. 4.

14. Alasdair MacIntyre, *After Virtue* (Notre Dame: University of Notre Dame Press, 1981), p. 71.

15. R. D. Hackett and R. M. Guion, "A Reevaluation of the Absenteeism-Job Satisfaction Relationship," *Organization Behavior and Human Decision Processes* 35 (June 1985): 340-81; L. H. Peters, D. D. Hartke, and J. T. Pohlman, "Fiedler's Contingency Theory of Leadership: An Application of the Meta-Analysis Procedures of Schmidt and Hunter," *Psychological Bulletin*, 97 (March 1985): 274-85; S. L. Premock and J. P. Wanous, "A Meta-Analysis of Realistic Job Preview Experiences," *Journal of Applied Psychology* 70 (November 1985): 706-19; J. L. Cotton and J. M. Tuttle, "Employee Turnover: A Meta-Analysis and Review with Implications for Research," *Academy of Management Review* 11 (January 1986): 55-70; G. M. McEvoy and W. F. Cascio, "Strategies for Reducing Employee Turnover: A Meta-Analysis," *Journal of Applied Psychology* 70 (May 1985): 342-53; R. P. Steel and N. K. Ovalle, "A Review and Meta-Analysis of Research on the Relationship between Behavioral Intentions and Employee Turnover," *Journal of Applied Psychology* 69 (November 1984): 673-86; M. T. Iaffaldano and P. M. Muchinsky, "Job Satisfaction and Job Performance: A Meta-Analysis," *Psychological Bulletin* 97 (March 1985): 251-73; B. T. Loher, R. A. Noe, N. L. Moeller, and M. P. Fitzgerald, "A Meta-Analysis of the Relation of Job Characteristics to Job Satisfaction," *Journal of Applied Psychology* 70 (May 1985): 280-89.

16. Herbert Simon, *Administrative Behavior* (New York: Macmillan Company, 1947, 1954), pp. 37, 42.

17. Loren Baritz. *The Servants of Power* (Middletown, CT: Wesleyan University Press, 1960).

18. As Gerald E. Frug commented, "A theory of democratic consent could validate every action taken by a bureaucratic organization." See Frug, "The Ideology of Bureaucracy in American Law," *Harvard Law Review* 97 (Spring 1984): 1354.

19. Bertrand de Jouvenel, *On Power* (Boston: Beacon Press, 1948, 1969), p. 378.

20. The sovereign immunity rule has been modified so that public sector executives are now more open to such legal actions, unlike their counterparts in the private sector.

21. MacIntyre, *After Virtue*, pp. 55-57.

22. This revision of the Bennis-Nanus slogan may be a way to resolve the "debilitating split" between leadership and management discussed by James Krantz and Thomas N. Gilmore, "The Splitting of Leadership and Management as a Social Defense," *Human Relations* 43, No. 2 (1990): 183-204.

23. Chester I. Barnard, "Methods and Limitations of Foresight in Modern Affairs," address to Thirtieth Annual Convention of the Association of Life Insurance Presidents, December 4, 1936, BL, Barnard Collection, carton 1, p. 17.

24. Alberto Guerreiro Ramos, *The New Science of Organization* (Toronto: University of Toronto Press, 1981).

25. Henry Mintzberg, *Structure in Fives: Designing Effective Organizations* (Englewood Cliffs, NJ: Prentice-Hall, 1983).

EPILOGUE: THE MANAGEMENT OF CRISIS AND TRIBULATION

1. Mindy Fetterman, "Autocratic Leaders Now Out of Step," *USA Today*, December 9, 1991, p. 2B.

2. Roberto Michels, *Political Parties* (Glencoe: Free Press, 1915, 1958), p. 418. Prefacing this famous statement, Michels wrote, "It is organization which gives birth to the dominion of the elected over the electors, of the mandatories over the mandators, of the delegates over the delegators. Who says organization, says oligarchy" (p. 418).

3. Peter F. Drucker, *America's Next Twenty Years* (New York: Harper and Brothers, 1955), p. 51.

Selected Bibliography

PRIMARY SOURCES

American Telephone and Telegraph Company Archives, Warren, NJ.
Baker Library, Graduate School of Business Administration, Harvard University, Barnard
  Collection, Boston, MA.
National Archives, Washington, D.C.
National Science Board Records, Washington, D.C.
New Jersey Bell Telephone Company Records, Newark, NJ.
Northfield-Mount Hermon School Archives, Northfield, MA.
Rockefeller Archive Center, North Tarrytown, NY.

SECONDARY SOURCES

Selected General References

Adams, Henry. *The Education of Henry Adams: An Autobiography.* Boston: Houghton
  Mifflin, 1918, 1961.
Adams, J. S. "Inequity in Social Exchange." In L. Berkowitz, ed., *Advances in Experi-
  mental Social Psychology*, pp. 267-99. Vol. 2. New York: Academic Press, 1965.
Adelstein, Richard P. " 'The Nation as an Economic Unit': Keynes, Roosevelt, and the
  Managerial Ideal." *Journal of American History* (June 1991): 160-87.
Alchon, Guy. *The Invisible Hand of Planning.* Princeton: Princeton University Press,
  1985.
Barber, Bernard, ed. *L. J. Henderson on the Social System.* Chicago: University of
  Chicago Press, 1970.
Baritz, Loren. *The Servants of Power.* Middletown, CT: Wesleyan University Press,
  1960.
Beard, Miriam. *A History of the Business Man.* New York: Macmillan Company, 1938.
Bellah, Robert N., et al. *Habits of the Heart.* Berkeley: University of California Press,
  1985.
Bem, D. J. "Self Perception Theory." In L. Berkowitz, ed., *Advances in Experimental
  Social Psychology*, pp. 1-62. New York: Academic Press, 1972.

217

Bendix, Reinhard. *Work and Authority in Industry: Ideologies of Management in the Course of Industrialization.* New York: Wiley, 1956.

Bennis, Warren, and Burt Nanus. *Leaders: The Strategies for Taking Charge.* New York: Harper and Row, 1985.

Berle, Adolf A., Jr. *The 20th Century Capitalist Revolution.* New York: Harcourt, Brace and Company, 1954.

Berle, Adolf A., Jr., and Gardiner C. Means. *The Modern Corporation and Private Property.* New York: Macmillan Company, 1933.

Borkenau, Franz. *Pareto.* New York: John Wiley and Sons, 1936.

Bramel, D., and R. Friend. "Hawthorne, the Myth of the Docile Worker, and Class Bias in Psychology." *American Psychologist* 36 (August 1951): 867-78.

Brown, Junius F. *Psychology and the Social Order.* New York: McGraw-Hill Book Company, 1936.

Burnham, James. *The Managerial Revolution: What Is Happening in the World.* New York: John Day Company, 1941.

Chandler, Alfred D., Jr. *The Visible Hand: The Managerial Revolution in American Business.* Cambridge, MA: Belknap Press of Harvard University Press, 1977.

————. *Strategy and Structure: Chapters in the History of American Industrial Enterprise.* Cambridge, MA: MIT Press, 1962.

Commons, John R. *Institutional Economics.* New York: Macmillan Company, 1934.

Coon, Horace. *American Tel and Tel.* New York: Longmans, Green and Co., 1939.

Copeland, Melvin T. *And Mark an Era.* Boston: Little, Brown and Company, 1958.

Copley, Frank B. *Frederick W. Taylor: Father of Scientific Management.* New York: Harper and Brothers, 1923.

Cuff, Robert D. *The War Industries Board.* Baltimore: Johns Hopkins University Press, 1973.

Cunningham, William J. "Scientific Management in the Operation of the Railroads," in Clarence B. Thompson, ed., *Scientific Management*, pp. 580-99. Cambridge, MA: Harvard University Press, 1914.

Davis, Ralph C. *Industrial Organization and Management.* New York: Harper and Brothers, 1928, 1940.

de Jouvenel, Bertrand. *On Power.* Boston: Beacon Press, 1948, 1969.

De Voto, Bernard. "Sentiment and the Social Order." *Harpers Monthly Magazine* 167 (October 1933): 569-81.

Diamond, Sigmund. *The Reputation of the American Businessman.* Cambridge, MA: Harvard University Press, 1955.

Donham, Wallace B. "The Failure of Business Leadership and the Responsibility of Universities." *Harvard Business Review* 11 (July 1933): 418-35.

————. "The Social Significance of Business." *Harvard Business Review* 5 (July 1927): 406-19.

Drucker, Peter F. *America's Next Twenty Years.* New York: Harper and Brothers, 1955.

————. *The Practice of Management.* New York: Harper and Brothers, 1954.

————. *The New Society: The Anatomy of the Industrial Order.* New York: Harper and Brothers, 1950.

Edwards, Lyford P. *The Natural History of Revolution.* Chicago: University of Chicago Press, 1927, 1970.

England, Merton. *A Patron for Pure Science.* Washington, D.C.: National Science Foundation, 1982.

Ehrlich, Eugene. *Fundamental Principles in the Sociology of Law.* Translated by Walter L. Moll. Cambridge, MA: Harvard University Press, 1936.

Fausold, Martin L. *The Presidency of Hoover.* Lawrence: University Press of Kansas, 1985.

Fayol, Henri. *General and Industrial Management.* London: Pitman, 1949.

Fearon, Peter. *War, Prosperity, and Depression.* Oxford: Philip Allan Publishers, 1987.

Festinger, L. *A Theory of Cognitive Dissonance.* Evanston: Row, Peterson, 1951.

Fiorina, M. P. "Flagellating the Federal Bureaucracy." *Society* 20 (March–April 1983): 66–73.

Follett, Mary Parker. "Constructive Conflict (Chapter 1 of *Dynamic Administration*)" in *Some Classical Contributions to Professional Management*, pp. 97–110, vol. 1 (New York: General Electric, 1956).

———. "The Process of Control." In Luther Gulick and Lyndall Urwick, eds., *Papers on the Science of Administration*, pp. 159-69. New York: Columbia University Press, 1937.

———. *Dynamic Administration.* London: Pitman, 1926, 1941.

Fosdick, Raymond B. *The Story of the Rockefeller Foundation.* New York: Harper and Brothers, 1952. New Brunswick, NJ: Transaction Publishers, 1989.

Fox, Charles J., and Clarke C. Cochran. "Discretion Advocacy in Public Administration Theory: Toward a Platonic Guardian Class?" *Administration and Society* 22 (August 1990): 249-71.

Franke, R. H. "The Hawthorne Studies Revisited." *American Sociological Review* 44 (1979): 861-67.

Frug, Gerald E. "The Ideology of Bureaucracy in American Law." *Harvard Law Review* 97 (Spring 1984): 1277-1388.

Galbraith, John Kenneth. *The New Industrial State.* 3d ed. Boston: Houghton Mifflin, 1978.

Gilbreth, Frank B. *Primer of Scientific Management.* London: Constable and Company, 1912.

Gilbreth, Lillian. *The Psychology of Management.* New York: Sturgis and Walton, 1914.

Graicunas, V. A. "Relationships in Organization," in Luther Gulick and Lyndall Urwick, eds., *Papers on the Science of Administration*, pp. 181-87. New York: Columbia University Press, 1937.

Grant, James. *Bernard M. Baruch: The Adventures of a Wall Street Legend.* New York: Simon and Schuster, 1983.

Greenberg, Jerald. "Looking Fair vs. Being Fair." In B. M. Staw and L. L. Cummings, eds., *Research in Organizational Behavior*, pp. 111-57. Vol. 12. Greenwich, CT: JAI Press, 1990.

Grumwald, A. G. "The Totalitarian Ego." *American Psychologist* 35 (1980): 603-18.

Gulick, Luther, and Lyndall Urwick, eds., *Papers on the Science of Administration.* New York: Columbia University Press, 1937.

Harr, John E., and Peter J. Johnson. *The Rockefeller Century.* New York: Charles Scribner's Sons, 1988.

Hart, David K., and William G. Scott. "The Philosophy of American Management." *Southern Review of Public Administration* 6 (1982): 240-52.

Hawley, Ellis W., ed. *Herbert Hoover as Secretary of Commerce.* Iowa City: University of Iowa Press, 1981.

———. *The Great War and the Search for a Modern Order.* New York: St. Martin's Press, 1979.

Henderson, Lawrence J. *Pareto's General Sociology.* Cambridge, MA: Harvard University Press, 1935.

Herzberg, F. *Work and the Nature of Man.* Cleveland: World Publishing Company, 1966.

Hickson, D. J. et al. "Operations Technology and Organization Structure: An Empirical Reappraisal." *Administrative Science Quarterly* 14 (September 1969): 378-97.

Homans, George C. *Coming to My Senses*. New Brunswick, NJ: Transaction Books, 1984.

Homans, George C., and Orville T. Bailey. "The Society of Fellows, Harvard University, 1933-1947." In Crane Brinton, ed., *The Society of Fellows*, pp. 1-37. Cambridge, MA: Harvard University Press, 1959.

Homans, George C., and Charles P. Curtis, Jr. *An Introduction to Pareto*. New York: Alfred A. Knopf, 1934.

Hoover, Herbert. *The Ordeal of Woodrow Wilson*. New York: McGraw-Hill, 1958.

——. *The Challenge to Liberty*. New York: Charles Scribner's Sons, 1934.

——. *American Individualism*. New York: Doubleday, Page and Company, 1922.

Johnson, Paul. *Modern Times*. New York: Harper and Row, 1983.

Karl, Barry Dean. *Charles E. Merriam and the Study of Politics*. Chicago: University of Chicago Press, 1974.

——. *Executive Reorganization and Reform in the New Deal*. Cambridge, MA: Harvard University Press, 1963.

Koffka, Kurt. *Principles of Gestalt Psychology*. New York: Harcourt, Brace and Company, 1935.

Krantz, James, and Thomas N. Gilmore. "The Splitting of Leadership and Management as a Social Defense." *Human Relations* 43, no. 2 (1990): 183-204.

Langer, E. J. "The Illusion of Control." *Journal of Personality and Social Psychology* 32 (1977): 311-28.

Laumann, Edward O., and David Knoke. *The Organizational State: Social Change in National Policy Domains*. Madison: University of Wisconsin Press, 1987.

Lawrence, P. R. and J. W. Lorsch. *Organization and Environment: Managing Differentiation and Integration*. Boston: Division of Research, Harvard Graduate School of Business Administration, 1967.

Lippmann, Walter. *The Method of Freedom*. New York: Macmillan Company, 1934.

Lipset, Seymour M., and William Schneider. *The Confidence Gap: Business, Labor, and Government in the Public Mind*. New York: Free Press, 1983.

McClosky, Herbert, and John Zaller. *The American Ethos*. Cambridge, MA: Harvard University Press, 1984.

MacIntyre, Alasdair. *After Virtue*. Notre Dame: University of Notre Dame Press, 1981.

Mansfield, Harvey C., Jr. *Taming the Prince: The Ambivalence of Modern Executive Power*. New York: Free Press, 1989.

Mayo, Elton. *Social Problems of an Industrial Civilization*. Boston: Division of Research, Graduate School of Business Administration, Harvard University, 1945.

——. *The Human Problems of an Industrial Civilization*. Cambridge, MA: Harvard University Press, 1933.

Michels, Roberto. "Authority." In E. R. A. Seligman, ed., *Encyclopaedia of the Social Sciences*, pp. 319-21. New York: Macmillan Company, 1930.

Miller, L., and R. Hamblin. "Interdependence, Differential Rewarding and Productivity." *American Sociological Review* 28 (1963): 768-78.

Miller, Peter, and Ted O'Leary. "Hierarchies and American Ideals, 1900-1940." *Academy of Management Review* 14 (April 1989): 250-65.

Mintzberg, Henry. *Structure in Fives: Designing Effective Organizations*. Englewood Cliffs, NJ: Prentice-Hall, 1983.

Mooney, James D., and Alan C. Reiley. *Onward Industry*. New York: Harper and Brothers, 1931.

Norton, David L. *Democracy and Moral Development*. Berkeley: University of California Press, 1991.

———. *Personal Destinies*. Princeton: Princeton University Press, 1976.

Orwell, George. *James Burnham and the Managerial Revolution*. London: Socialist Book Center, 1946.

Pareto, Vilfredo. *The Mind and Society*. Translated by Andrew Bongiorno and Arthur Livingstone. New York: Harcourt, Brace and Company, 1935.

Parsons, Talcott. *The Social System*. London: Free Press of Glencoe, 1951.

———. *The Structure of Social Action*. 2d ed. Glencoe: The Free Press, 1949.

Pateman, Carole. *Participation and Democratic Theory*. Cambridge: Cambridge University Press, 1970.

Peters, Thomas J., and Richard H. Waterman, Jr. *In Search of Excellence*. New York: Harper and Row, 1982.

Pincoffs, Edmund L. *Quandaries and Virtues: Against Reductivism in Ethics*. Lawrence: University Press of Kansas, 1986.

Rabin, Jack, and Gerald J. Miller. "Moral Code, Compliance with Authority, and Productivity." *Public Productivity Review* 12 (Summer 1989): 423-35.

Ramos, Alberto Guerreiro. *The New Science of Organization*. Toronto: University of Toronto Press, 1981.

Ripley, William Z. *Main Street and Wall Street*. Boston: Little, Brown and Company, 1927.

Roethlisberger, Fritz J. *Management and Morale*. Cambridge, MA: Harvard University Press, 1941.

Roethlisberger, Fritz J., and William J. Dickson. *Management and the Worker*. Cambridge, MA: Harvard University Press, 1939.

Rohr, John A. *To Run a Constitution*. Lawrence: University Press of Kansas, 1986.

Schaar, John H. "Legitimacy in the Modern States." In Philip Green and Sanford Levinson, eds., *Power and Community*, pp. 276-327. New York: Pantheon Books, 1970.

Simon, Herbert. *Administrative Behavior*. New York: Macmillan Company, 1947.

Skowronek, Stephen. *Building a New American State*. Cambridge: Cambridge University Press, 1982.

Stegner, Wallace. *The Uneasychair: A Biography of Bernard De Voto*. New York: Doubleday and Company, 1974.

Taylor, Frederick W. "The Principles of Scientific Management." In *Scientific Management*, pp. 1-144. New York: Harper and Brothers, 1911, 1939, 1947.

———. "A Piece-Rate System." *Transactions*, 16, pp. 856-903, ASME, 1895.

Thayer, Frederick C. *An End to Hierarchy and Competition*. New York: New Viewpoints, 1981.

Thompson, James P. *Organizations in Action*. New York: McGraw-Hill Book Company, 1967.

Towne, Henry. "The Engineer as an Economist." *Transactions*, 7, pp. 428-32. ASME, 1886.

Trahair, Richard S. C. *The Humanist Temper*. New Brunswick, NJ: Transaction Books, 1984.

Tugwell, Rexford. *Industrial Discipline*. New York: Columbia University Press, 1933.

Useem, Michael. "The Social Organization of the American Business Elite and Participation of Corporate Directors in the Governance of American Institutions." *American Sociological Review* 44 (August 1979): 553-72.

Van Dusen, Henry P., ed. *The Spiritual Legacy of John Foster Dulles*. Philadelphia: Westminister Press, 1960.

Waldo, Dwight. *The Administrative State*. 2d ed. New York: Holmes and Meier, 1984.
———. *The Enterprise of Public Administration*. Navato, CA: Chandler and Sharp, 1980.
Weber, Max. *Theory of Social and Economic Organization*. Translated by Talcott Parsons and A. K. Henderson. New York: Oxford University Press, 1947.
Weick, Karl E. "Cognitive Processes in Organizations." In B. M. Staw, ed., *Research in Organizational Behavior*, pp. 41-74. Greenwich, CT: JAI Press, 1979.
Whitehead, Alfred North. *Process and Reality*. New York: Macmillan Company, 1929.
Whitehead, T. N. *The Industrial Worker*. Cambridge, MA: Harvard University Press, 1938.
Whyte, William H., Jr. *The Organization Man*. New York: Simon and Schuster, 1956.
Wilson, Woodrow. "The Study of Administration." *Political Science Quarterly* 2 (June 1887): 197-222.
Wolin, Sheldon S. "Political Theory as a Vocation." *American Political Science Review*. 63 (December 1969).
———. *Politics and Vision*. Boston: Little, Brown and Company, 1960.
Woodward, Joan. *Industrial Organization: Theory and Practice*. London: Oxford University Press, 1965.
Wrege, Charles D., and Ronald G. Greenwood. *Frederick W. Taylor, The Father of Scientific Management: Myth and Reality*. Homewood, IL: Irwin Business One, 1991).

Interpretations of Barnard's Work

Andrews, Kenneth. "Introduction" to the Thirtieth Anniversary Edition of Chester I. Barnard, *The Functions of the Executive*, pp. 3-9. Cambridge, MA: Harvard University Press, 1968.
Copeland, Melvin T. "The Job of an Executive." *Harvard Business Review* 17, no. 2 (Winter 1940): 148-60.
Litzinger, William D., and Thomas Schaefer. "Perspective: Management Philosophy Enigma." *Academy of Management Review* 9, no. 4 (December 1966): 337-43.
Mitchell, Terrence R. and William G. Scott. "The Barnard-Simon Contribution: A Vanished Legacy." *Public Administration Quarterly* 12, no. 3 (Fall 1988): 348-68.
———. "The Universal Barnard: His Micro Theories of Organization Behavior." *Public Administration Quarterly* 9, no. 3 (Fall 1985): 239-59.
Perrow, Charles. *Complex Organizations, A Critical Essay*, pp. 62-76. 3d ed., New York: Random House, 1986.
Rabin, Jack, and Gerald J. Miller. "Moral Code, Compliance with Authority, and Productivity." *Public Productivity Review* 13, no. 4 (Summer 1989): 423-35.
Sayre, Wallace S. "Organization as Social Process." *Public Administration Review* 9, no. 1 (Winter 1949): 45-50.
Scott, William G. "Chester I. Barnard as Rockefeller Foundation President, 1948-1952," *Research Reports from the Rockefeller Archive Center*, Spring, 1990, pp. 3-5.
———. "Barnard on the Nature of Elitist Responsibility." *Public Administration Review* 42 (May-June 1982): 197-201.
Scott, William G. and Terrence R. Mitchell. "The Universal Barnard: His Meta Concepts of Leadership in the Administrative State." *Public Administration Quarterly* 13, no. 3 (Fall 1989): 295-320.
———. "The Universal Barnard: His Macro Theory of Organization." *Public Administration Quarterly* 11, no. 1 (Spring 1987): 34-58.
Vaughn, Jacqueline. "The Functions of the (Chief) Executive: How Chester Barnard Might View the Presidency." *Presidential Studies Quarterly* 8, no. 1 (1978): 18-27.

Wells, Lloyd M. "The Limits of Formal Authority: Barnard Revisited." *Public Administration Review* 23, no. 3 (1963): 161–66.

Williamson, Oliver E., ed. *Organization Theory from Chester Barnard to the Present and Beyond.* New York: Oxford University Press, 1990.

Wolf, William B. *The Basic Barnard.* ILR Paperback No. 14. Ithaca, NY: Cornell University, 1974.

———. *Conversations with Chester I. Barnard*, ILR Paperback No. 12. Ithaca, NY: Cornell University, School of Industrial and Labor Relations, 1973.

BARNARD'S BOOKS, MONOGRAPHS, ARTICLES, AND MANUSCRIPTS:
A SELECTED CHRONOLOGICAL LIST*

"Status of the Government Ownership Movement." Memorandum to H. B. Thayer, May 15, 1914. ATTA, box 47, folder marked "Government Ownership."

"Provision of Circuits for Connection to Radio Broadcasting Apparatus." *Commercial Letter #218*, April 11, 1922, ATTA, folder marked "Radio Bulletin #4," Radio Telephony, box 62.

"The Development of Executive Ability." Sackett's Industrial Conference, 1925, Pennsylvania State College, BL, Barnard Collection, carton 1.

"Our Task and Opportunity." *The New Jersey Bell*, October 1927, NJBTR.

"Address by Chester I. Barnard after having been presented by the National Exchange Club with a medallion in recognition of distinguished service to the city of Newark during 1931-1932." June 14, 1932, BL, Barnard Collection, carton 1. Mimeographed.

"Moving Forward to Higher Standards." *The New Jersey Bell*, October 1932, NJBTR.

"Summary of President Barnard's Talk to Employee and Management Representatives." August 18, 1933, NJBTR.

"Business Integration Essential to Stabilized Progress." Interview in *Journal of Industry and Finance*, 1934, ATTA, 5S-05-01-09.

"Persistent Dilemmas of Social Progress." Address at the Newark College of Engineering, June 12, 1936, BL, Barnard Collection, carton 1.

"What Other Purpose?" Commencement address, The Polytechnic Institute of Brooklyn, June 19, 1936, BL, Barnard Collection, carton 1.

"Methods and Limitations of Foresight in Modern Affairs." Address to Thirtieth Annual Convention of the Association of Life Insurance Presidents, December 4, 1936, BL, Barnard Collection, carton 1.

Early draft of manuscript for chapter 1 of *The Functions of the Executive*, "Introduction." 1936, BL, Barnard Collection, carton 1.

The Functions of the Executive. Cambridge, MA: Harvard University Press, 1938.

"Notes on Some Obscure Aspects of Human Relations." A speech given to Professor Philip Cabot's business executive group at the Harvard Graduate School of Business Administration, March 6, 1939, BL, Barnard Collection, carton 1.

"Observations and Reflections on a Brief Call at Leningrad and Moscow." Privately published pamphlet, July 1939, BL, Barnard Collection, carton 1.

"Requirements of Leadership in a Democratic Society." Presentation at a conference on

*A longer list of Barnard's papers may be found in William B. Wolf, *The Basic Barnard*, ILR Paperback No. 14, Ithaca: Cornell University, 1974. This inventory, while extensive, is not complete as it lacks reference to many of his papers located in the RAC, ATTA, NSBA, and NJBTR.

the Cooperative Study of Teacher Education, October 24, 1940, BL, Barnard Collection, carton 1.

"The Requirements of Leadership in Democratic Societies." Excerpt from draft of notes, October 1940, BL, Barnard Collection, carton 1.

"The Future Will Test the Fibre and Loyalty of all of us . . . ." *The New Jersey Bell*, October 1940, NJBTR.

"Concerning the Theory of Modern Price Systems." Privately published pamphlet, March 10, 1941, BL, Barnard Collection, carton 1.

"Nine Weeks in the United States Treasury: October 6 to December 11, 1941." Unpublished manuscript of personal recollections in the possession of Julia Welch.

"A Memorandum on the Nature of the Social Sciences." Submitted to the Board of Trustees of the Rockefeller Foundation, 1942, RAC Policy and Progress Reports, 1942-1943. Mimeographed.

"Education for Executives." *Journal of Business* 18 (October 18, 1945): 175-82.

"Review of Barbara Wootton's *Freedom Under Planning.*" *Southern Economic Journal* 12 (January 12, 1946): 290-300.

"Report of the Special Committee on Policy and Programs." December 3 and 4, 1946, RAC, box 28, series 900, folder 155.

"Memorandum on Modern Problems of Morals and Ethics." Manuscript, 1946, RAC, series 900, box 56, folder 303.

"The History and Economics of the Dial Program of the New Jersey Bell Telephone Company." Memorandum for the Supervisory Organization of the Company, September 2, 1947, ATTA, folder marked "C.I. Barnard-110-11-01-02."

"Starting Our Third Decade." *The New Jersey Bell*, October 1947, NJBTR.

Memorandum to Henry P. Van Dusen, August 31, 1948, RAC, series 900, box 56, folder 303.

"President's Review." The Rockefeller Foundation *Annual Report 1948*, RAC.

First Annual Report to the Rockefeller Foundation. RAC, 1949.

Organization and Management. Cambridge, MA: Harvard University Press, 1949.

"Skill, Knowledge, and Judgement." An address to MIT graduating class, 1950, RAC, RG3-910, box 10.

Minutes of Second Meeting of NSB. January 3, 1951, NSBA.

Memorandum to Dean Rusk. June 11, 1952, RAC, series 900, box 56, folder 304.

"Memorandum to Members of the National Science Board." September 22, 1955, NSBA, file marked "Reflections on the 35th Meeting of the NSB," record numbers 165 and 166.

"Elementary Conditions of Business Morals." *California Management Review* 1 (Fall 1958): 1-13.

Index

Accountability, 36, 81, 142, 143-44, 145-46, 150, 167, 168, 175, 177-78, 184
Adams, Henry, 10
Adelstein, Richard P., 2
Administrative Behavior (Simon), x, 127, 143, 203(n36)
Administrative state, 189(n1). *See also* Managerial state
Alberts, William, xiii, 11, 190(n13)
Alchon, Guy, 3, 9, 15, 50
Alder, Allan, 172
Aldrich, H. E., 125
Alpert, Harry, 82-83
American Association of Collegiate Schools of Business, 51
American Civil Liberties Union, 172
American dialectic, 158, 160
American Economic Review, 50
American Individualism (Hoover), 17-18
American Magazine, The, 28, 29
American Society of Mechanical Engineers, 26-27
American Telephone and Telegraph, xi, 8, 61, 63, 64-66, 68, 71, 72, 74-75, 83, 85-86, 100, 109, 167
  associated companies, 163
  company archives, xiv
  and managerialism, 38, 136
  Plan of Employee Representation, 70
Andrews, Kenneth, 6
Arensburg, Conrad, 43
Aristotle, 105, 149, 157, 164
Asceticism, 139
Associational specialization, 61, 91
Aston group, 125
Atomic Energy Commission, 71
Authority, 96-98, 113, 115, 118, 123, 124, 130-32, 162, 183, 186 (*see also* Moral authority)
  expert, 174
  centralization of, 33
  legitimate, 59
  objective, 149, 159
"Authority," article in *Encyclopedia of the Social Sciences* (Michels), 92, 97

Bailey, Orville T., 41-42
Baker Library, Graduate School of Business Administration, Harvard University, xiv
Barber, Bernard, xiv, 46, 194(n3), 196(n33)
Baritz, Loren, 175
Barnard, Chester I., ix-xii, xiii-xiv, 7, 13, 19, 24, 145-46, 185-87, 194(n8), 196(n33) 204(nn60, 8), 210(nn17, 24), 211(n27)
  and ATT, 61-74, 77, 83-87
  and attributes of the managerial elite, 134-44
  and behavioral control, 104-17
  biographical sketch of, 61-87
  and cooperative systems, 119-33
  and epistemology of the social sciences, 88-103
  and Ethics and Morals Project, Rockefeller Foundation, 151-55
  and exhaustion of managerialism, 169-84
  and existentialism, 147-50
  and formation of the managerial state, 2-8
  and Harvard Circle, 40-60
  and Hoover's cooperative ideal, 5, 18
  and informal executive organization, 37
  and management revolution, 25, 33, 35, 36-37
  and moral authority, 23
  and moral deficit, 151-56

Barnard, Chester, *continued*
  and NJBT, 66–74, 76, 77, 83–87
  and public service, 74–83, 87
  and revolution in political science, 157–68
  and Rockefeller Foundation, 63, 74, 77–79,
    80, 81, 83, 87, 101–3
  and theory of authority, 130–32
  and theory of exchange, 125, 126–30
  and theory of formal organization, 123–26,
    132–33
  and war system, 15
Barton, Bruce, 28
Baruch, Bernard M., 14–15, 19, 74
Batty, Linda, xiv
Beard, Miriam, 209(n4)
Behavioral control, 89, 104–17
  behavioral model of persons, 111–12
  behavioral sciences, 33, 108, 124, 186
  group dynamics, 112–16, 133 (*see also*
    Communication; Group process; Informal
    organization)
  human behavior, 25, 105–8, 111, 116, 117,
    133, 138 (*see also* Free will; Individuals
    and persons; Limited choice; Internal and
    external causes; Reverse causality; tension
    reduction)
  See also Motivation; Social sciences; Social
    engineering
Bellah, Robert N. 171
Bell System, 6, 59, 61, 65, 66, 67, 72, 74, 84,
  86–87, 89, 163. *See also* American
  Telephone and Telegraph Co.
Bem, D. J., 108
Bendix, Reinhard, 205(n30)
Bennis, Warren, 134, 149, 178, 180, 182, 185
Bentham, Jeremy, 136
Berle, Adolph A., Jr., 19, 23, 38–39, 141
Bernard, Claude, 46
Bolshevism, 12
Bounded rationality, 98
Brandeis, Louis D., 28
Brown, Junius F., 93, 101
Brownlow, Louis, 21
Brownlow report, 21, 33
Bureaucracy, 88, 89, 162. *See also* Classical
  organization theory; Formalization;
  Formal Organization
Burnham, James, 23–24, 25, 38–39
Bush, Vannevar, 81
Business-government relationships, xi, 53,
  160–61, 163

Cabot, Richard, 40
Camus, Albert, 148
Capitalism, 12, 13, 23, 24, 49
Carnegie, Andrew, 10

Carter, Jimmy, 170
Casey, William, 172
Central Intelligence Agency, 172
Chandler, Alfred D., Jr., 1, 9, 126
China Medical Board, 212(n19)
Christian absolutism, 147
Circulation of the elite, 36, 45, 48–49
Civilian Conservation Corps (CCC), 76
Classical organization theory, 7, 33–35, 99,
  118–19
  and assembly line, 33
  and centralization of authority, 33, 34
  and coordination, 9, 15, 21, 34, 75, 98, 118,
    124, 125, 126, 161, 162, 185, 186
  and division of labor, 33, 34, 126
  and organizational hierarchy, 34
  and scalar principle, 34
  See also Management revolution: structural-
    ists' approach
Collectivism, 2, 13, 15, 175–76
  absolute, 5, 187
  free, 4, 187
Colorado Public Service Commission, 65
Committee for Administrative Management
  (Brownlow Committee), 21, 191(n39). *See*
  also Brownlow Report
Committee on a Just and Durable Peace, 151
Commons, John R., 92, 94–95, 110, 142
Communication, 95, 99, 113, 114, 115–16,
  124, 125, 131, 200(n52)
Communism, 13, 16, 46, 90, 154
Competency, 134
Complex organizations, 7, 8, 89, 125, 126, 141
Complex reasoning, 139–41
Conant, James B., 41, 80
Concrete Sociology. *See* Sociology 23
Consent theory of authority, 7, 96–98, 130,
  131–32
  zones of indifference, 6, 98, 131–32
Contingency theory, 148
Cook, Morris L., 27
Coolidge, Calvin, 17
Coon, Horace, 38
Cooperation, xi, 6, 7, 13, 17, 21, 23, 52, 55,
  58–59, 70, 74, 88–89, 90, 91, 96, 98, 104,
  105, 108, 111–12, 113, 114–16, 119–22,
  123, 124–25, 126, 129–30, 133, 135, 136,
  147, 148, 156, 163, 165, 167, 168, 175,
  182–84, 186, 187, 201(n68)
  bankruptcy of, 175–76
  morality of, 147
  theory of, 33, 93–94
  voluntary, 14, 18–19, 75
Cooperative systems, 89, 96, 104, 109, 119–23,
  126, 130, 133, 148, 149, 158, 159, 167,
  168, 176
  theory of, 107

Coordination, 34, 98, 118, 124, 125, 126, 161, 186
  industrial, 9, 21, 162, 185
  institutional, 15
  national, 75
Copeland, Melvin T., 50, 53
Corporatism, 13-16, 17, 18, 20
  corporative state, 17
Coughlin, Father, 54
Cuff, Robert D., xv, 15
Culture, 43, 99, 113, 116-17
Curtis, Charles P., Jr., 22
  and Harvard Circle, 42, 47, 48
Cutler, Henry F., 62, 64

Darman, Richard G., 173
Davis, Kingsley, 47
Davis, Ralph C., 33
Day, Edmond, 31
Deane, Herbert A., 155
Deaver, Michael, 172
Decision Theory, 94-95, 128
  and decisionmaking, 118, 119, 127, 140, 142-43, 147, 186
Declaration of Independence, 158
de Jouvenel, Bertrand, 157, 176, 187
Delaware and Atlantic Telegraph and Telephone Company, 66-67
Deming, W. Edwards, 191(n31)
Dennison Manufacturing Companies, 56
Department of Commerce, 50
Determinate hierarchy, 34, 193(n28)
de Tocqueville, Alexis, 158
DeVinney, Lelund C., 213(n38)
De Voto, Bernard, 47
Dewey, John, 136
Dial system, 68, 72, 86
Dickson, William J., 47, 55, 92, 93, 96, 99, 112
Discretionary power, 7, 12, 156, 177
  discretion or discretionists, 145, 146, 149, 156, 157, 163, 165, 167, 168, 176, 177-78, 183, 204(n9), 211(n37)
Dissonance theory, 108
Donham, Wallace B., 12, 22, 23, 31, 89, 90, 179, 182, 196(n42)
  and Harvard Circle, 40, 41, 47, 48-55, 57-58, 59
Dove, Hazel, xiv
Drucker, Peter, x, 1, 9, 173, 180, 186, 190(n6)
Dulles, John Foster, 78, 79, 150-55, 156, 212(n21)
Durkheim, Emil, 98

Education of leaders, 137-38
Edwards, Lyford P., 169
Effectiveness, 96, 109, 110, 120, 125, 138, 176
  organizational, 115

Effectiveness and efficiency, Barnard's theory of, 6, 96, 109, 120
Efficiency, 11, 25, 32, 95, 109, 118, 120, 161, 162, 173, 179
  economic, 162
  Henry Towne on, 26-27
  organizational, 34
  and scientific management movement, 27-29
  social, 17
Ehrlich, Eugene, 92, 97, 99
Einstein, Albert, 88
Eliot, T. S., 63
Emerson, Harrington, 27
Emerson Piano Company, 62
Engineering Foundation, 30
English Villagers of the Thirteenth Century, The (Homans), 42
Enterprise of Public Administration (Waldo), 189(n1)
Equilibrium, 45, 52-53, 58, 90, 96, 120, 121, 122
  dynamic, 120
  internal, 121
  organic, 52-53
  social, 45, 48, 54, 90
  systems and, 43, 45, 46, 47-48, 58
Ethics, 49, 146, 148-49, 172-73, 181-82
  and morals, 146, 151-55
  quandary, 150
Exchange theory. See Theory of exchange
Executive functions. See Theory of formal organizations
External validity, 102

Fascism, 12, 14, 16, 45, 46
Fayol, Henri, 32-33
Federal Council of Churches, 151, 152, 153
Federalist papers, 158
Festinger, L., 108
Fiorina, Morris, 173
Follett, Mary Parker, 33, 91, 99, 112, 206(n49)
Food Administration, 14, 17
Force fields systems, 123
Formalization, 118, 119, 120-21, 125, 132
Formal organization, xi, 8, 109, 112, 113, 114, 115, 138, 147, 165, 176, 183
  consent in, 118-33
  theory of, 43, 98-99, 119, 123-26
Fosdick, Raymond B., 77-79, 81, 84, 101-2, 152, 153, 155, 156, 209(n7)
Franke, R. H., 197(n71)
Frankfurter, Felix, 19
Freud, Sigmund, 32, 136
Frick, Henry Clay, 10
Frug, Gerald E., 146, 216(n18)
Functionalism, 95-96

Functions of the Executive, The (Barnard), ix, x, 6, 24, 40, 93, 195(n10)
Fundamental Principles of the Sociology of Law (Ehrlich), 92, 97

Galbraith, John Kenneth, 189(n3)
Gantt, Henry, 27
Garibaldi, Giuseppe, 44
Geneen, Harold S., 172
General and Industrial Administration (Fayol), 32
General Electric, 56, 172
General Motors, 171
George H. Champlin Company, 62
George Orwell (Crick), 192(n50)
Gestalt, 114, 123
Giantism, 15
Gibbs, J. Willard, 46
Gifford, Walter S., 36, 61-66, 87, 152, 155, 156, 160-61, 198(n16), 200(n52)
   and ATT, 15, 38, 61, 63-66, 83, 167
   public service of, 15, 74-75, 77
   and WIB, 15, 74
Gilbreth, Frank, 27
Gilbreth, Lillian, 27, 116
Golembiewski, Robert T., 211(n32)
Governance, 119, 142
Graicunas, V.A., 92, 99, 125
   theorem of, 125
Gramsci, Antonio, 28
Great Depression, 52, 53, 70, 73, 74, 76, 85, 119, 122, 139, 161, 185. *See also* Hoover, Herbert; New Deal; Roosevelt, Franklin D.
Group process, 114-15, 116
Guardian class /guardianship, 3-4, 37, 138, 169, 187
   concept of, 3
   management and, 11, 149
Guardians, 3-4, 11, 24, 36, 59, 139, 169, 181, 186, 187
   management, 7
Guggenheim Foundation, 137
Gulick, Luther, 21, 34

Habits of the Heart (Bellah et al.), 171-72
Hamblin, R., 115
Harbord, Major-General James G., 130
Harding, Warren G., 17
Hart, David K., ix, xiii, xv
Harvard Business Review, 49, 52
Harvard Circle, 8, 39, 40-60, 90, 96, 99, 100, 104, 107, 111, 129, 133
   and Harvard Graduate School of Business, 49-55
   and Laboratory of Industrial Physiology, 55-58

national agenda of, 58-60
and Paretan Scholars, 43-49 (*see also* Henderson, Lawrence J.; Pareto, Vilfredo)
segments of, 41-42
and Society of Fellows, 42-43
Hawley, Ellis, 15
Hawthorne studies, 32, 40, 43, 45, 47, 48, 55-58, 59, 96, 100, 104-5, 133, 186, 205(n35)
   and Hawthorne effect, 57, 197(nn68, 71, 72)
   and Hawthorne researchers, 110, 113, 129
Henderson, Lawrence J., xiv, 31, 91-93, 96, 104, 110, 122, 123, 195(n27), 196(n33)
   and Fatigue Lab, 55-56
   and Harvard Circle, 40, 41-43, 45-49, 51-52
Hershey, H. Roy, xiv, 84
Herzberg, F., 128
High School Teachers Association, 28
History of the Business Man, A (Beard), 209(n4)
Hitler, Adolph, 12
Hobbes, Thomas, 119, 148-49
Hochheiser, Sheldon, xiv, 200(n52)
Hocking, William Earnest, 151-52, 153, 156
Homans, George C., 22
   and Harvard Circle, 40, 41-43, 46, 47, 48
Hoover, Herbert, 4, 5, 70, 75, 89, 121, 164, 166-67, 185
   and Belgian Relief, 75
   and cooperation, 21, 92, 93, 161, 163
   and the Food Administration, 14
   and government activism, 23
   and the Great Depression, 74
   and New Era, 9, 17-19
   political philosophy of, 58
   and Progressivism, 7, 10-11, 18
Hoveland, C. I., 115
Human interaction systems, 123
Human Problems of an Industrial Civilization, The (Mayo), 92, 93
Hutchins, John M., 31

Illinois Bell Telephone Co., 66, 86
Incentives, 105, 109, 125, 127, 128-29, 130, 131, 139
Individualism, xi, 12, 17-18, 58, 119, 166, 168, 183
Individuals and persons, differentiated, 105-6
Industrial Discipline (Tugwell), 21
Industrial Organization and Management (Davis), 33
Industrial Worker, The (Whitehead), 93
Informal organization, xi, 8, 43, 91, 99-100, 112-14, 205(n39)
   executive, 91
   and informal groups, 130-31

norms of, 59, 97, 99, 105, 113, 114, 116-17, 120, 131, 133, 145
roles of, 113-14, 116-17, 120
Informal systems, 113-14
In Search of Excellence (Peters and Waterman), 36, 113
Institutional Economics (Commons), 92, 94
Insull, Samuel, 38
Integration, 161
and stability, 7, 161
Interdependence, 43
Internal and external causes of behavior, 105, 106, 107
Internal validity, 102-3
International Telegraph and Telephone, 172
Interstate Commerce Commission, 28, 163

Johnson, Amory R., 137
Johnson, Gen. Hugh, 19
Jung, Carl Gustaf, 32
Justice, 164-66, 167, 168, 178
corrective, 164, 165-66
distributive, 164, 165-66
Justice ideal, 165-66

Kafka, Franz, 169
Kant, Emanuel, 117
Kierkegaard, Sören Aabye, 148
Kingsbury, N.C., 66
Klopsteg, Paul, 82
Kluckhohn, Florence, 43
Koffka, Kurt, 92, 94

Laboratory of Industrial Psychology (Fatigue Lab), 31-32, 51, 55-56
Labor in America (Dulles), 202(n3)
Langer, E. J., 107
Laura Spelman Rockefeller Memorial, 30-31. *See also* Rockefeller Foundation
Lawrence, P. R., 125
Laws (Plato), 157
Leadership, 53, 119, 125, 134-44, 157, 170-73, 175, 185, 187. *See also* Accountability; Asceticism; Complex reasoning; Decision theory: decision making; Education of leaders; Governance; Moral authority
Leadership elite. *See* Managerial elite
Leffler, Melvyn P., 17
Legitimacy, 4, 7, 20, 37, 98, 145, 169
leader, 3, 89, 187
management or managerial, 3, 11-12, 24, 28, 33, 59, 89, 91, 98, 121, 123, 131, 132, 133, 135, 137, 148, 171, 173, 177, 186
L. J. Henderson on the Social System (Barber, ed.), 194(n3), 196(n33)
Lenin, Nikolai, 13, 17, 28

Lewin, Kurt, 101
Liberty, 166-68
Lippmann, Walter, xi, 4-5, 63, 169, 173, 198(n16)
Limited choice, 98, 106
Locke, John, 119
Locus of power, 22
Long, Huey, 54
Lorsch, J. W., 125
Lowell, A. Lawrence, 40, 41, 42, 43
Lowes, John L., 42

McClosky, Herbert, 158,168
Machiavelli, Niccolo, 133, 159, 168
McRae, G. W., 76, 77, 83
MacIntyre, Alasdair, 173, 178
Management and the Worker (Roethlisberger and Dickson), 92, 93
Management elite, 2, 3, 4, 18, 22-23, 36-37, 45, 49, 52-53, 58, 93, 96, 111-12, 155, 156, 168, 170, 175, 177, 180, 186, 194(n32)
Management functions, 25
Management governance, 164-68, 169
Management initiated grievance systems, 166
Management revolution, 7, 24, 25-39, 41, 169
(*see also* Progressivism)
class awareness of, 8, 25, 35-39
functionalists' approach to, 32-33, 35
professional awareness of, 8, 25-35, 39
and scientific management movement, 27-30, 35
and self-awareness, 25, 35, 51
structuralists' approach to, 33-35
Management virtues, xi, 138, 141, 144, 157, 187
Managerial class, 3, 11-12, 22-23, 35, 36-37, 49, 70, 80, 169
Managerial Revolution, The (Burnham), 23
Managerial state, 4, 7, 9, 11, 35, 36, 41, 49, 53, 59, 130, 133, 134, 135, 136, 144, 160, 163, 168, 175, 176, 185, 186-87, 189(n1)
(*see also* Corporatism)
definition of, 2
in early Roosevelt era, 19-21
in Hoover era, 17-19
modern opinion of versus reality, 21-24
post-World War I, 16-17
and search for political formula, 12-13
and war system, 14-16
Managerialism, ix, 2, 7, 8, 23, 24, 49, 136, 145, 158, 186-87
competency and rationality of, 178-80, 182
discretion and accountability of, 177-78
exhaustion of, 169-84
foundations of, 15
ideology of, 9-13

Managerialism, *continued*
  integrity and moral character of, 180–82
  and management legitimacy, 7
  and restoration of confidence, 177–84
  and war system, 15
Mansfield, Harvey C., Jr., 133, 146, 159
Marx, Karl, 13, 38, 45, 47
Marxism, 51, 59, 166
Mayo, Elton, 30, 31, 90, 91–94, 104, 110, 111,
  112, 116, 130, 133
  and Harvard Circle, 40, 42, 43, 46, 47, 48–
  49, 51–52, 55–57, 59
Means, Gardiner C., 23, 38–39
Mee, John F., x
Meno (Socrates), 181
Mental processes, logical and nonlogical, 100
Merriam, Charles E., 21, 31
Merton, Robert K., 41, 43, 47
Metaphysics (Aristotle), 157
Michels, Roberto, 92, 97–98, 186, 216(n2)
Milkis, Stanley M., 21
Mill, John Stuart, 136
Miller, Gerald J., 208(n54)
Miller, L., 115
Miller, Peter, 53
Mills, C. Wright, 194(n32)
Mind and Society, The (Pareto), 92, 93
"Mind in Everyday Affairs, The" (Barnard),
  211(nn27, 34)
Mintzberg, Henry, 183
Mitchell, James M., 84
Mitchell, Terence R., x, xiii, xv
Modernization, 9
Moe, Henry A., 137
Modern Corporation and Private Property, The
  (Berle and Means), 23
Moffett, Guy, 31
Moody, Dwight Lyman, 62
Mooney, James D., 34, 98, 124
Moral authority, 2–3, 4, 5, 18, 19, 20–21, 22–
  23, 52, 58, 75, 90, 134, 135, 163–64, 173
Moral deficit, 79, 150–56, 180
Moral integrity, 4, 11, 25, 36, 49, 137, 175
Morality, 90, 134, 135, 146–47, 148, 152, 175,
  178, 182, 187
Moral minimalism, 149
Moral obligations of the elite, 106, 145–56,
  157, 170
Moral philosophy, 51, 63, 79, 94, 146, 148,
  150, 151–55, 157, 181–82, 186
Moral responsibility, xi, 8, 119, 134, 147, 148–
  49, 164, 173, 175
Moral virtues, 146, 151
Morgan, J. P., 10
Morgenthau, Henry, Jr., 76–77, 209(n6)
Mosca, Gaetano, 12
Motivation, 7, 30, 32, 55, 76, 105, 108–10,

111, 112, 113, 116, 126, 127, 139, 140,
  164
  and cooperation, 108, 110
  and cost-benefit analysis, 108, 109–10, 111,
  120, 127, 131
  and equity, 108, 110, 111, 114, 164
  and goal setting, 108–9
Motives, 45, 105, 108, 116, 133, 159
  and motivators, 128–29
Mountain States Telephone and Telegraph
  Company, 65
Mount Hermon School. *See* Northfield-Mt.
  Hermon School
Mulherin, James, 56, 197(n68)
Munsterberg, Hugo, 116
Mussolini, Benito, 12–13, 16, 17
Mutual causality, 101
Mutuality of interests, 7, 28, 96, 117, 130, 133,
  159–60, 170, 192(n8)

Nanus, Burt, 134, 149, 178, 180, 182
National Academy of Science, 30
National Archives, xiv
National Education Association, 28
National Federation of Telephone Workers, 72
National governance, 134, 135
National Industrial Recovery Act, 20, 21
National Recovery Administration, 19, 20, 69
National Research Council, 30
  Division of Engineering and Research, 56
National Science Board, 79–83, 87
  archives of, xiv
National Science Foundation, 79–82, 84
National socialism, 12
National Unemployment Council, 74
Nazism, 46
Newark College of Engineering, 121
Newark Exchange Club, 119, 139
Newcomer, Mabel, 36, 190(n12)
New Deal, 15, 16, 19–21, 31, 53, 75–76, 160,
  161
New Industrial State, The (Galbraith), 189(n3)
New Jersey Bell Telephone Company, xiii, xiv,
  66–74, 76, 77, 83–87, 162
New Jersey Board of Public Utility Commis-
  sioners, 71, 86
New Jersey Emergency Relief Administration,
  75, 138, 159, 206(n2)
New Jersey Exchange Club, 75
New managerial order, 8, 15, 39, 137
New order of national power and organizational governance, 157–68
  and distribution of national power, 160–64
  individuality and community of, 158–60,
  168
  justice ideal of, 165–66
  liberty ideal of, 166–68

order and freedom, 158-60, 164, 165, 166-68
Newton, Isaac, 46
New York Telephone Company, 66-67, 86
Nisbett, R. F., 107
Noera, Grace F., 61
Nonlogical language and behavior, 45
Northfield-Mt. Hermon School, xiv, 62-63, 64
Norton, David L., xiii, 4, 148

Office of Scientific Research and Development, 80
Office of the Navy, 80
Office of War Information, 82
O'Leary, Ted, 53
Onward Industry (Mooney and Reiley), 34, 98
Open systems theory, 91-93. See also Systems theory
Organizational governance, 122, 157-68, 178, 184
Organizational power, xi
Organizational structure, 25, 33, 125
Organizational Values in America (Scott and Hart), ix, xiii
Orwell, George, 6, 18, 24, 160

Papers on the Science of Administration (Gulick and Urwick, eds.), 34
Pareto, Vilfredo, 36, 41, 43, 91-93, 96, 98, 99, 100, 117, 138, 191(n26), 195(n27)
    and Harvard Circle, 43-49, 52, 54
    and Mazzini political party, 43-44
    Paretan optimality of, 44
    Paretan sociology of, 91
    and theory of the elite, 45
Pareto's General Sociology (Henderson), 92
Parsons, Talcott, 92, 95-96, 98, 139, 195(n27)
    and Harvard Circle, 40, 43, 46, 47
Peirce, Charles Sanders, 5-6
Peking Union Medical College, 212(n19)
Pennsylvania Bell Telephone Company, 66
Perrow, Charles, 135, 136, 209(n3)
Persistent aggregates, 54
Persuasion, 105, 109, 125, 127, 129-30, 131, 139
Peters, Thomas J., 113, 117
Phillips, Kevin, 2-3
Pincoffs, Edmond L., 150
Plato, 3-4, 157. See also Guardians
Pluralism, 2, 22, 164, 183
Pluralistic groups, 145
Pluralistic network, 22
Political Parties (Michels), 216(n2)
Pope John XXIII, 78, 79
Population, 201(n68)
Positivism, 46
Power Elite, The (Mills), 194(n32)

Practice of Management, The (Drucker), x, 190(n6)
Principles of Gestalt Psychology (Koffka), 92, 94
Private cupidity, 23-24, 39
Privatism, 7, 185
Process and Reality (Whitehead), 92, 93
Progressivism, x, 2, 7, 10-11, 18, 25, 39, 61, 185
    ideals of, 11, 24, 35, 91, 169, 173-75
    and origins of management's professionalism, 26-27
Psychology and the Social Order (Brown), 93
Psychology of Management, The (Gilbreth), 27-28
Public Administration Clearing House, 31

Rabin, Jack, xv, 208(n54)
Radiotelephony, 75
Ramos, A. G., 183-84
Rathenau, Walter, 28
Rationalism, 46
Rationality, 11, 25, 27, 28, 36, 58, 173, 175, 180, 187
Rational-legal systems, 123
Reagan, Ronald, 170, 172
Reconstitution, 9
Reconstruction, 9
Reiley, Alan C., 34, 98, 124
Residues and Derivations, 45, 46, 48, 54, 96, 100, 106-7, 117, 128, 138, 195(n28)
Responsibility, 33, 91, 93, 94, 142, 149, 154, 157, 159, 165, 182
Reverse causality, 105, 106, 107-8
Ripley, William Z., 23
Robinson, Dwight, 20
Rockefeller, John D., 10, 154
Rockefeller, John D., Jr., 77-79, 146, 150, 152, 155, 156
Rockefeller, John D. III, 151
Rockefeller, Laura Spelman. See Laura Spelman Rockefeller Memorial
Rockefeller Archive Center, xiv, 84
Rockefeller Foundation, xi, 30, 31, 58, 63, 74, 77-79, 80, 81, 83, 101-3, 104, 111, 115, 122, 138, 146, 150, 156, 174, 182
    and moral deficit, 151-55
    philanthropies of, 30-32
    Social Science Division, 31, 78, 154
Roethlisberger, Fritz, 91, 92, 93, 96, 99, 112
    and Harvard Circle, 41, 46, 47, 48, 55
Rohr, John, 23, 214(n6)
Roosevelt, Franklin D., 2, 4, 15, 22-23, 41, 53-54, 75, 160
    and the New Deal, 15, 16, 19-21, 53
Roosevelt, Theodore, 10, 61
Rousseau, J. J., 119

Rule creativeness, 150
Rule responsibility, 149, 150
Ruml, Beardsly, 30-31
Rusk, Dean, 78, 154, 155-56

Sartre, Jean Paul, 148
Satisficing, 128, 204(n8)
Schaar, John H., 12
Schumpeter, Joseph, 47
Scientific management movement. *See*
    Management revolution
Scott, Walter Dill, 30, 116
Shartle, Carroll L., 78, 201(n67)
Simon, Herbert, x, 7, 9, 98, 127, 128, 136, 143,
    167, 173, 203(n36), 204(n8)
Sinclair, Upton, 29
Skinner, B. F., 41, 42
Skowronek, Stephen, 28
Social enclaves, 183
Social engineering, 2, 24, 54, 89, 105, 116,
    176, 186, 187
Socialism, 23, 24
Social Science Citation Index, 6
Social Science methodology, 100-101
Social Science Research Council, 31
Social sciences, 8, 30-32, 35, 43, 46, 77, 88-
    103, 129, 138, 155, 174, 180
  anthropology, 100
  and behavioral control, 104-17
  importance of to management, 9, 51-55, 57,
    59, 103-17
  industrial psychology, 30, 31, 56, 111, 116,
    175
  and NSF and NSB, 80-83
  organizational behavior, 108
  psychology, 108, 157
  social psychology, 7, 100, 101, 112, 164,
    205(n35)
  sociology, 115, 157
Social system, 45
Social System, The (Parsons), 195(n27)
Sociology 23, 47, 196(n33)
Socrates, 181
Sorokin, Pitirim, 43, 55, 197(n66)
Southern Bell Telephone Co., 86
Sovereign immunity rule, 216(n20)
Spencer, Herbert, 136
Spiritual Legacy of John Foster Dulles, The
    (Van Dusen), 212(n21)
Stalin, Joseph, 13, 16, 17
Statism, 15, 17
Steffens, Lincoln, 13
Stegner, Wallace, 47
Stempel, Ralph C., 171. *See also* General
    Motors
Stewardship, 74

corporate, 24
national, 22
rational, 4
Stewart, Walter W., 77, 78. *See also* General
    Motors
Structural-functional analysis, 95-96
Structuralism in management theory, 33-35
Structure of Social Action, The (Parsons), 92
Subsidiarity, 183
Systems and equilibrium, 43, 45, 46, 47-48,
    58
Systems theory, 96, 101

Tarbell, Ida, 10
Taylor, Frederick W., 5, 25, 27, 28-29, 30, 32,
    37, 139
Technology, 120, 122, 125, 128, 167
Telephone Pioneers of America, 71
Thayer, Harry B., 65
Theory of authority, 130-32. *See also* Consent
    theory of authority
Theory of cooperative systems. *See* Coopera-
    tive systems
Theory of exchange, 94-95, 125, 126-30, 132,
    142
  coercion, 95, 129
  economy of incentives, 127
  inculcation of motives, 129, 130
  inducements and contributions, 127-28,
    131
  method of incentives, 127, 128-29
  method of persuasion, 95, 105, 109, 127,
    129-30
  rationalization of opportunity, 129-30
Theory of formal organization, 43, 98-99,
    123-26
  and executive functions, 124-25
  and span of control, 99, 125
  and structural design, 126
Theory of opportunism, 94, 95, 142
  and limiting factor, 94, 95
  and strategic factor, 94, 95, 142, 143
Theory of Social and Economic Organization
    (Weber), 92
Theory of structural dynamics, 33
Thompson, James D., 142
To Run a Constitution (Rohr), 214(n6)
Towne, Henry, 26-27, 61, 173
Townsend, Dr., 54
Trade-off theory of freedom, 159
Trattato di Sociologia Generale (Pareto), 44,
    46, 47
Truman, Harry S., 77, 79, 80
Tugwell, Rexford, 19, 21
Twentieth Century Fund study of American
    ethos, 158

Unionization, 59, 69-70, 90
Union Theological Seminary, 79, 151, 153, 154-55
United Service Organization, 77, 78, 87
Unity of command, 34, 193(n28)
Urwick, Lyndall, 32-33, 34
Useem, Michael, 36
U.S. Telephone Administration, 74
Utility or utilitarianism, 29, 136
    utilitarian, 127-28

Vail, Theodore N., 64-65, 160-61, 198(n20)
Vanderbilt, Cornelius, 10
Van Dusen, Henry P., 79, 151, 153, 154, 155, 212(n21), 214(n44)
Veblen, Thorstein, 10, 11
Victor Emmanuel II (king of Italy), 44
Voluntarism, 4-5, 7, 17, 58, 70, 75, 119, 183, 185

Waldo, Dwight, 3, 9, 25, 39, 189(n1)
Walras, Anton, 44
War Industries Board, 14, 19, 74, 75
    Advisory Commission of the Council, 74
    Council of National Defense, 74
Warner, Lloyd, 41, 43, 113
War system, 14-16, 17, 30
Waterman, Alan T., 80, 82, 84
Waterman, Richard H., Jr., 113, 117
Weber, Max, 33, 88, 89, 92, 98, 123
    theory of bureaucracy, 33, 88, 89, 118

Weick, K. E., 108
Welch, Jared, xiv
Welch, Julia, xiv, 198(n14), 200(n54)
Western Electric Company, 32, 48, 55-57, 63, 112, 163
Wheeler, William Morton, 46, 52
Whitehead, Alfred North, 40, 42, 47, 51, 91-93
Whitehead, T. N., 47, 112
Whyte, William F., 41, 43
Willits, Joseph H., 77, 101-2, 115, 137, 152-53, 154-55, 156, 204(n60), 213(n38)
Wilson, T. D., 107
Wilson, Woodrow, 5, 10-11, 22-23, 61
    and Progressive movement, 10-11, 26
    and war system, 14, 121
Wolf, William B., xiv, 6, 60, 62, 84
Woodward, Joan, 125
Wootton, Barbara, 162
Work and Authority in Industry: Ideologies of Management in the Course of Industrialization (Bendix), 205(n30)
Work Projects Administration, 76

Yankee City Studies, 43
Yerkes, Robert M., 30, 116
Young Men's Christian Association, 151

Zaller, John, 158, 168
Zinsser, Hans, 47
Zones of indifference. *See* Consent theory of authority